Guitar Tabs & Lyrics Notebook

Dexter Lives

This Book Belongs to:

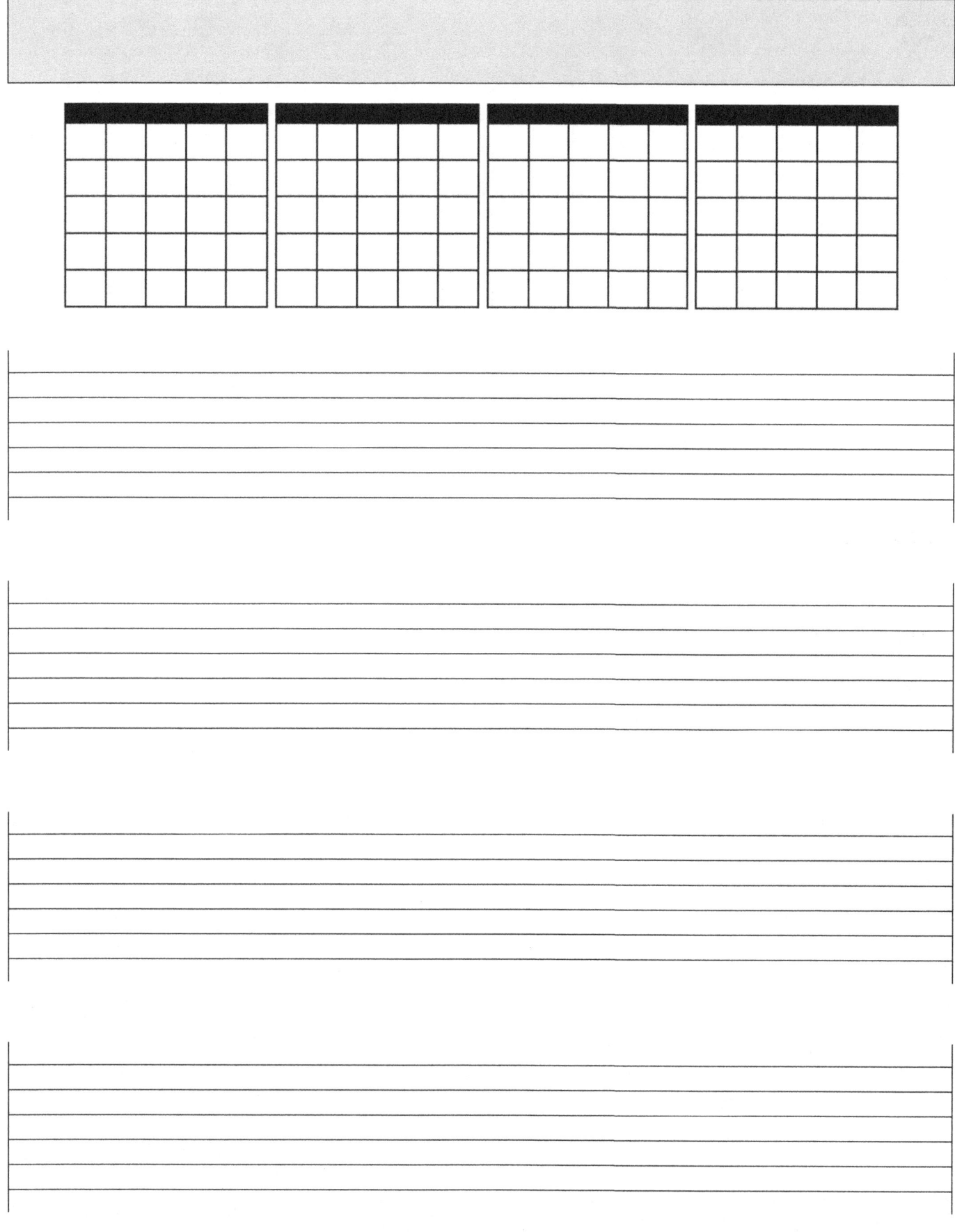

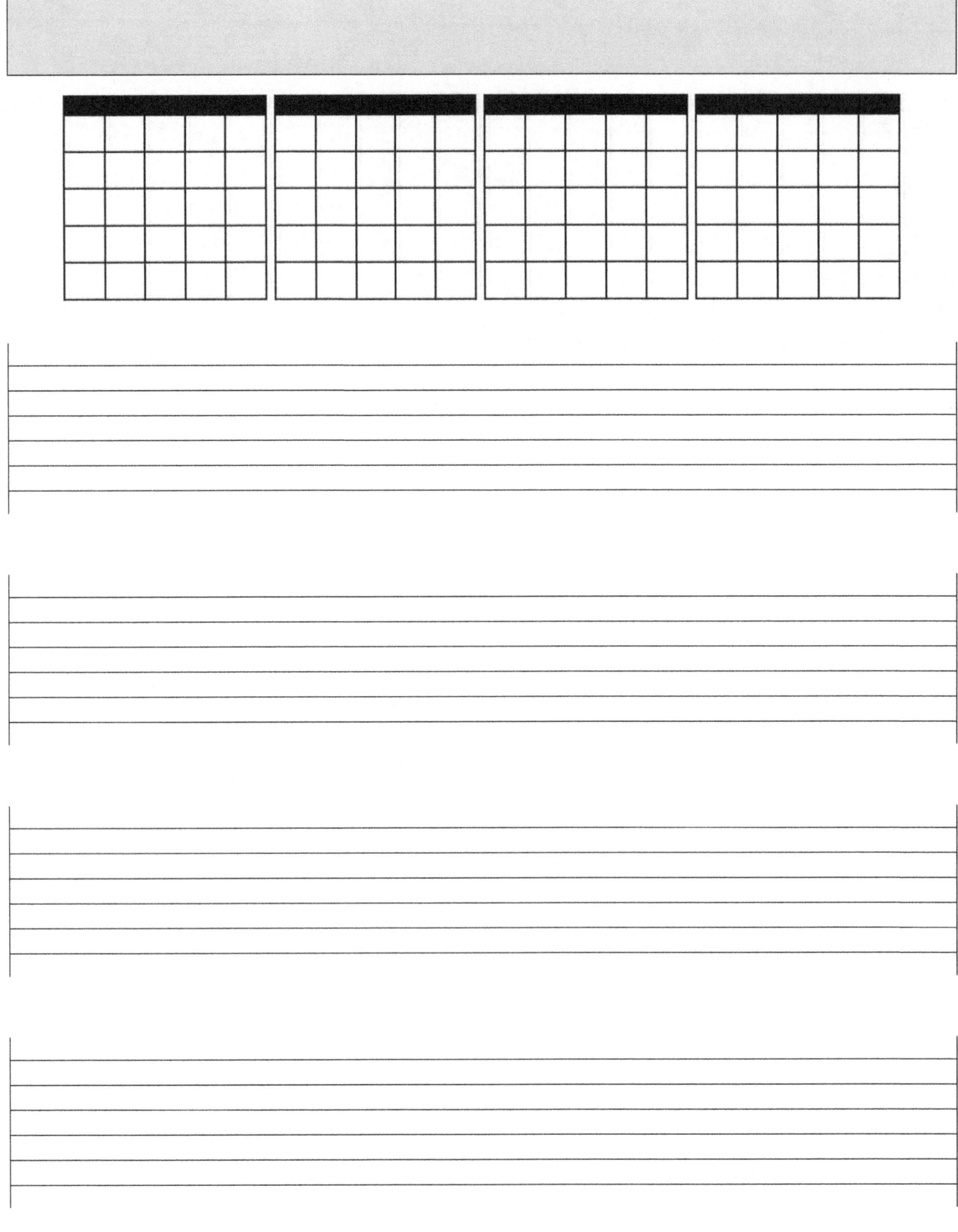

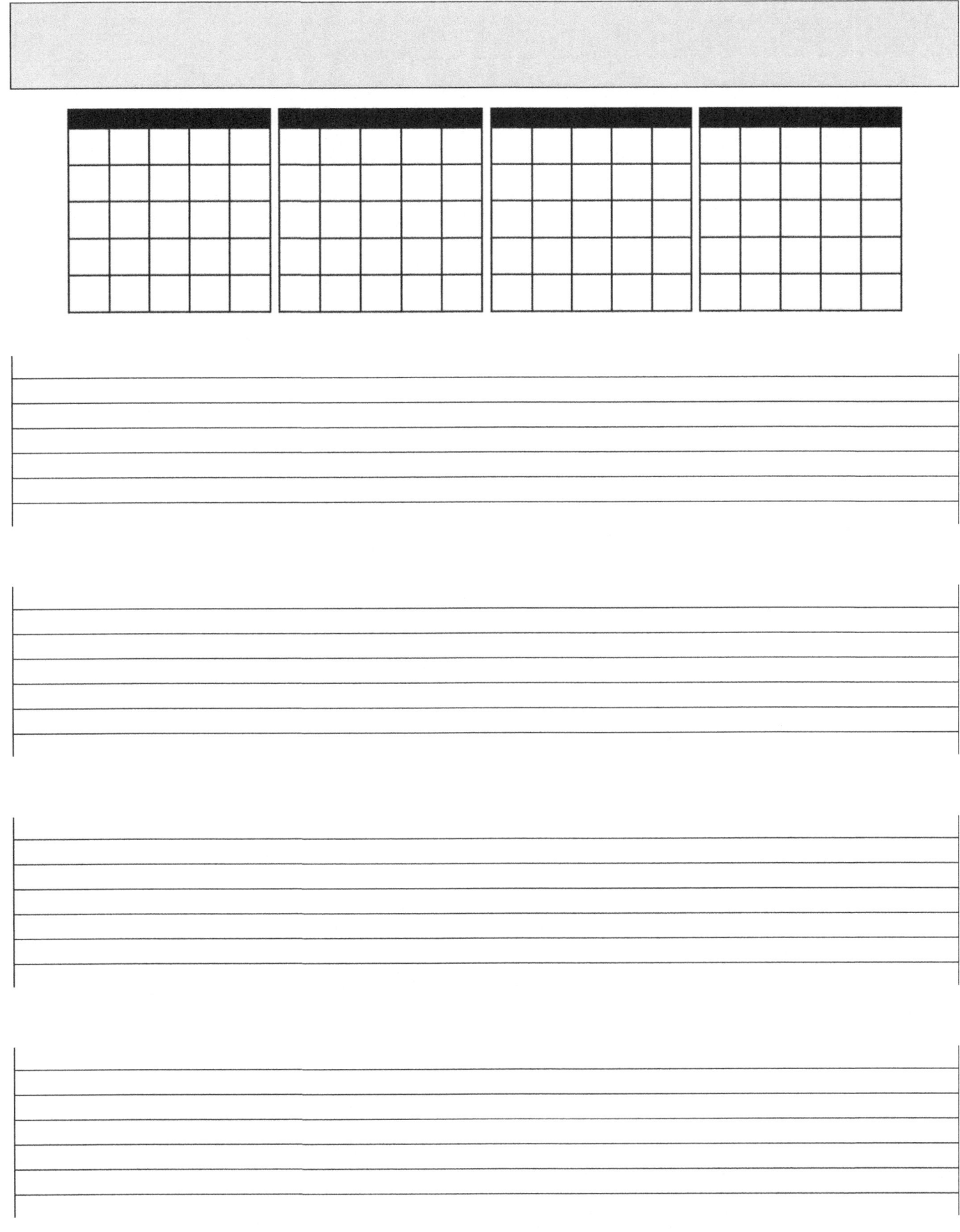

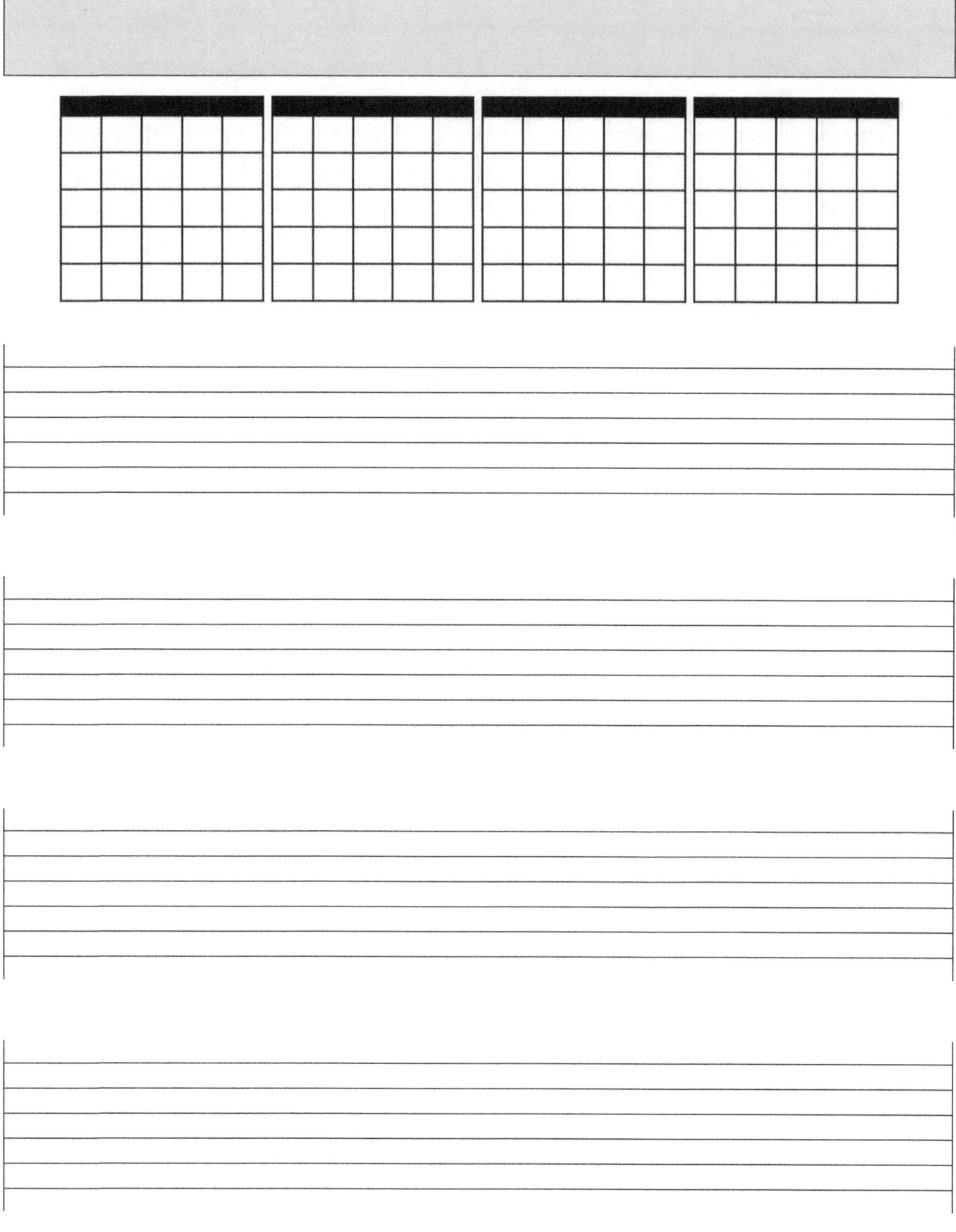

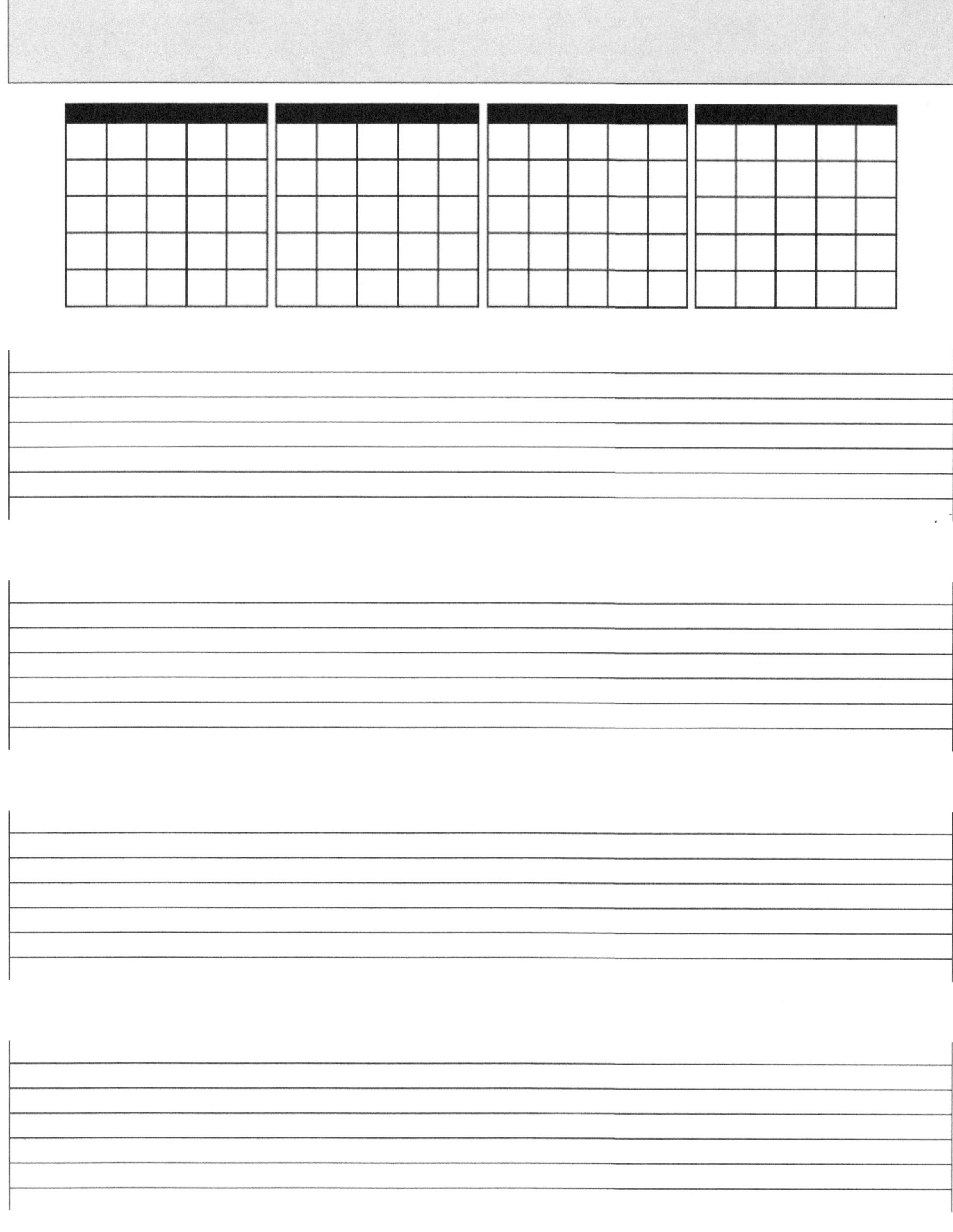

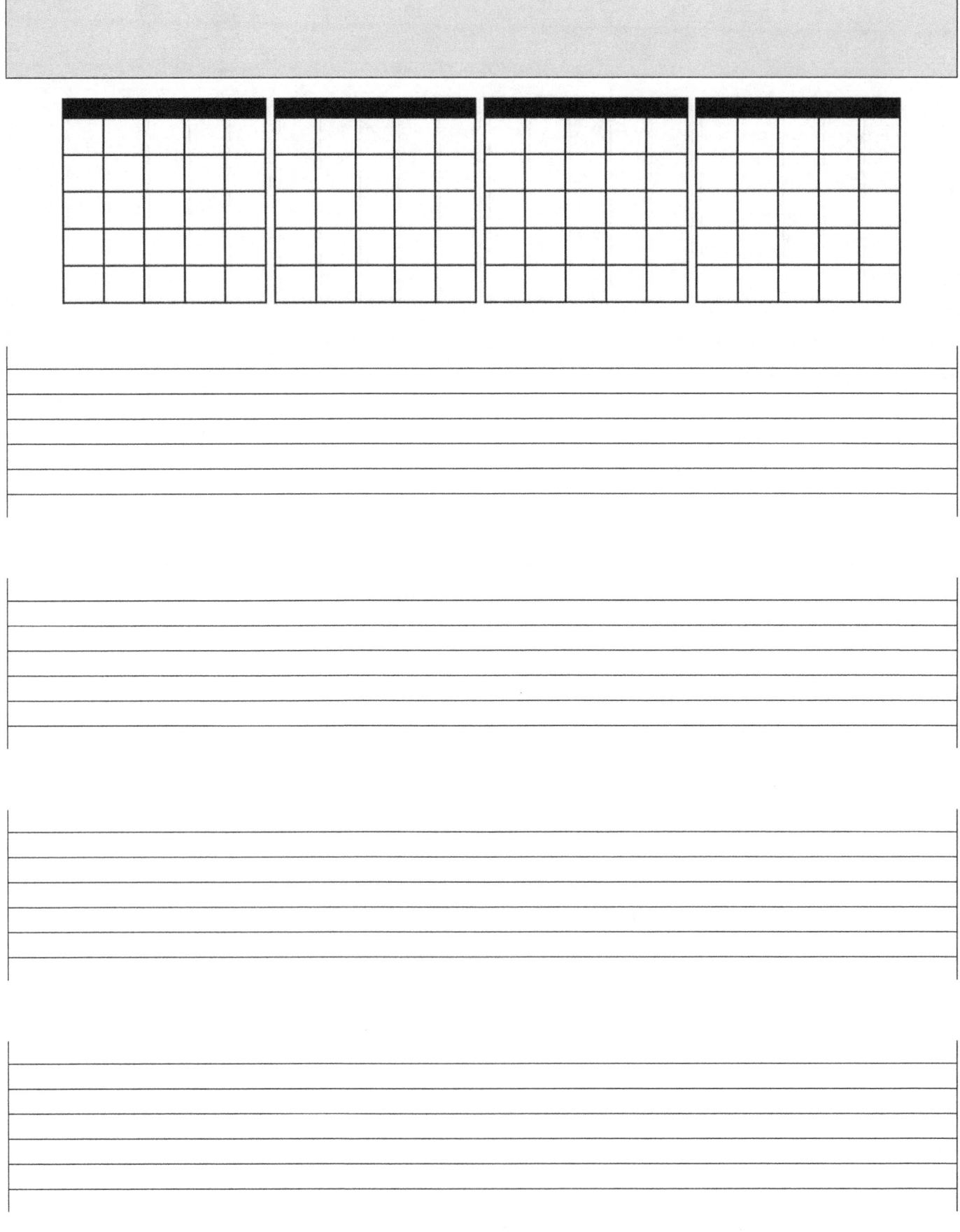

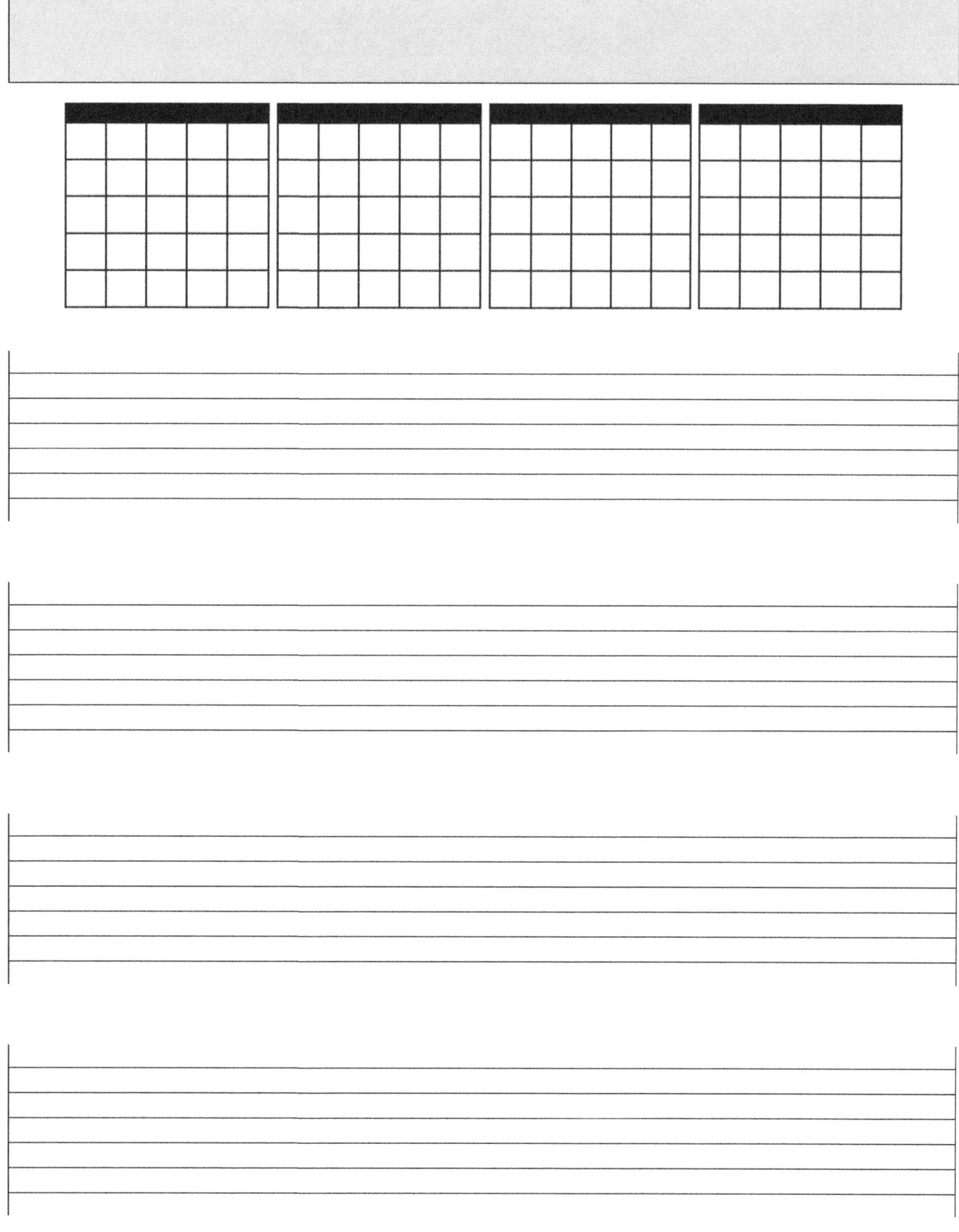

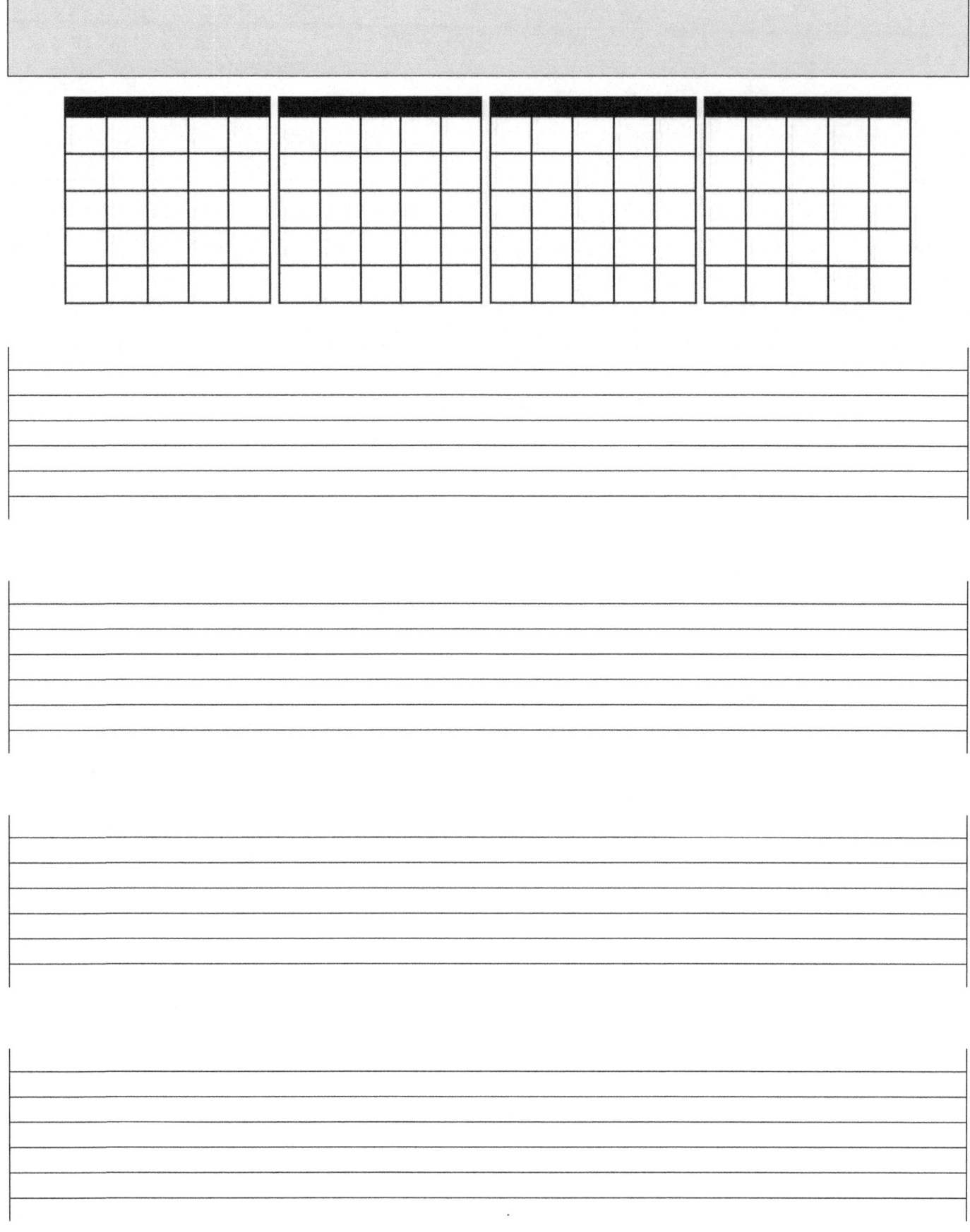

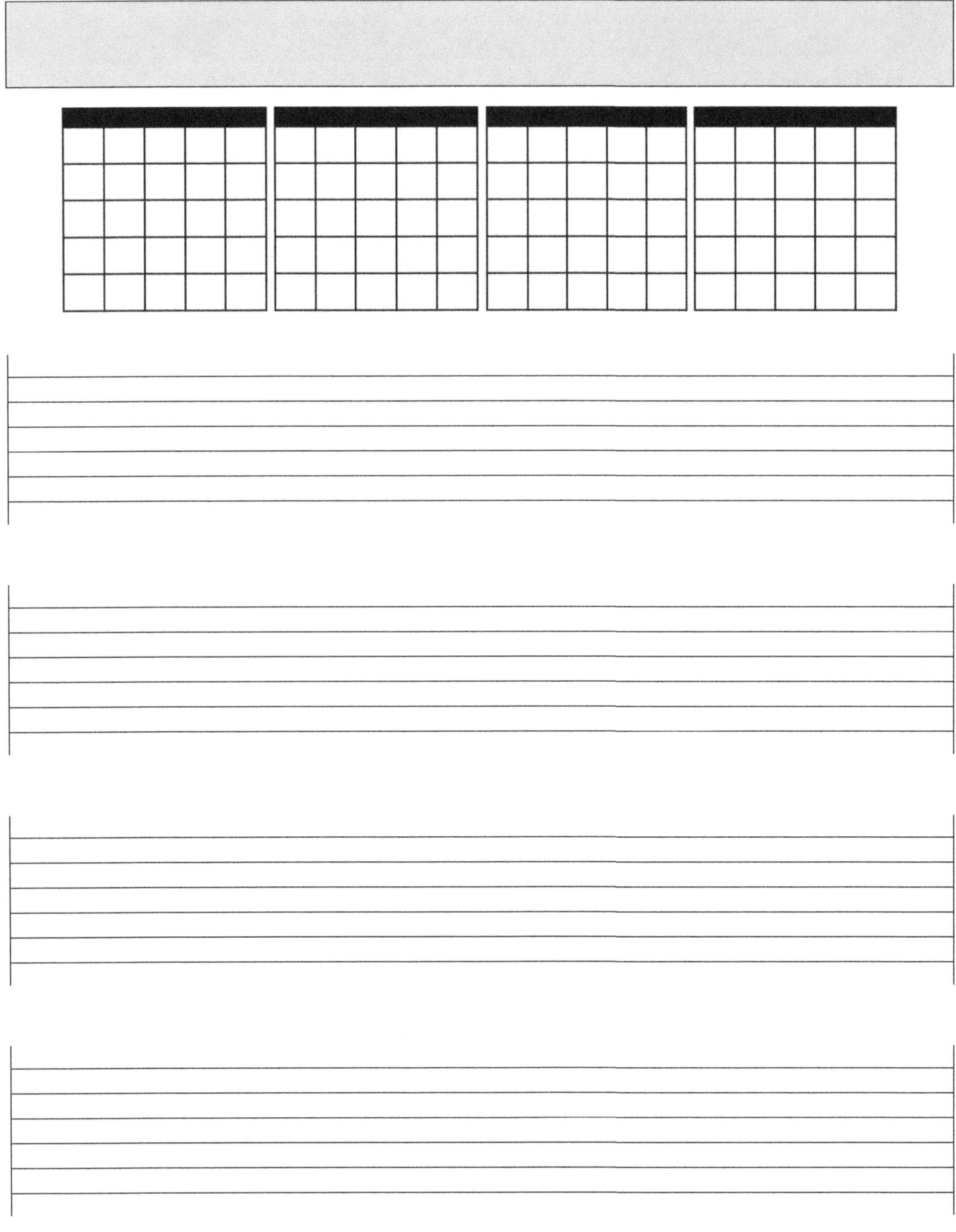

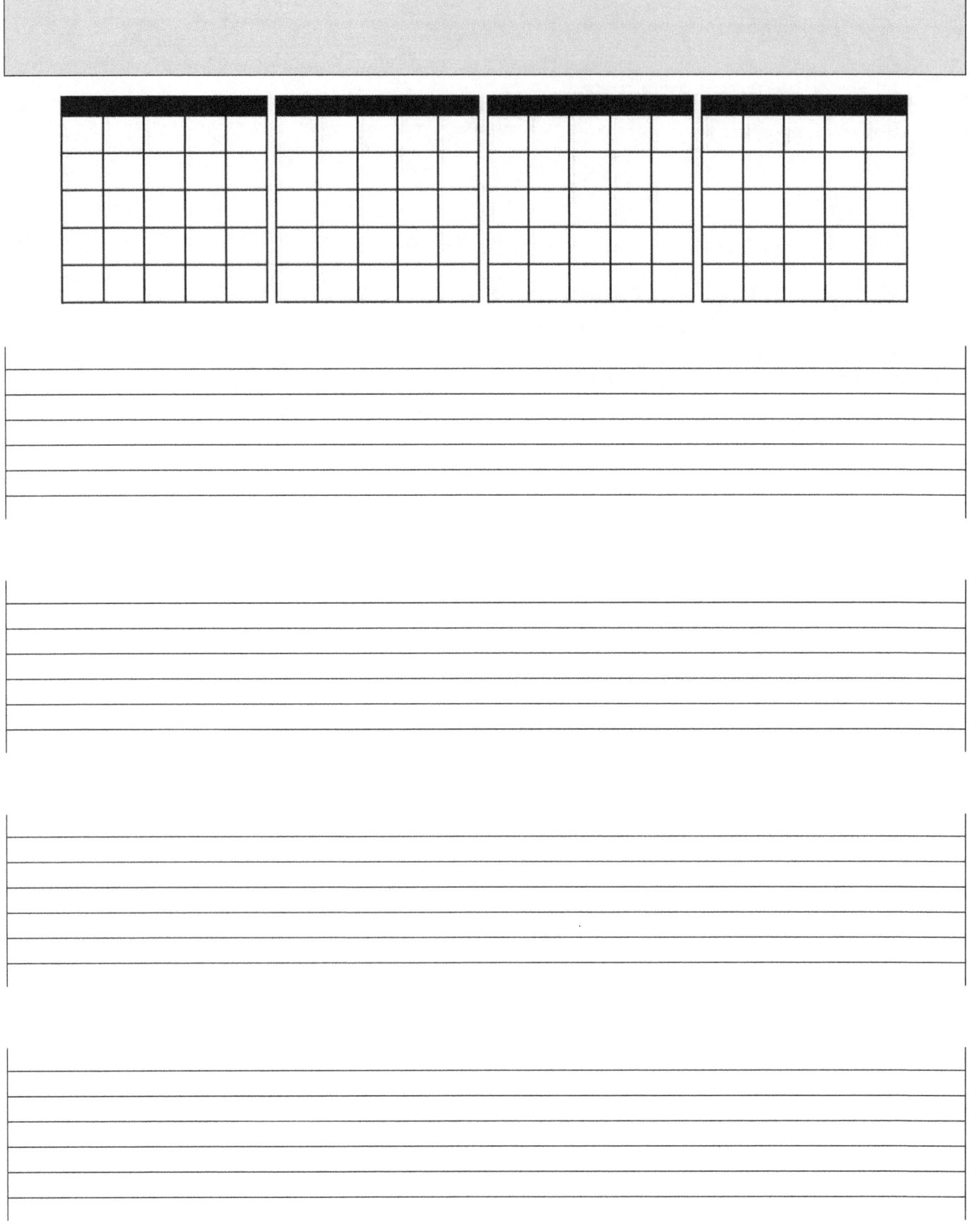

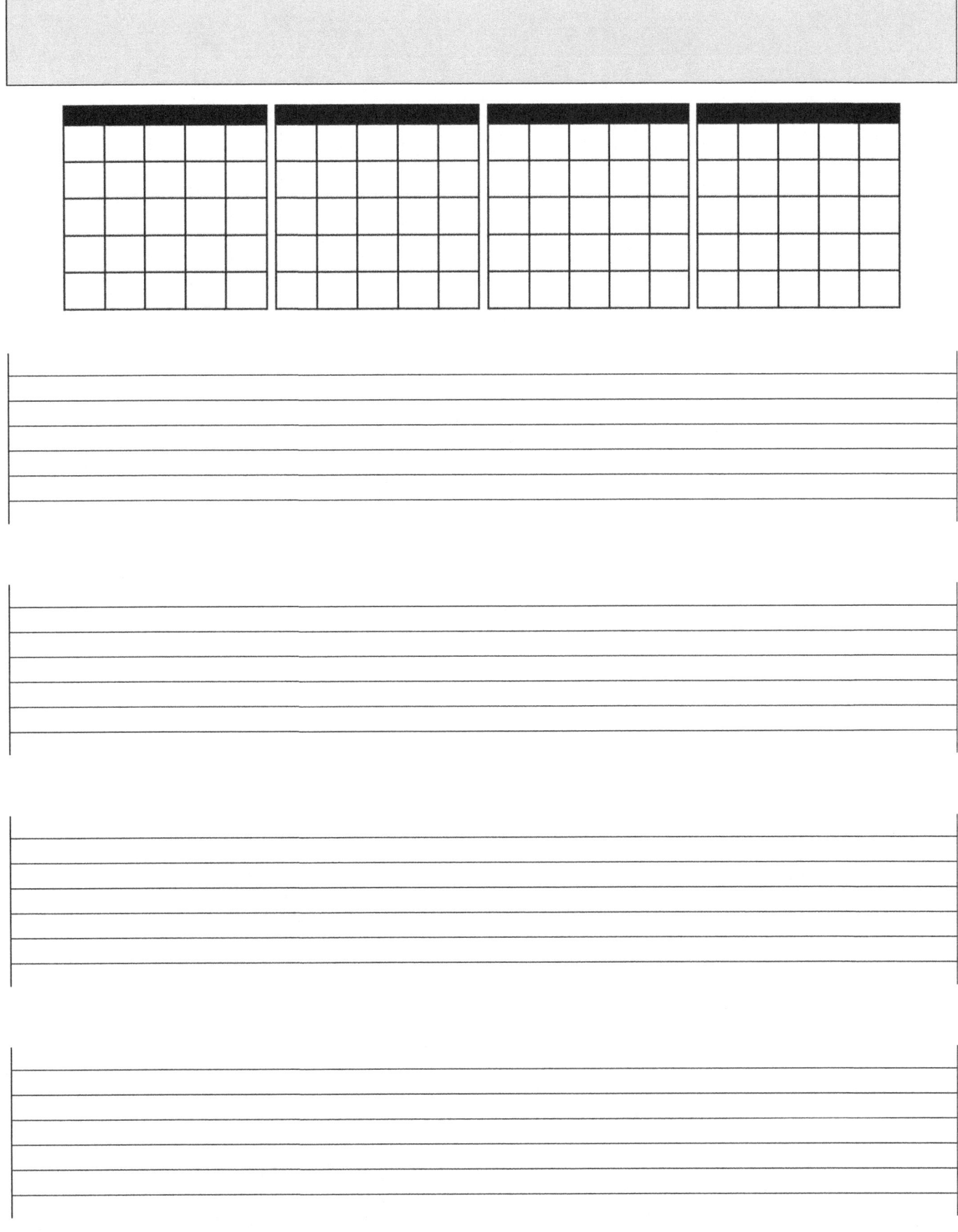

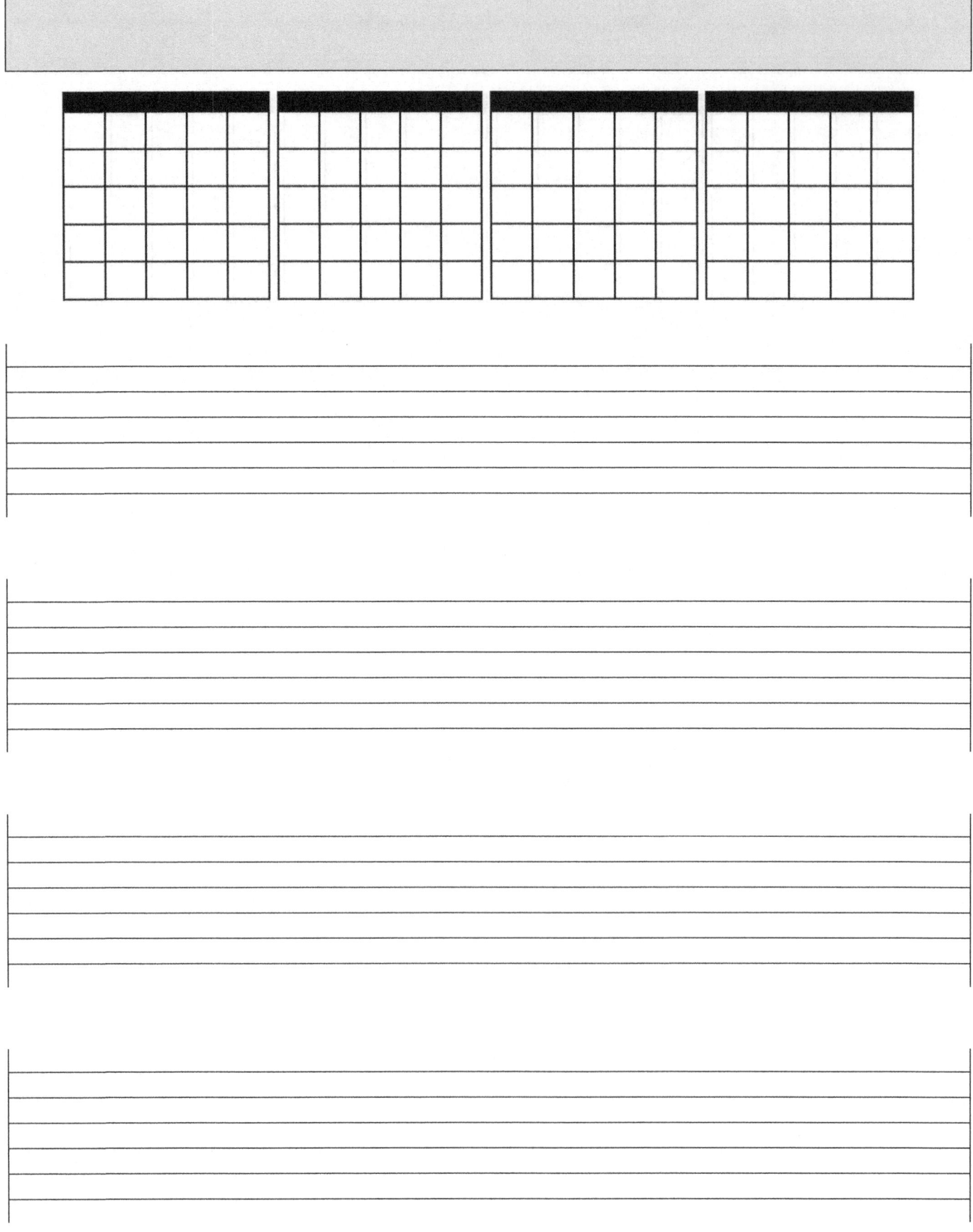

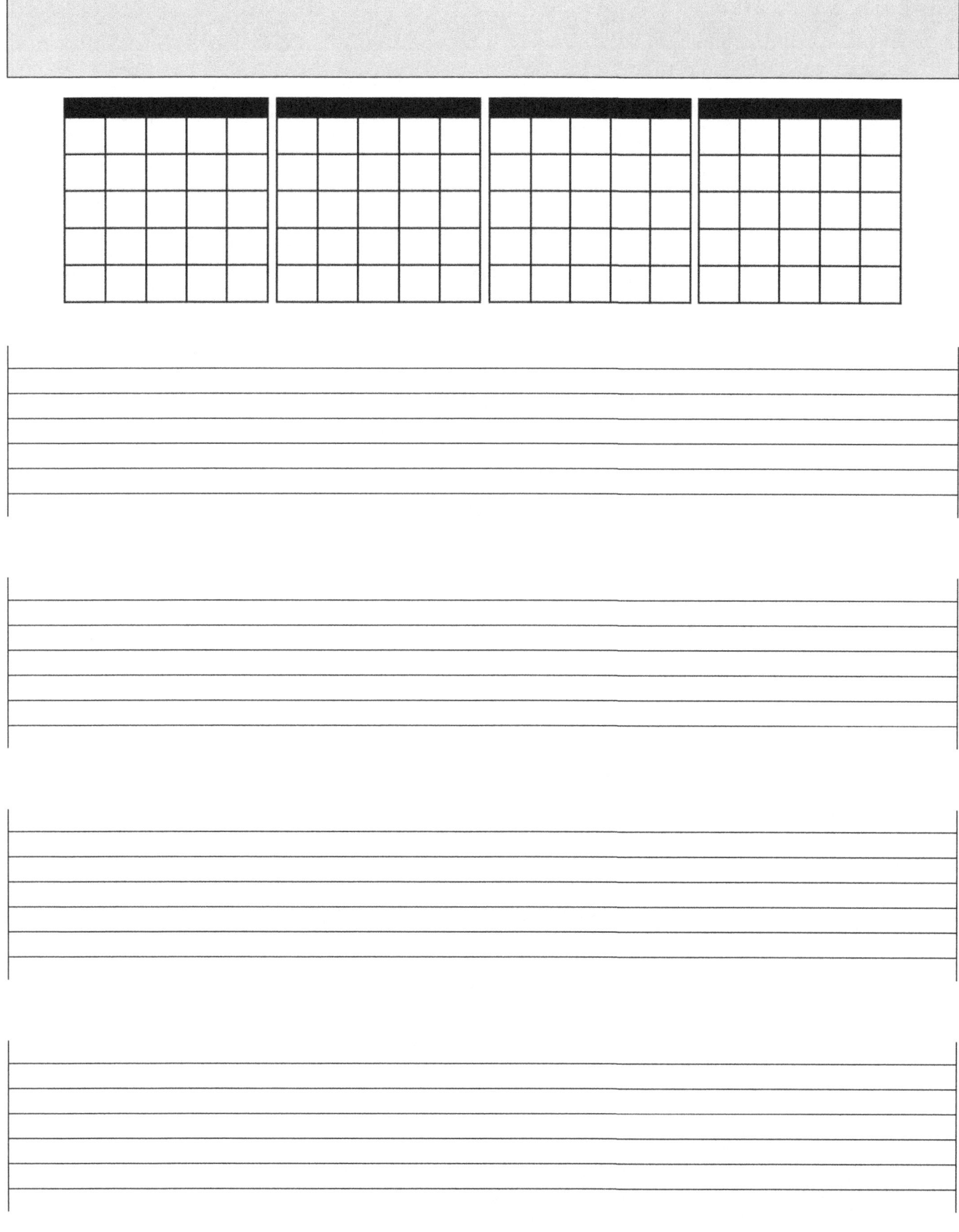

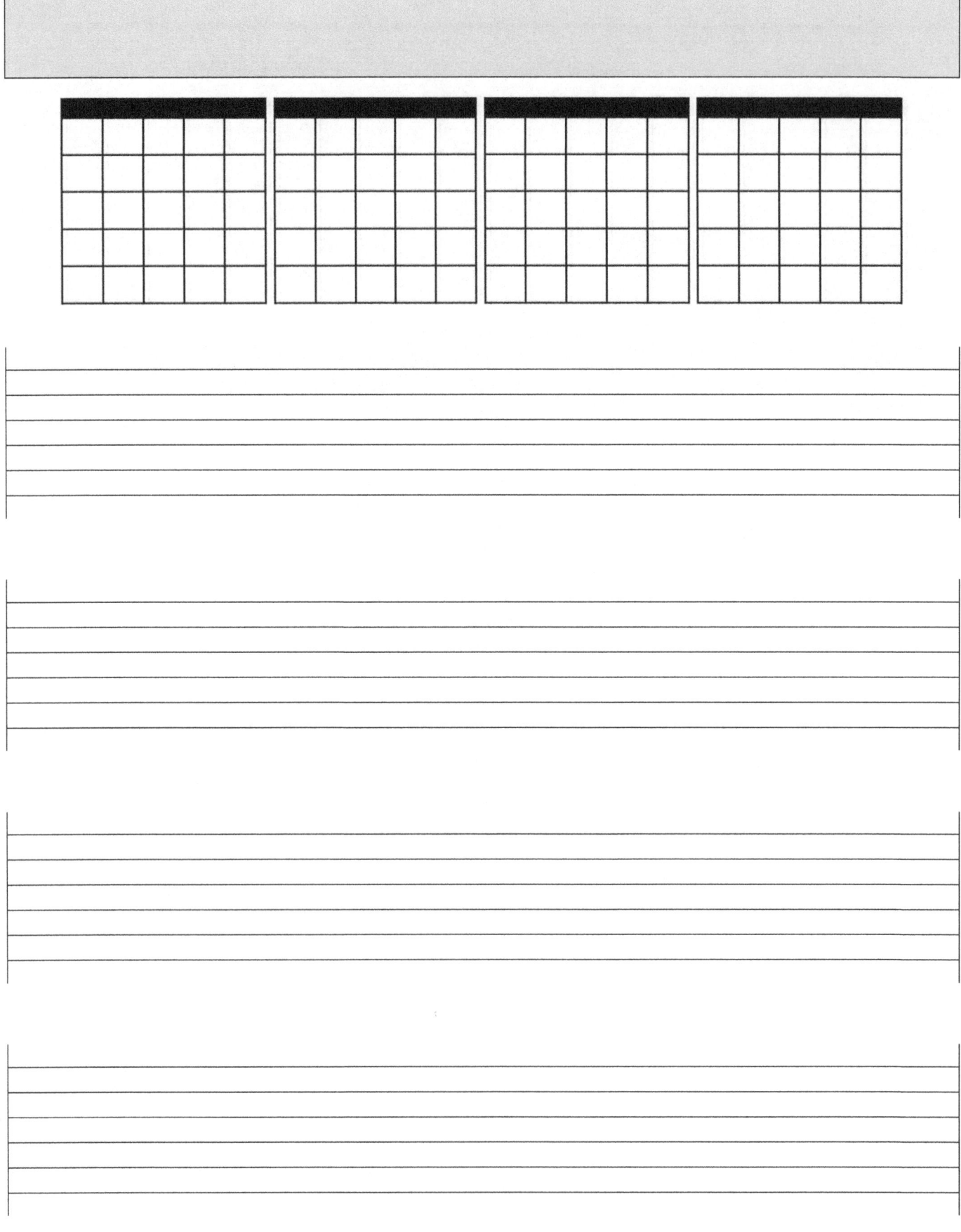

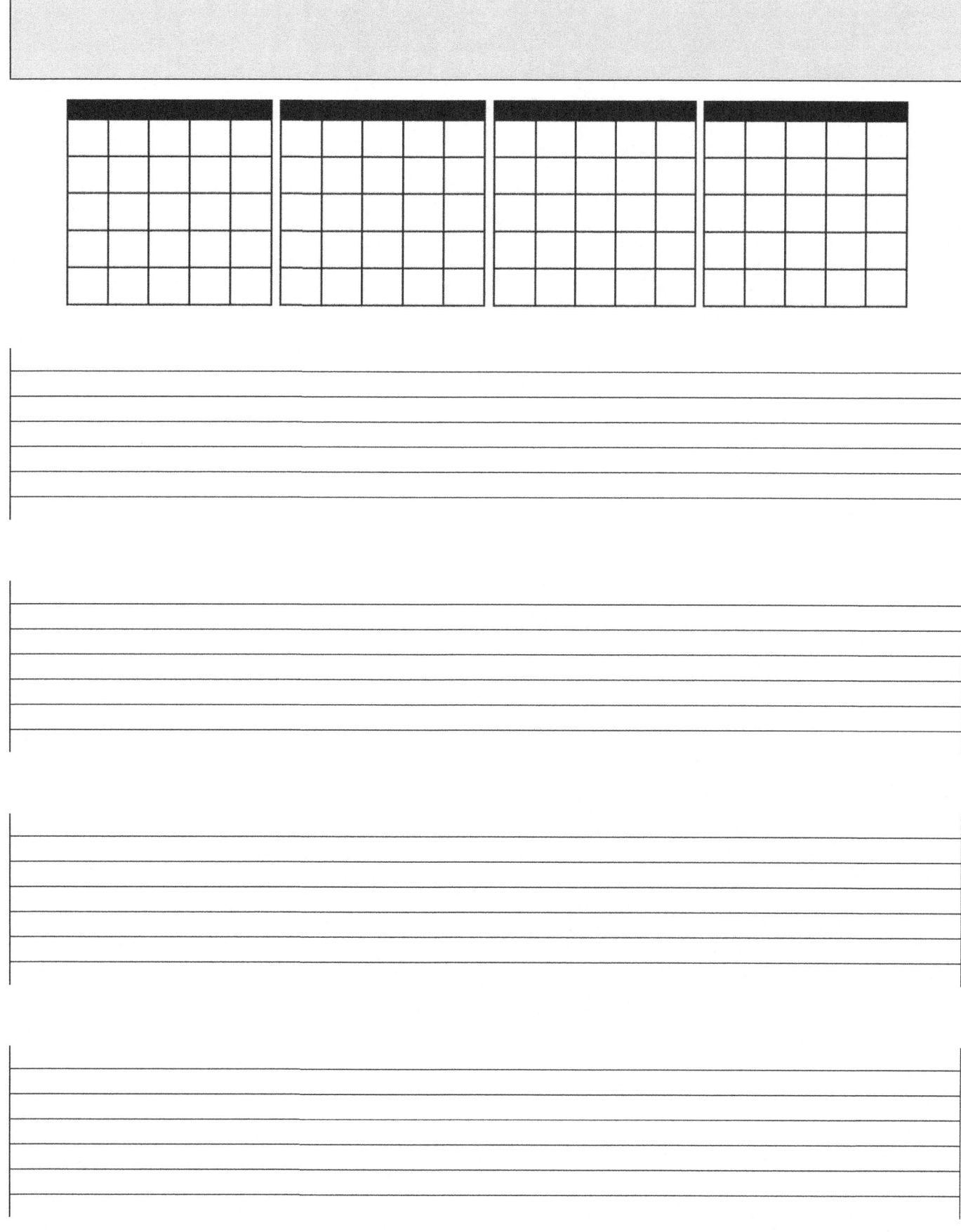

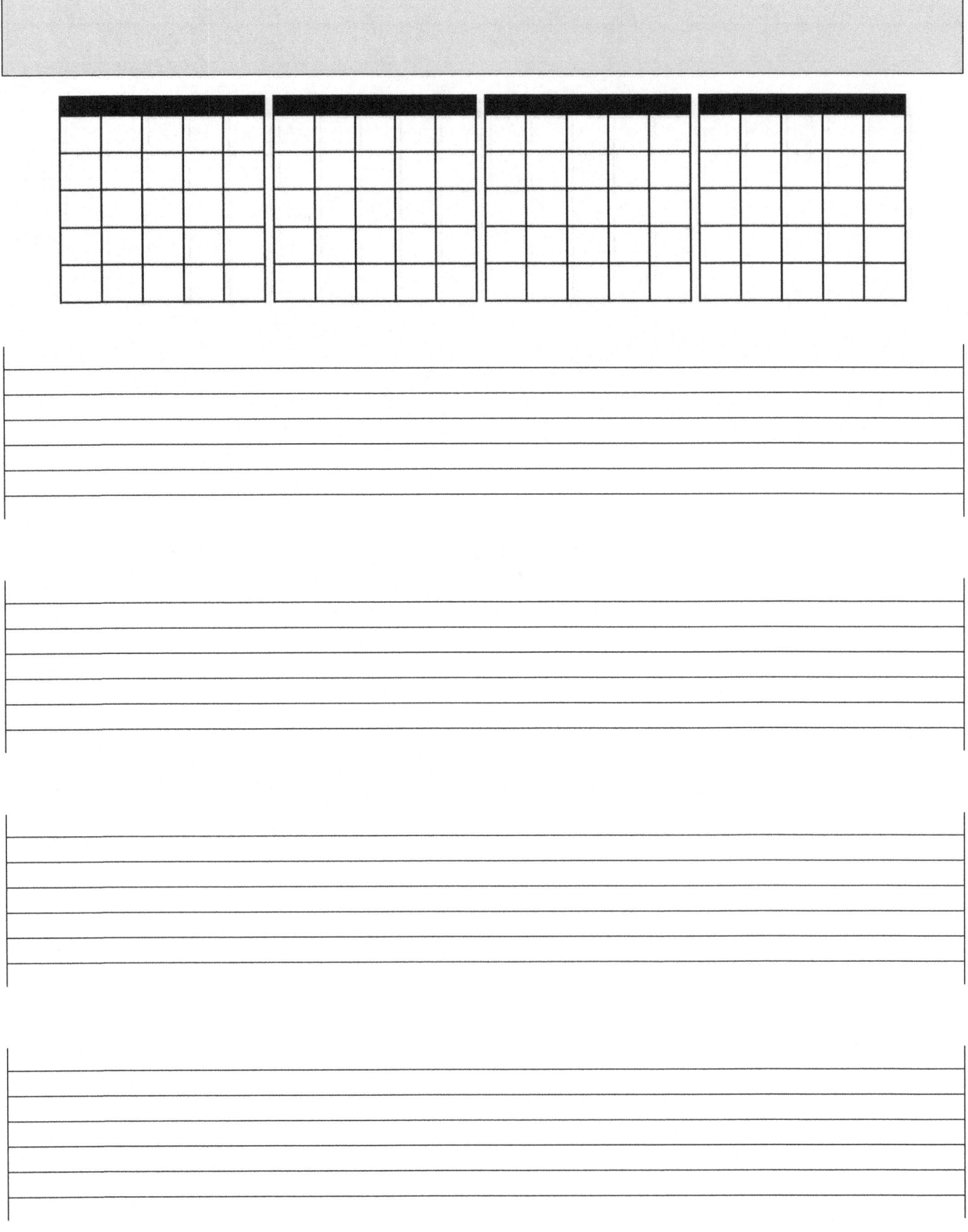

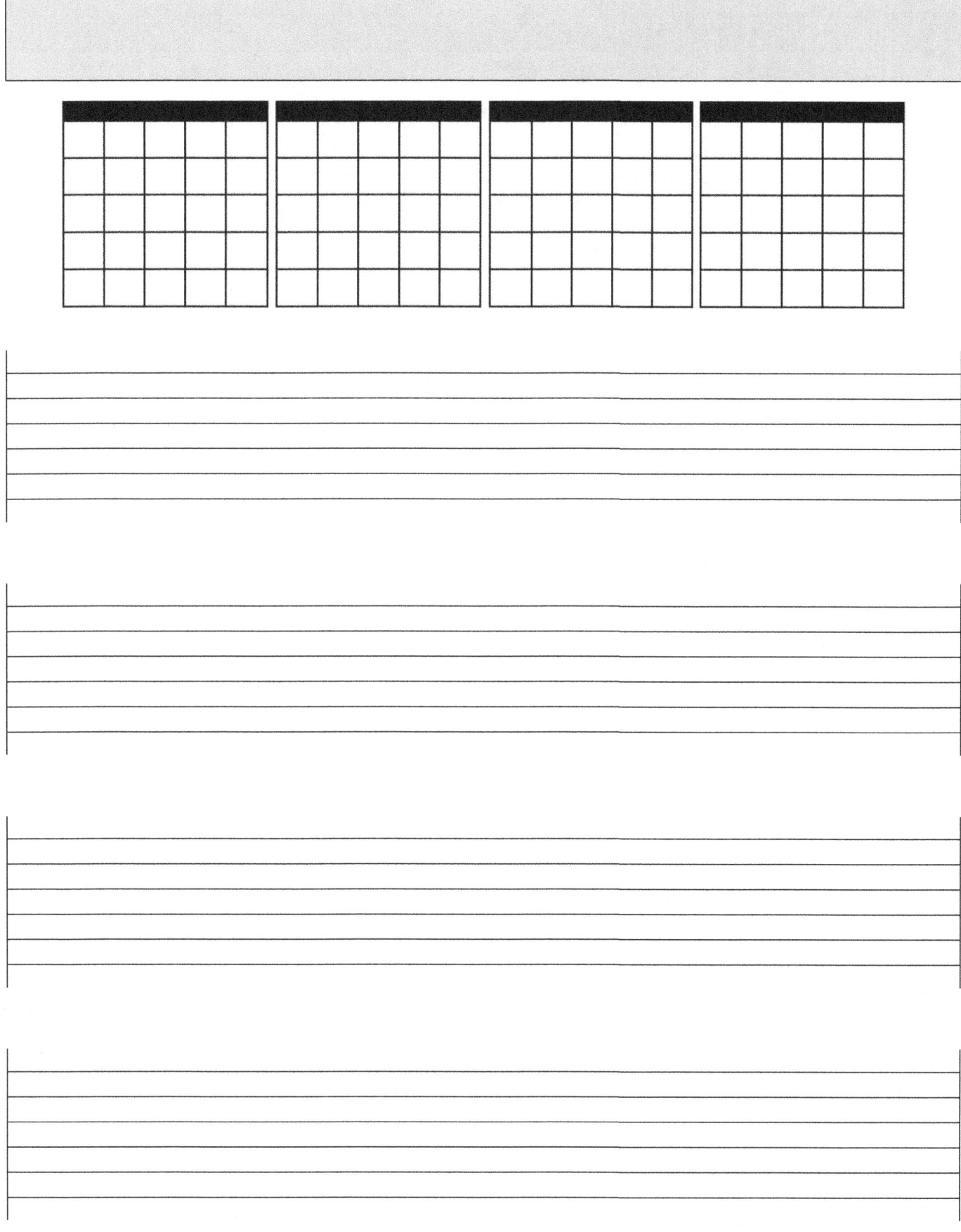

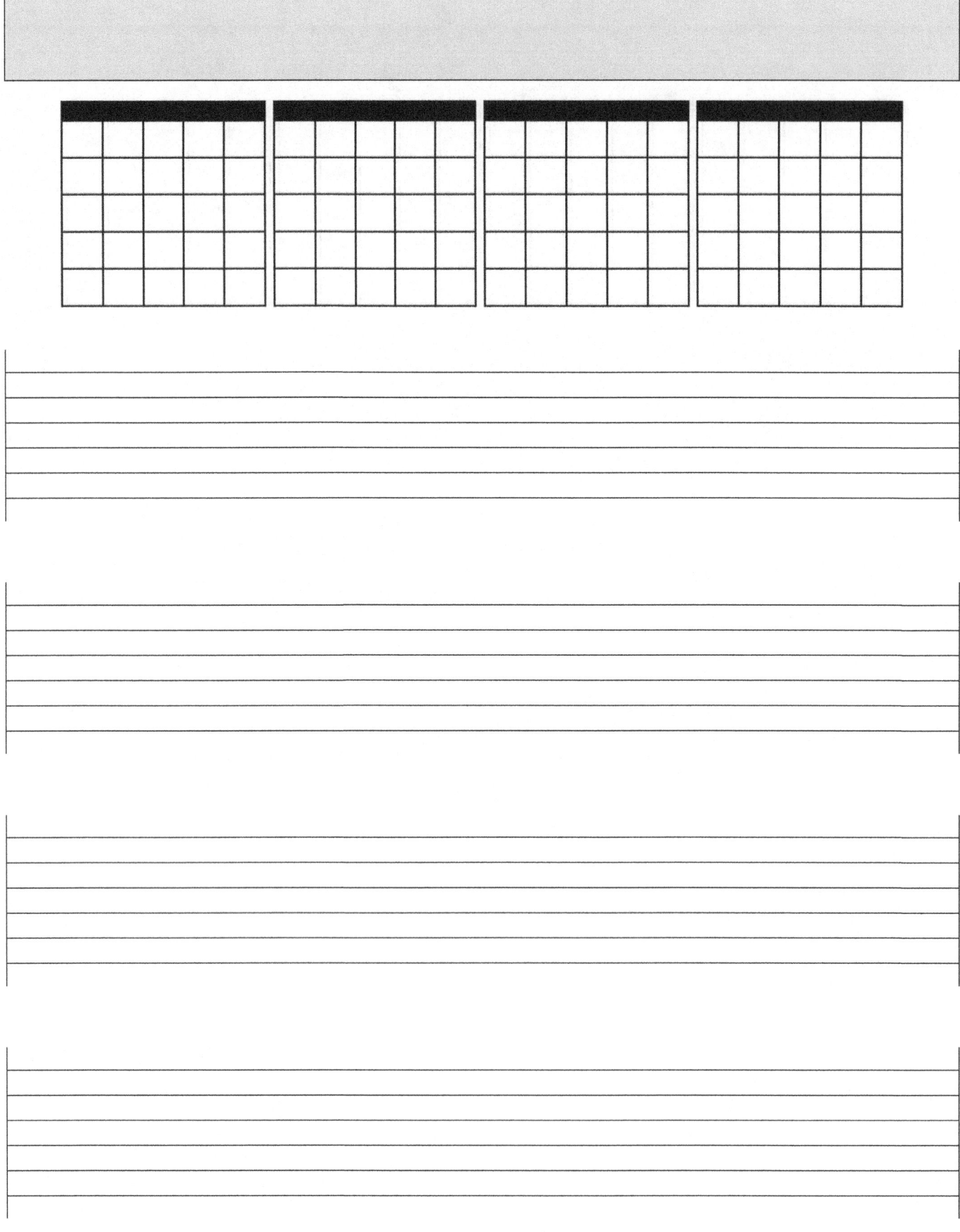

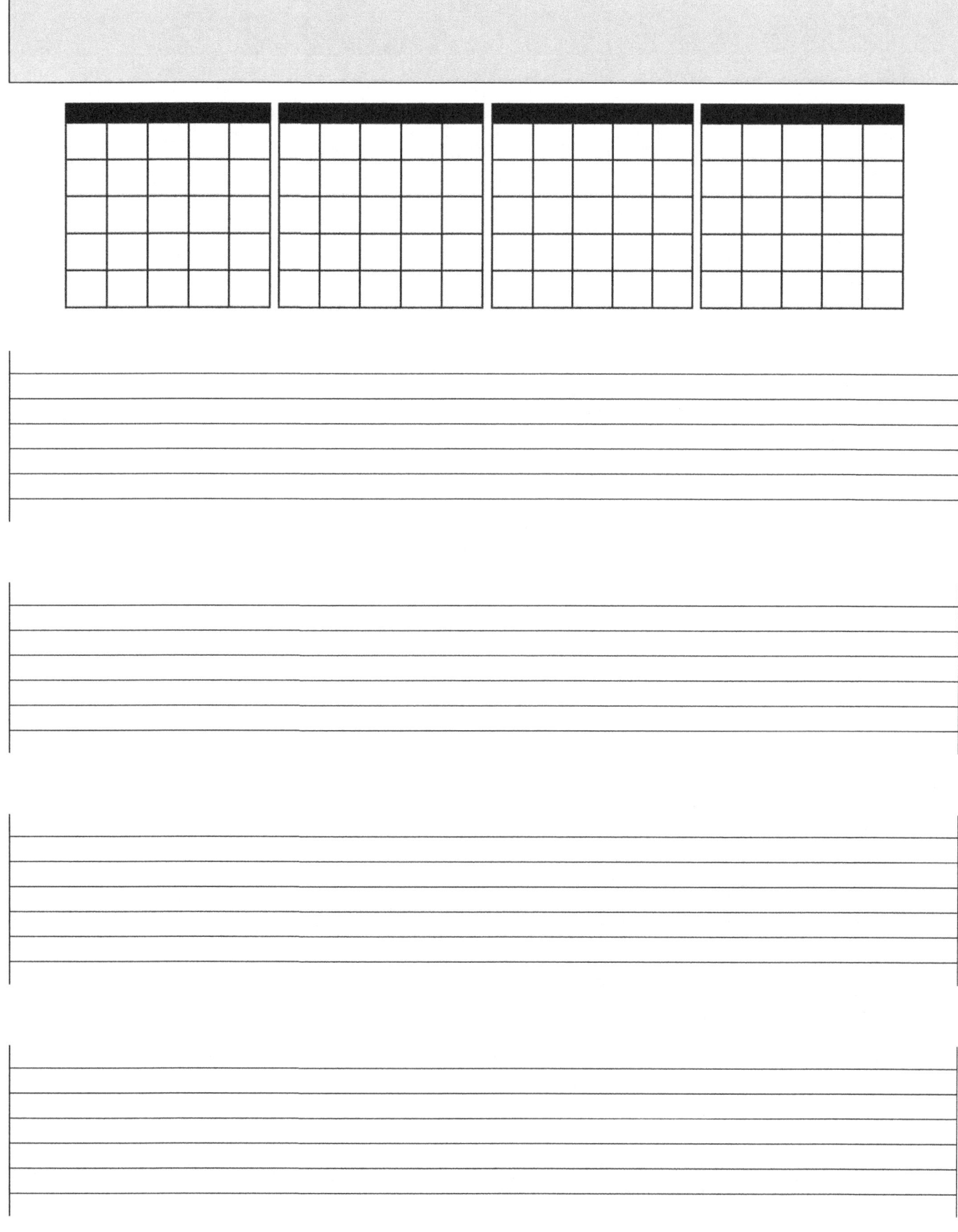

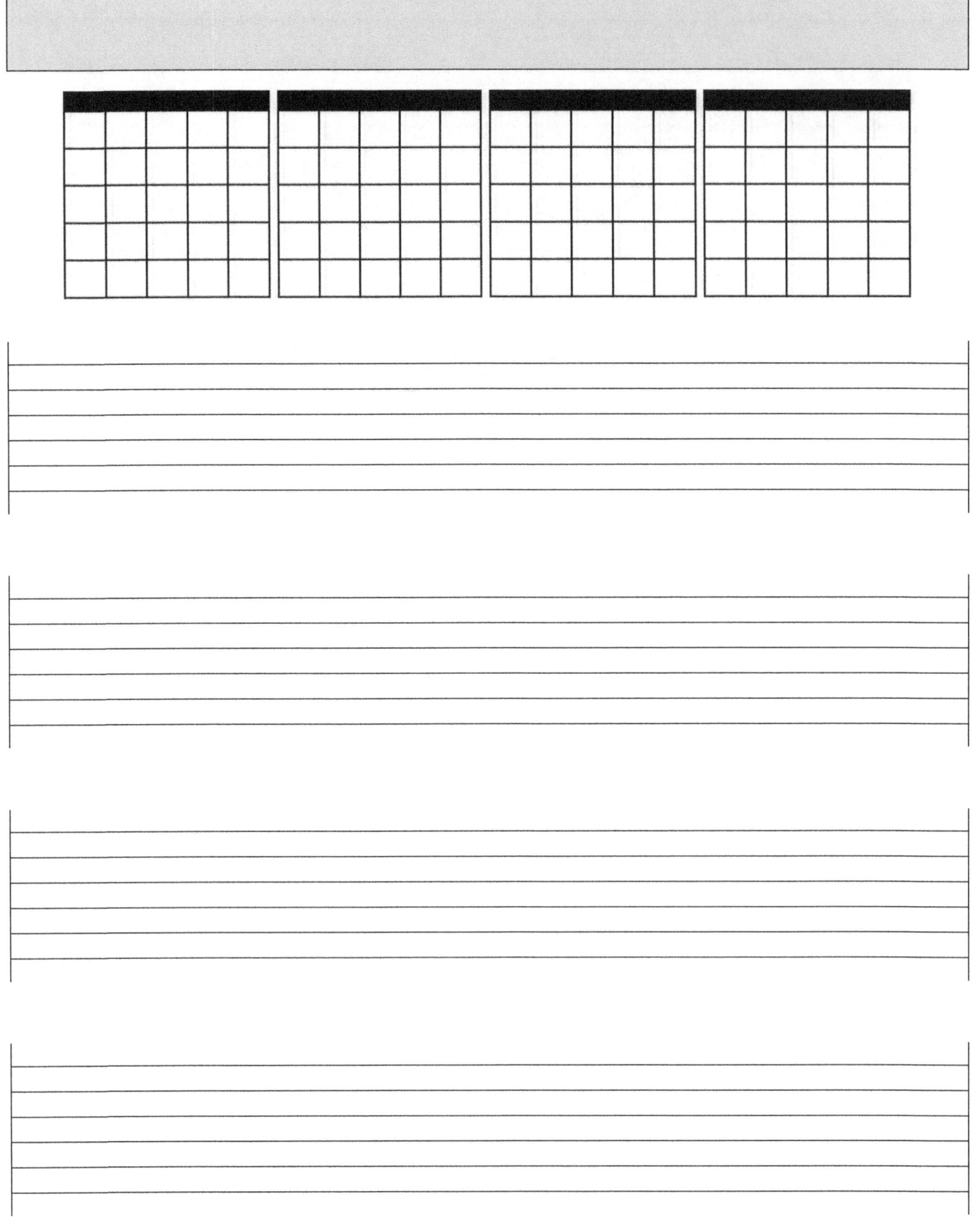

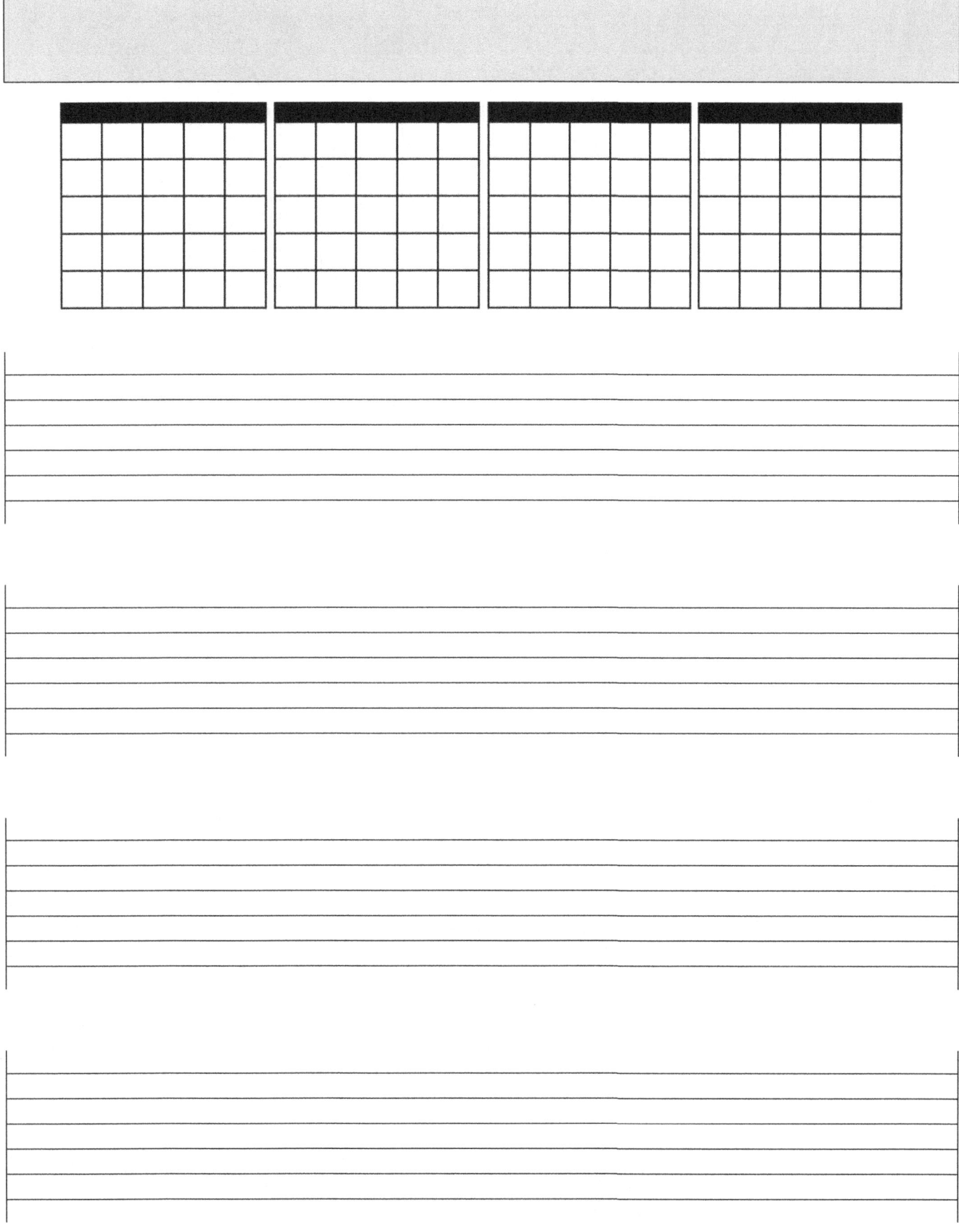

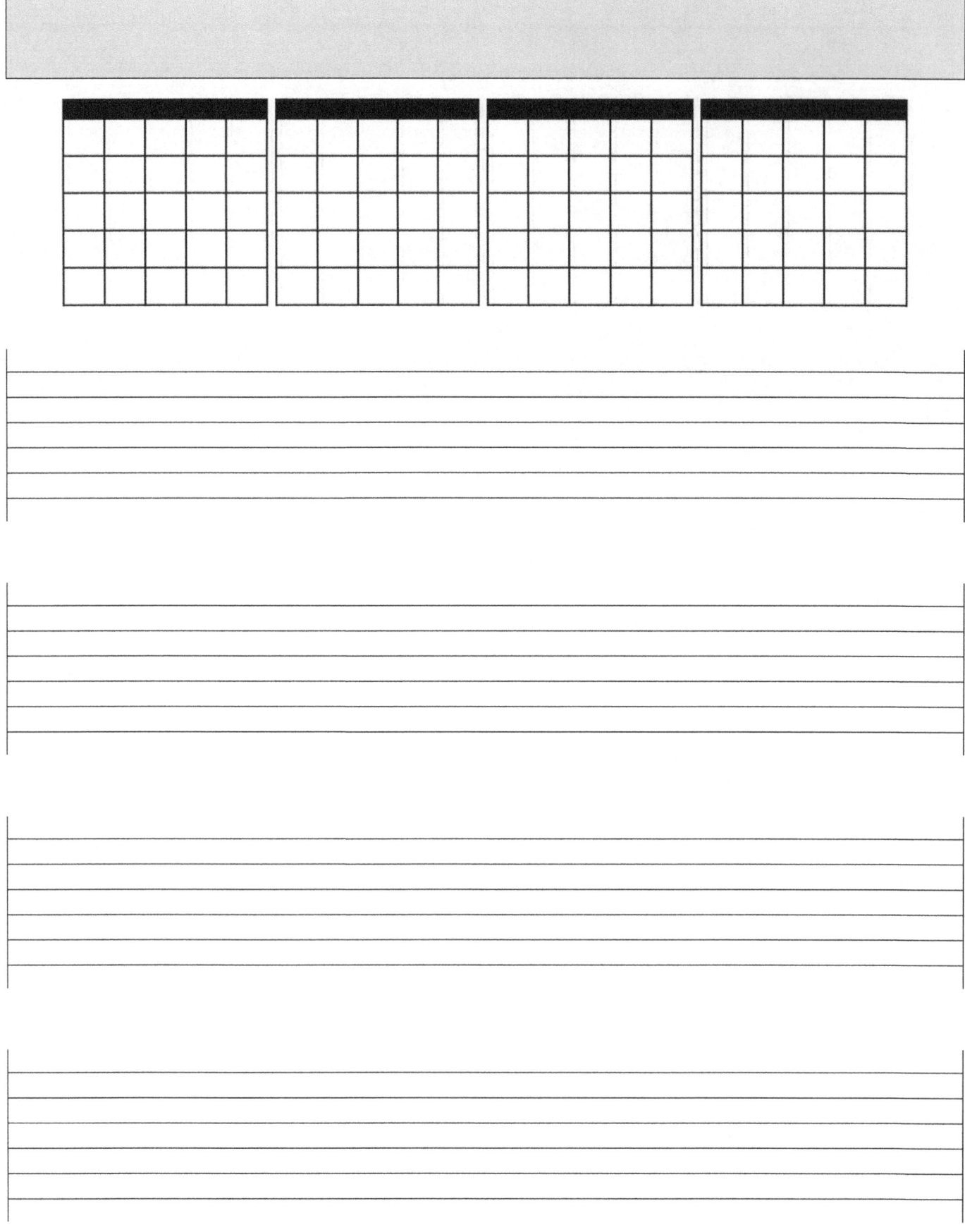

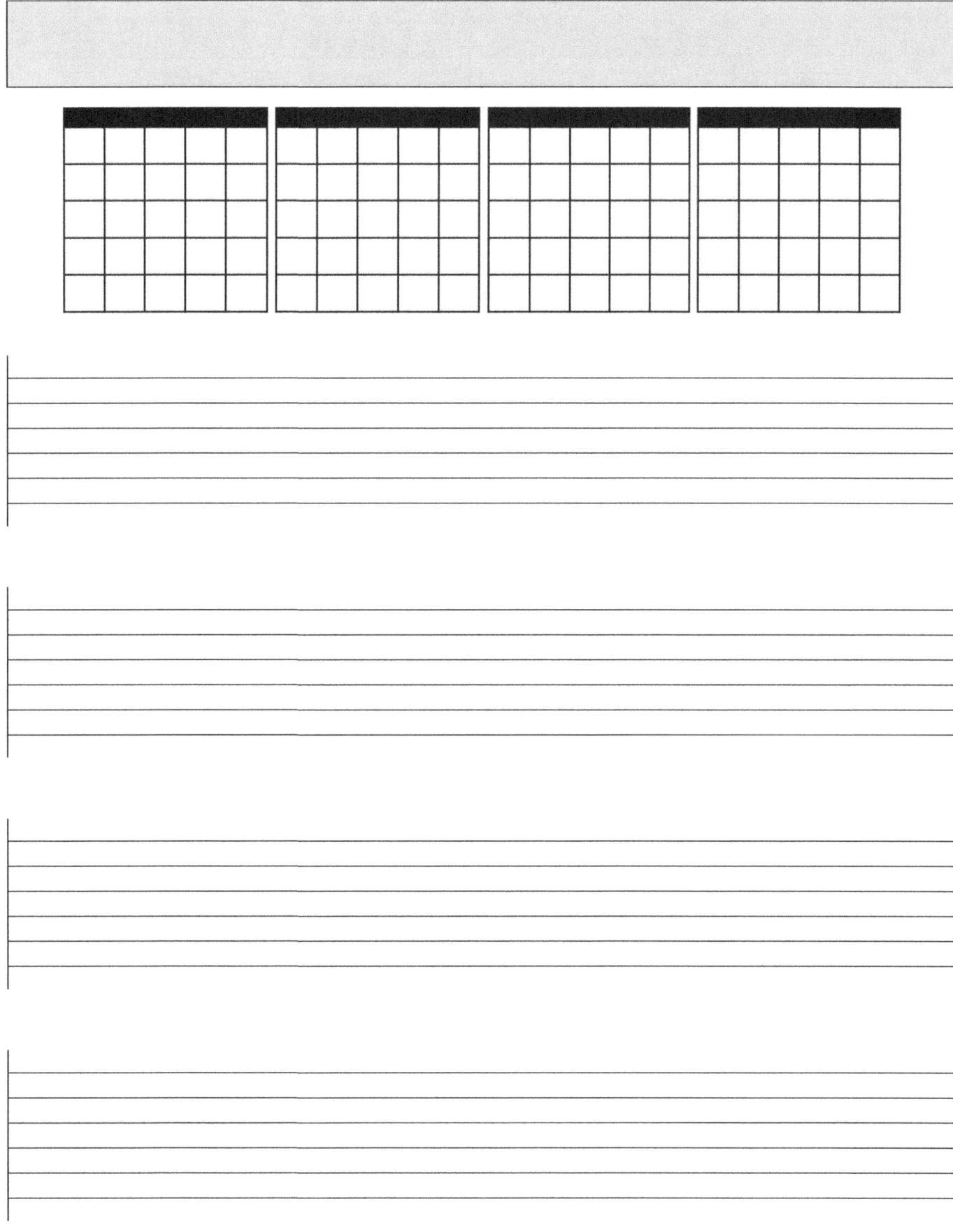

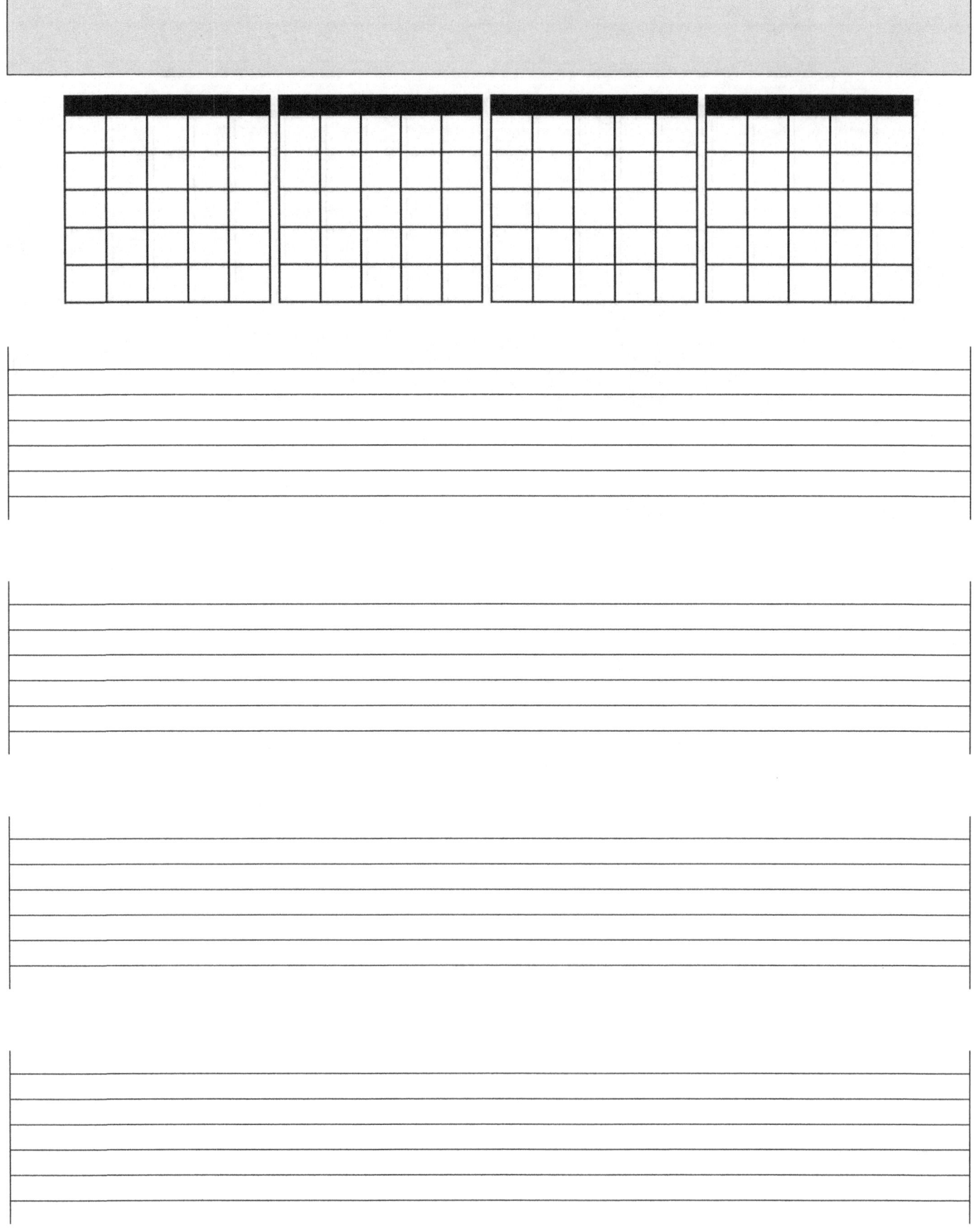

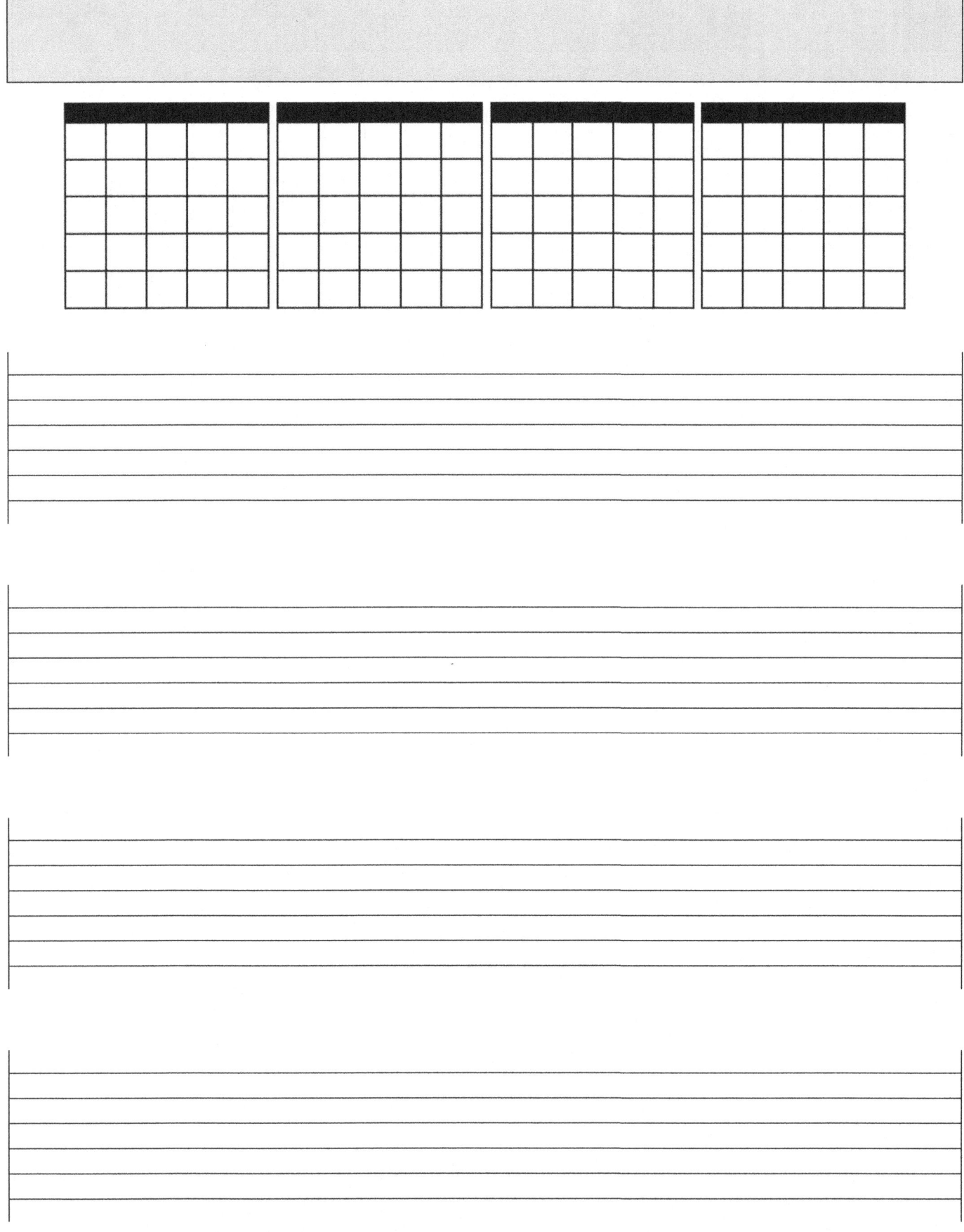

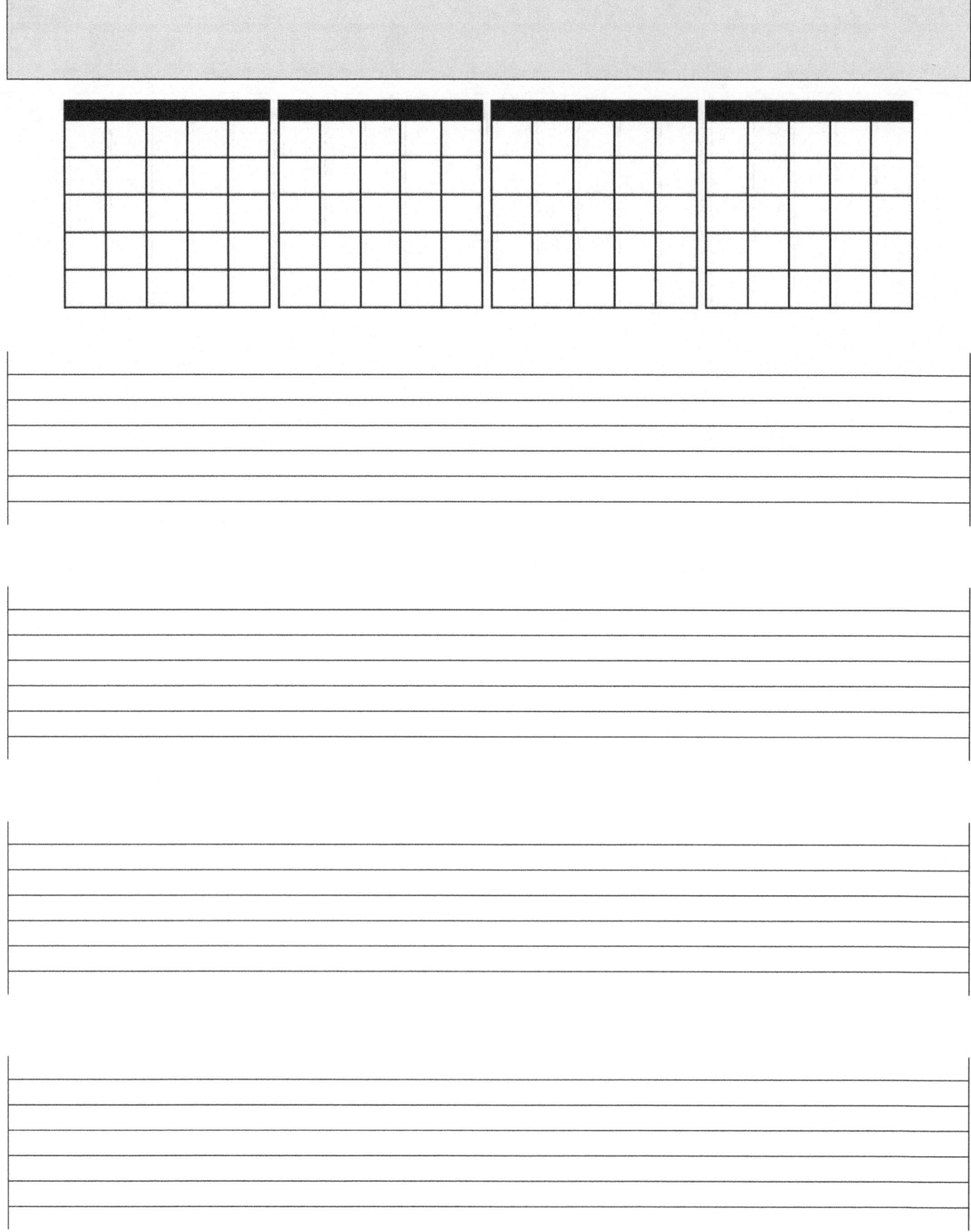

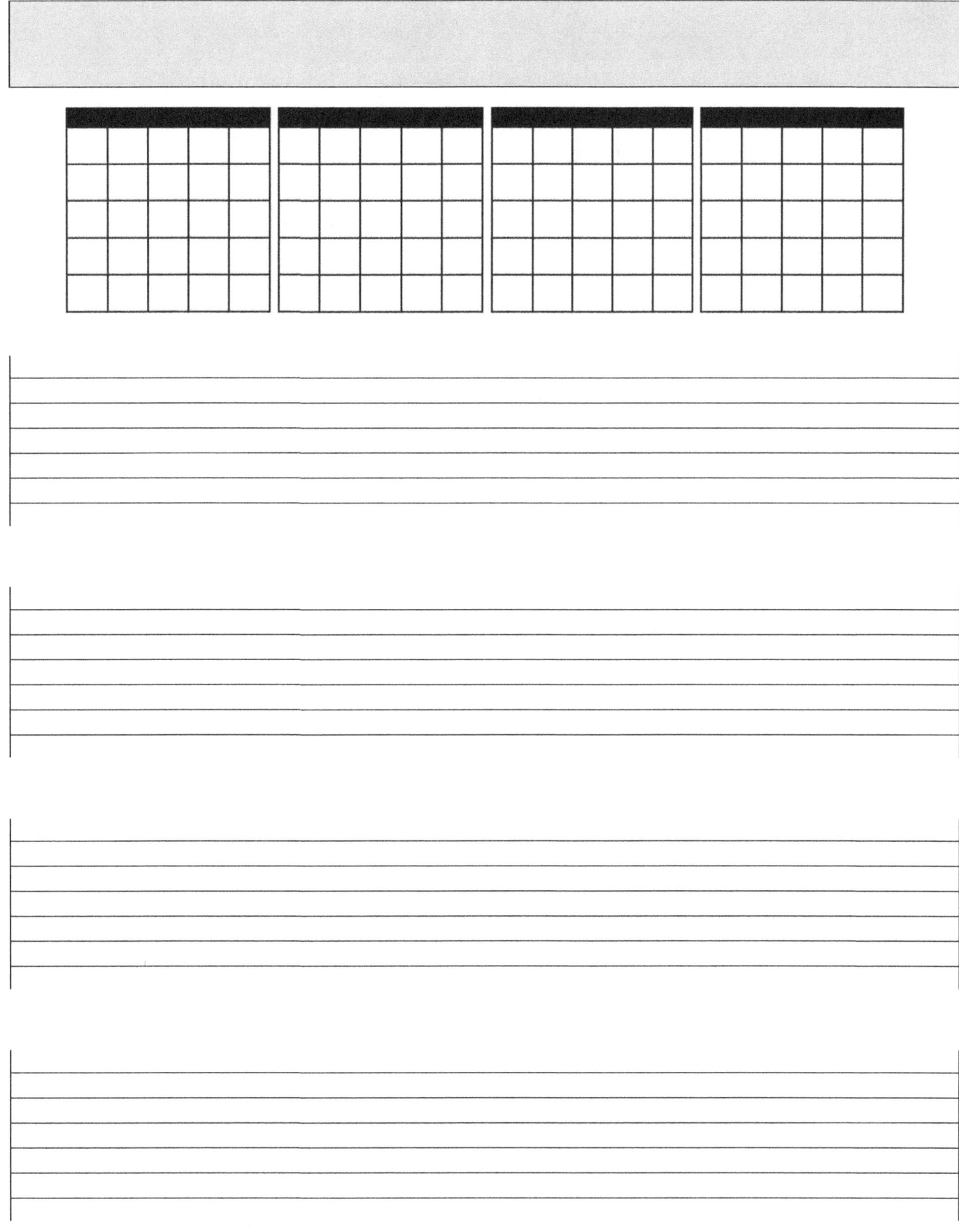

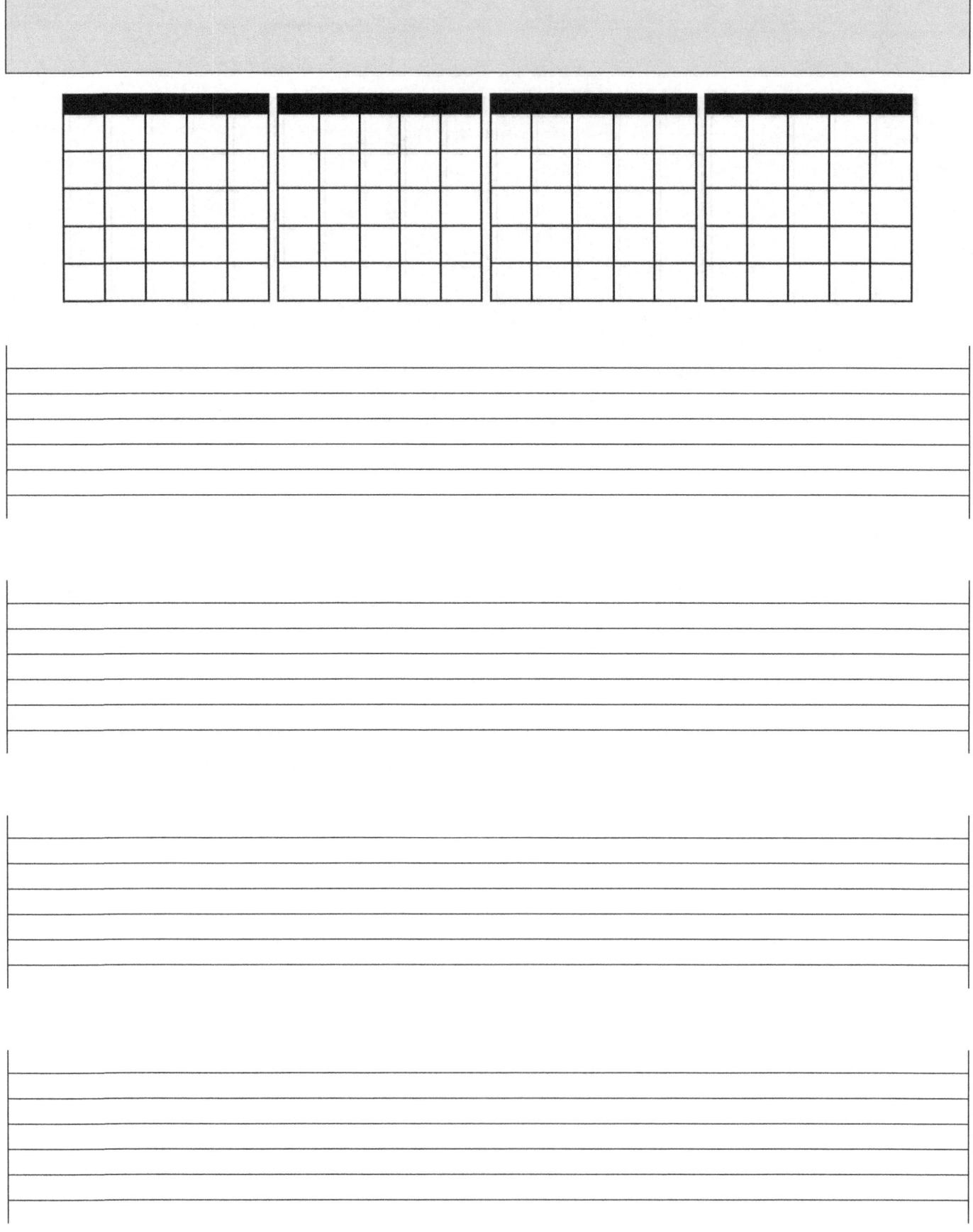

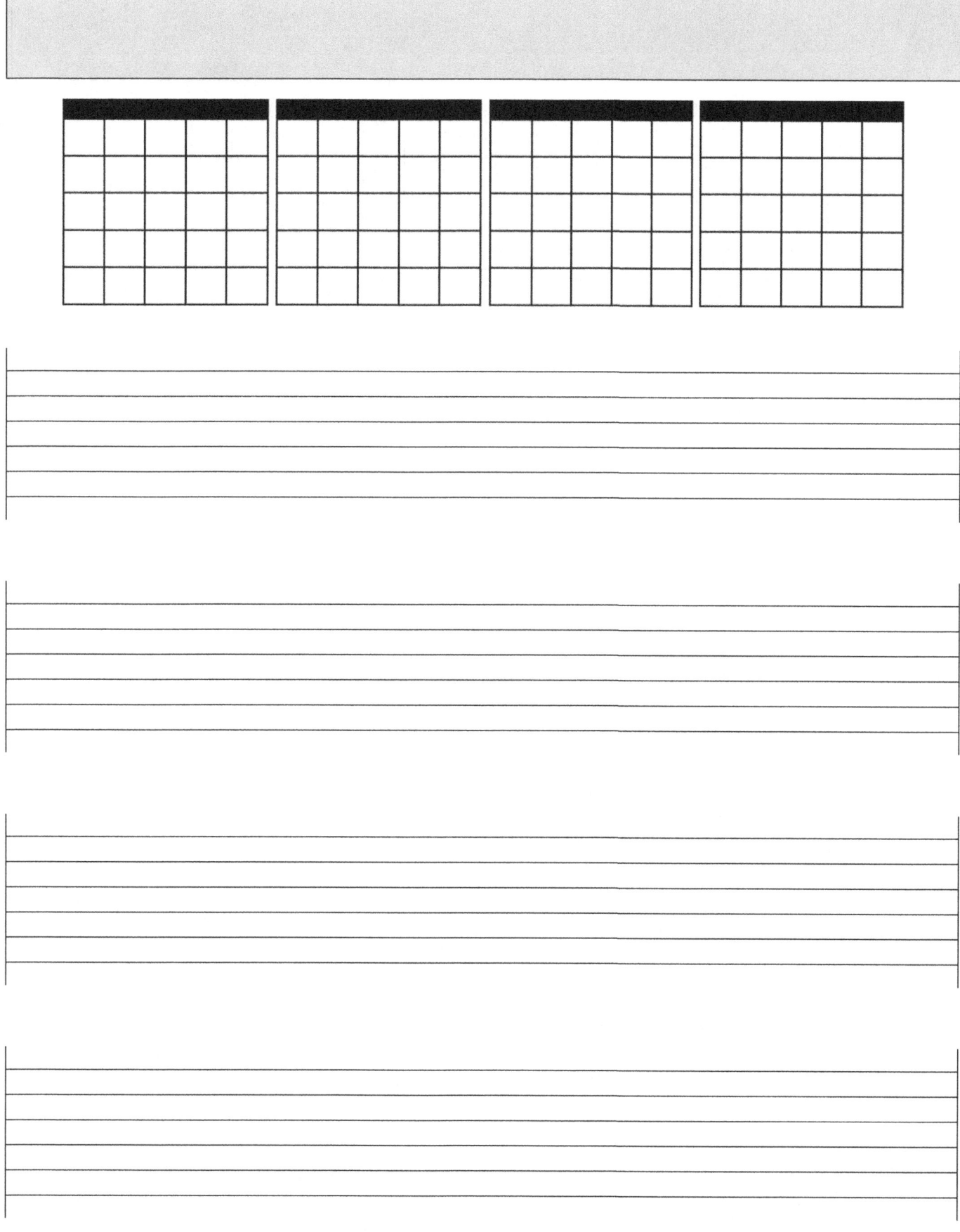

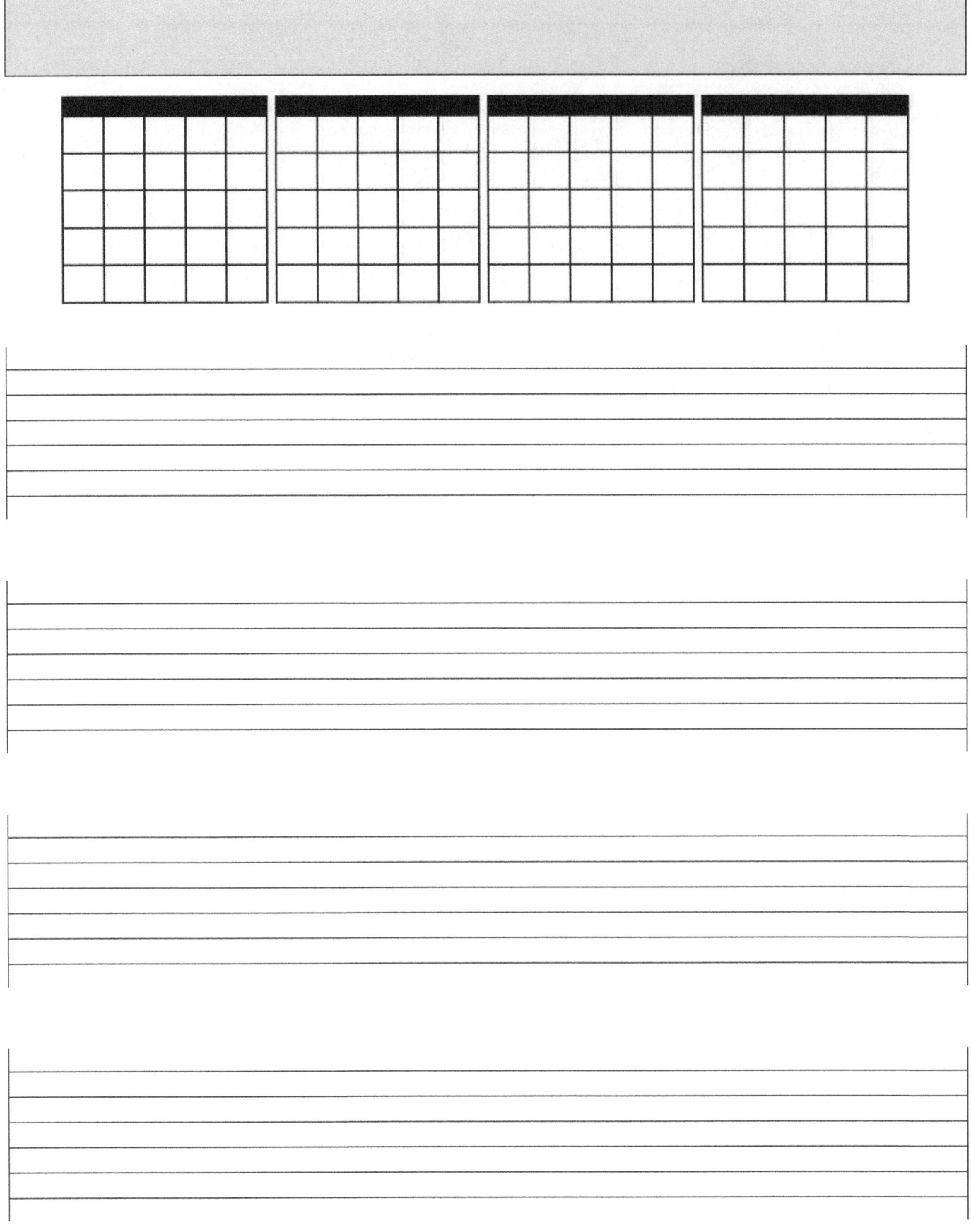

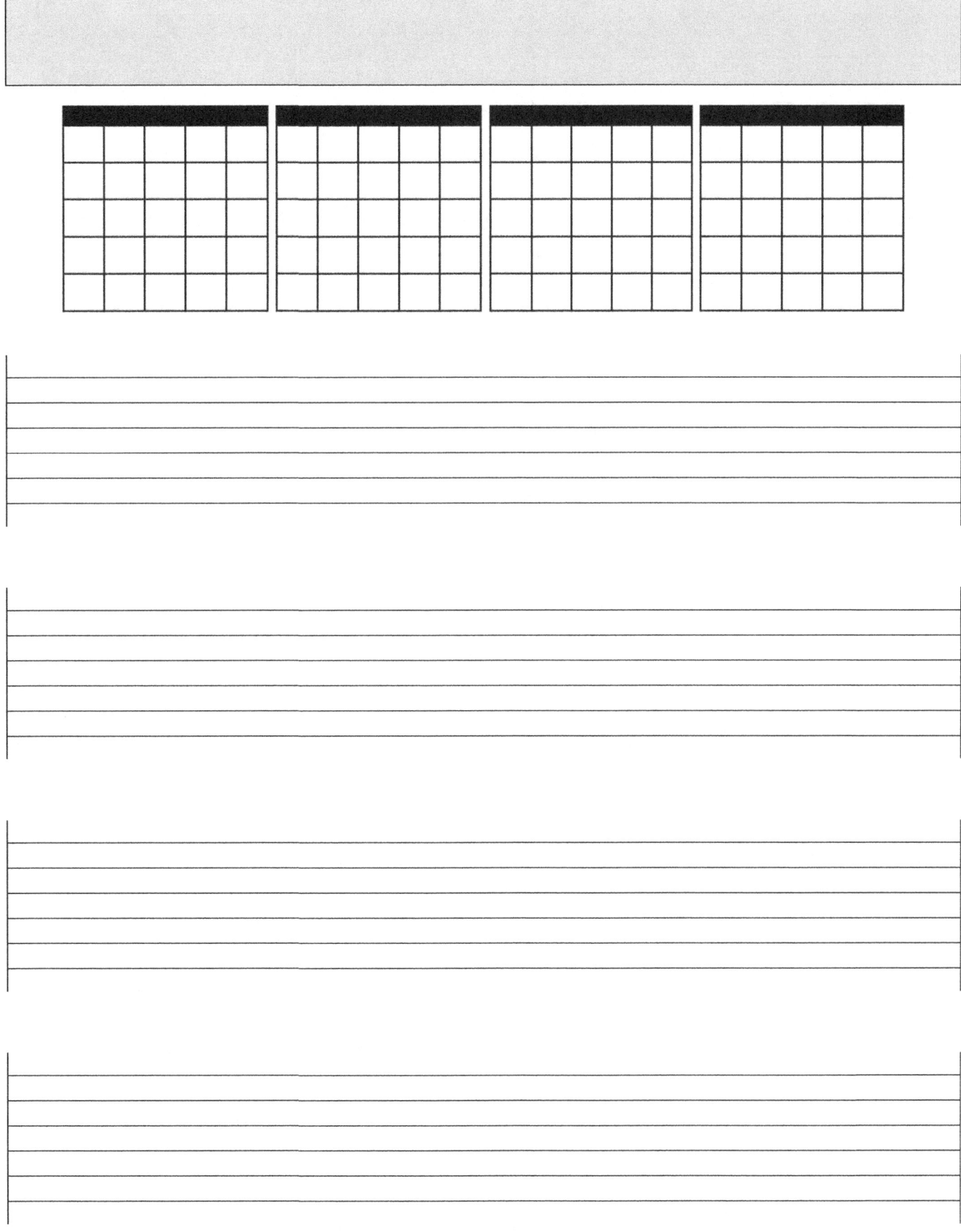

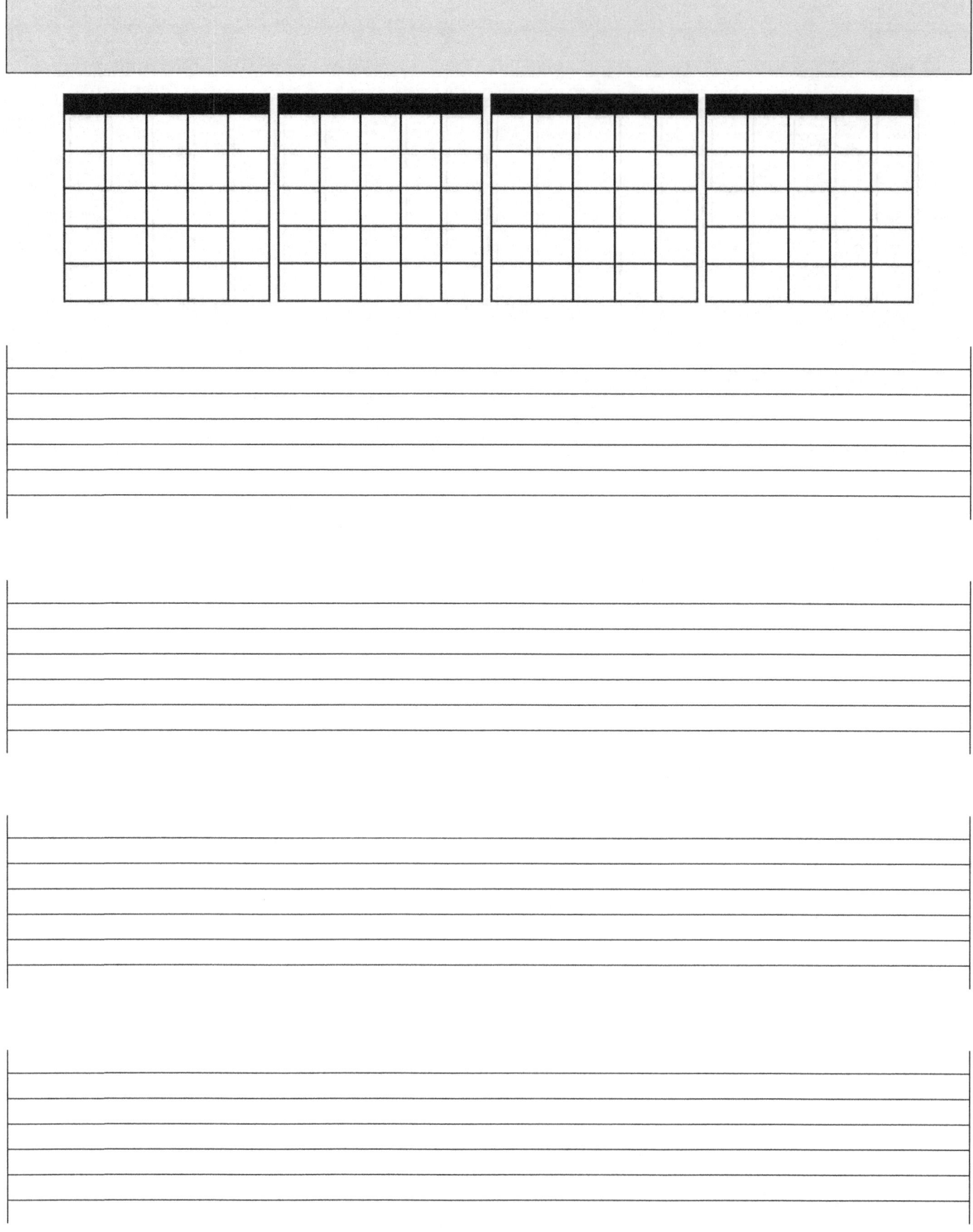

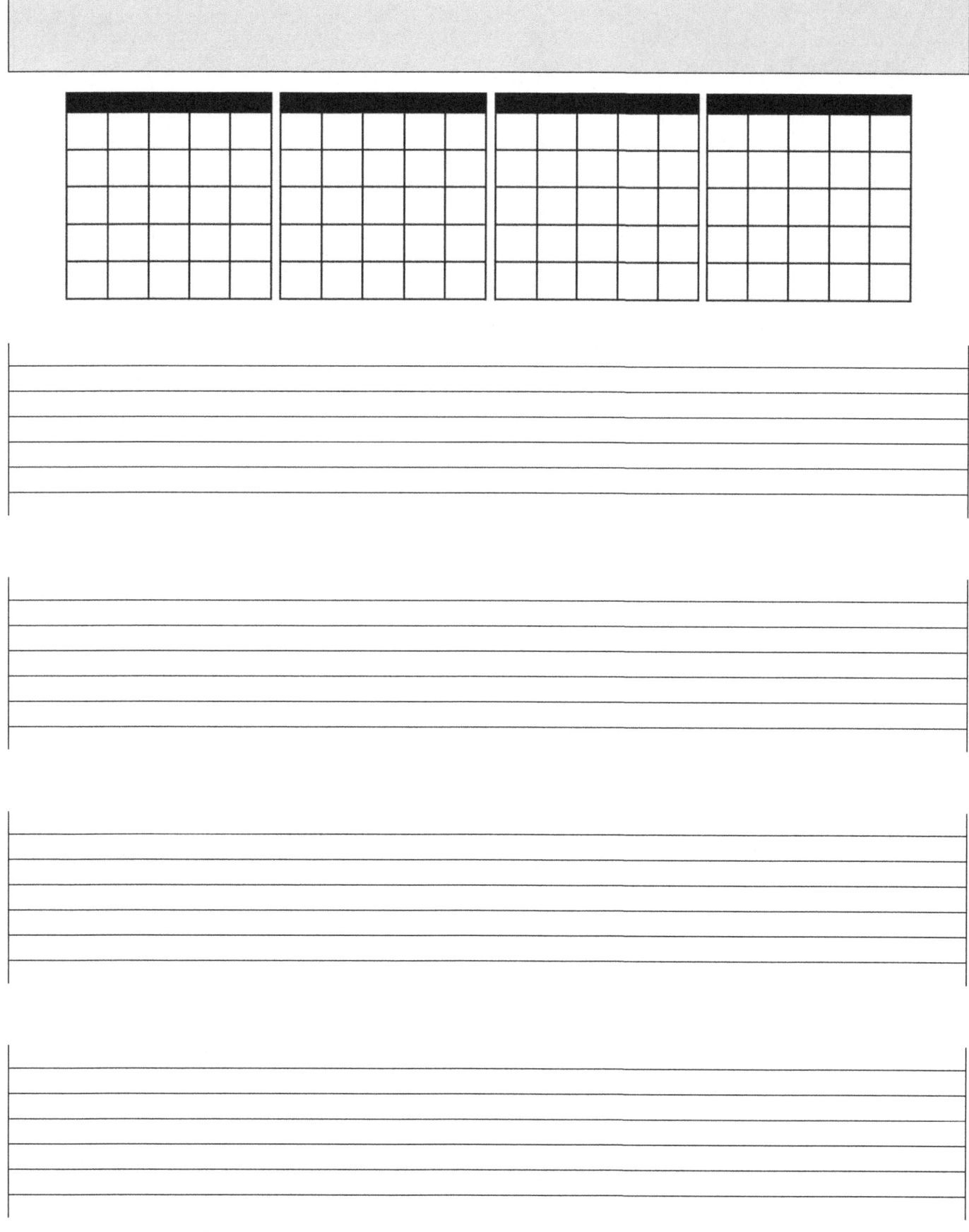

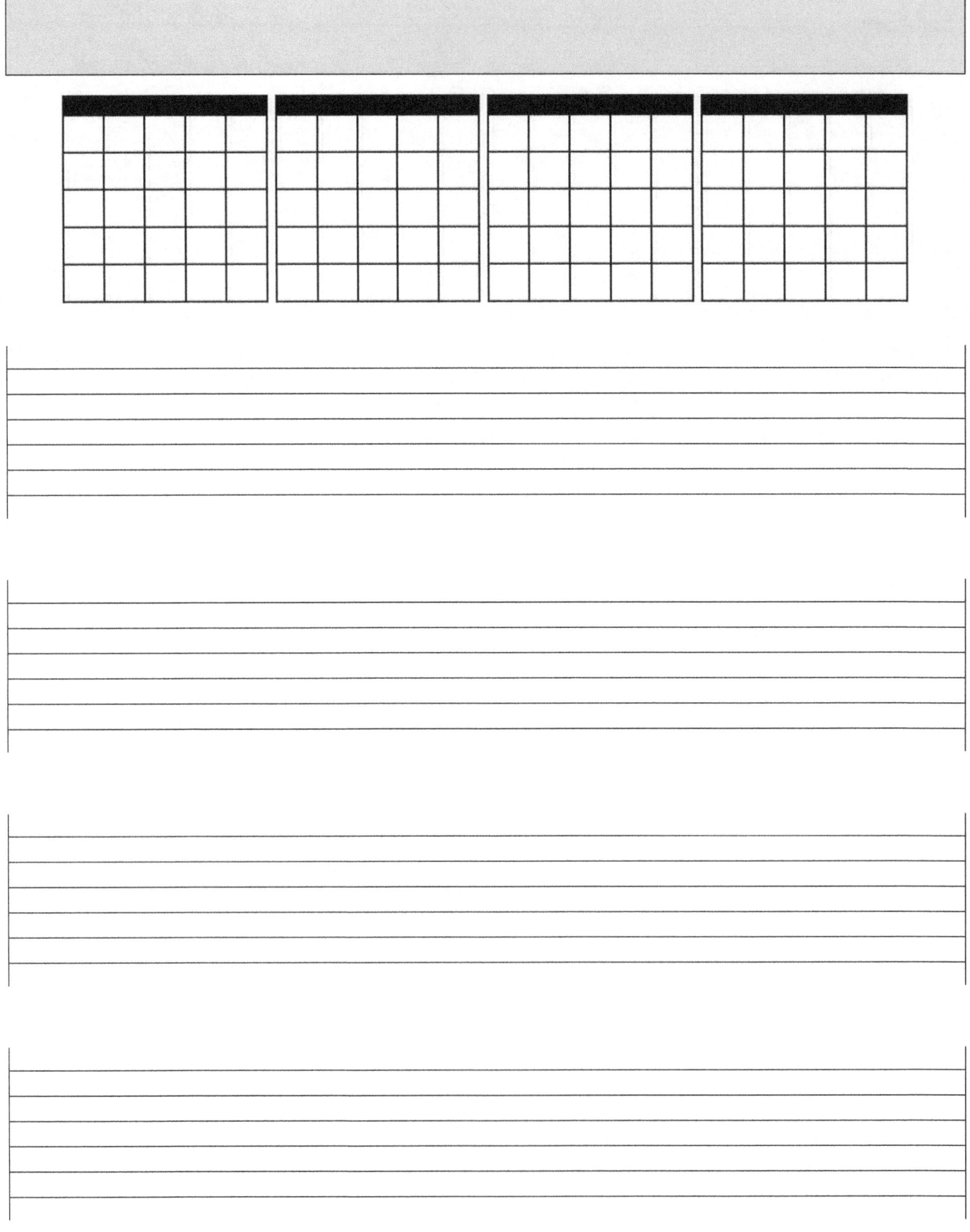

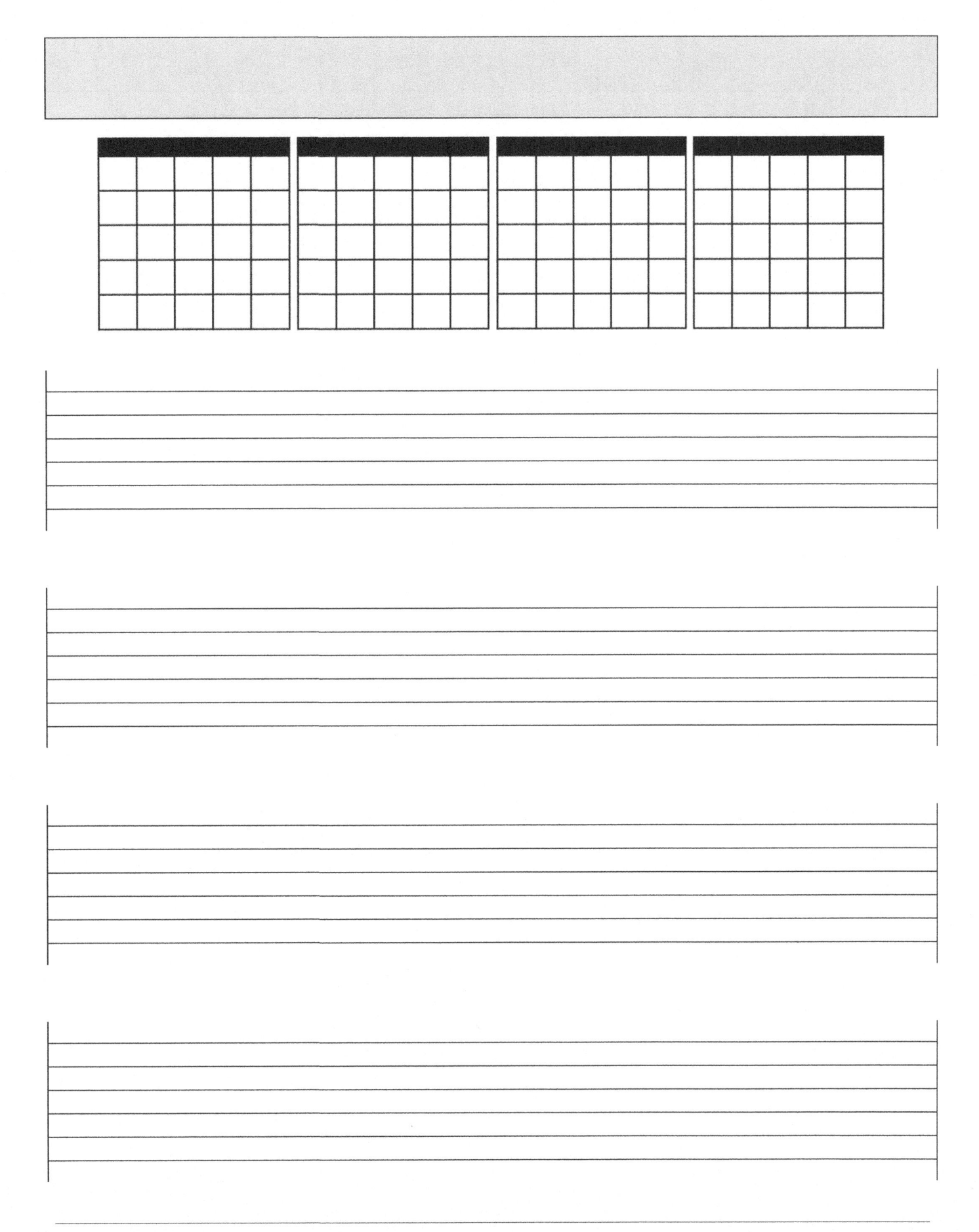

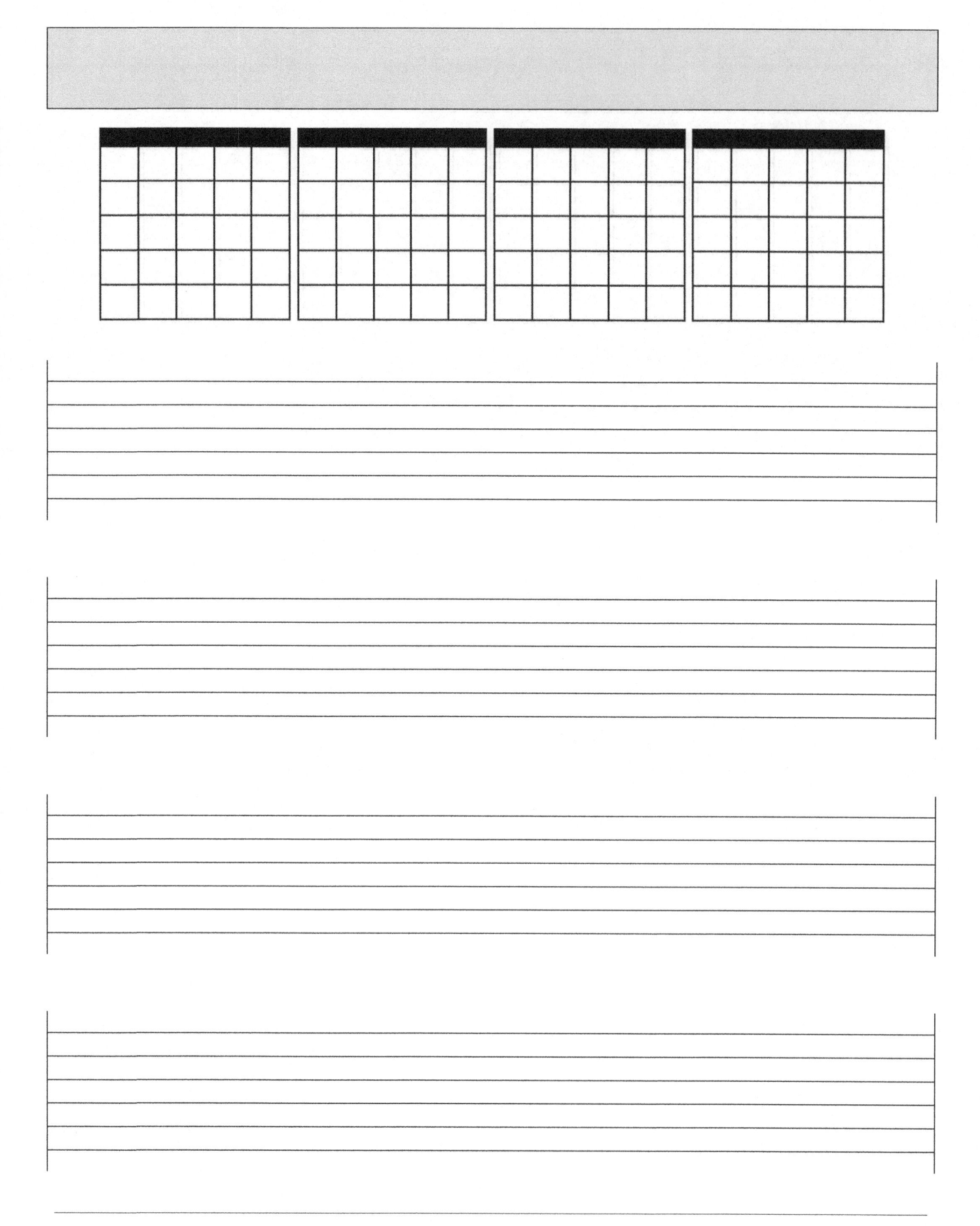

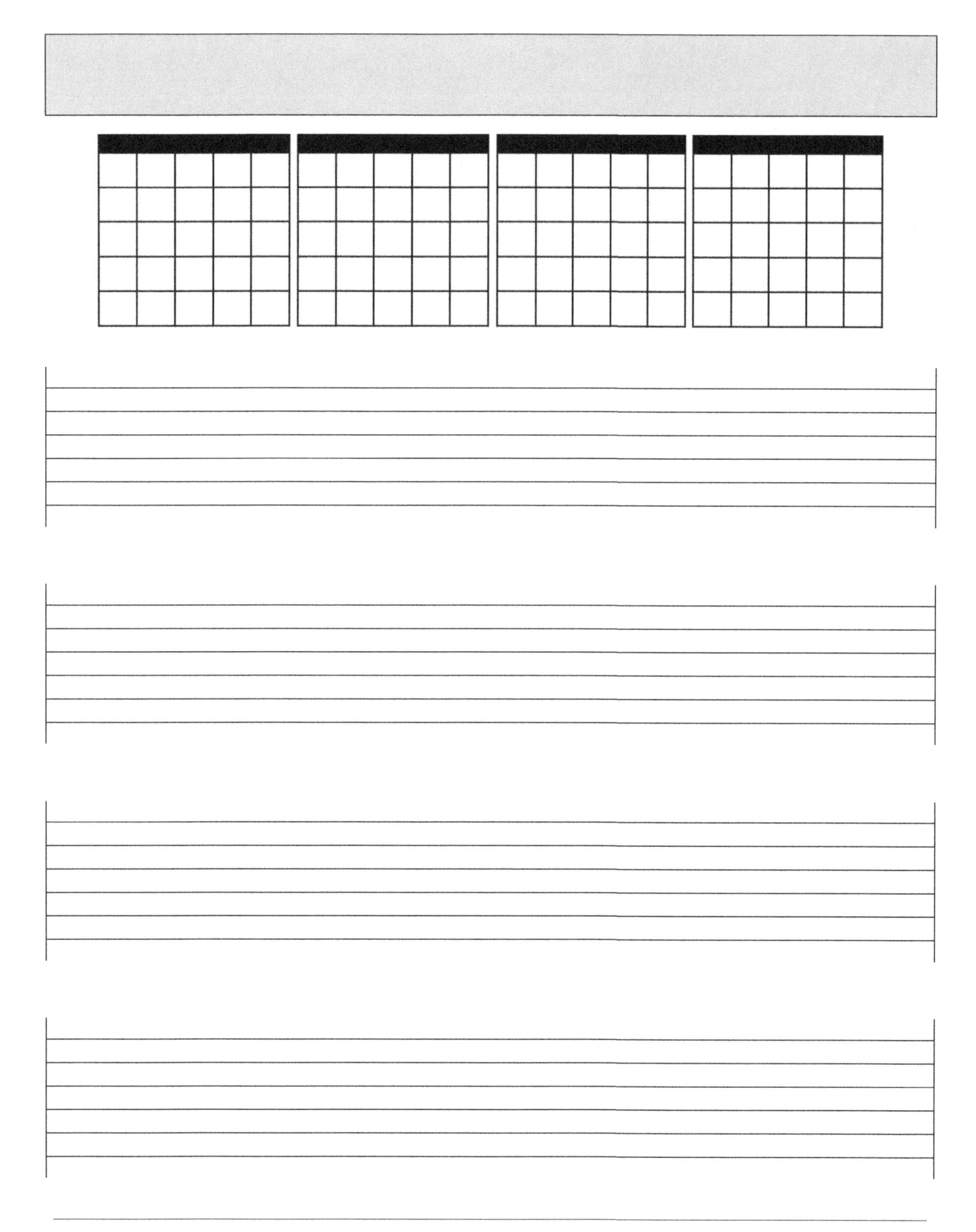

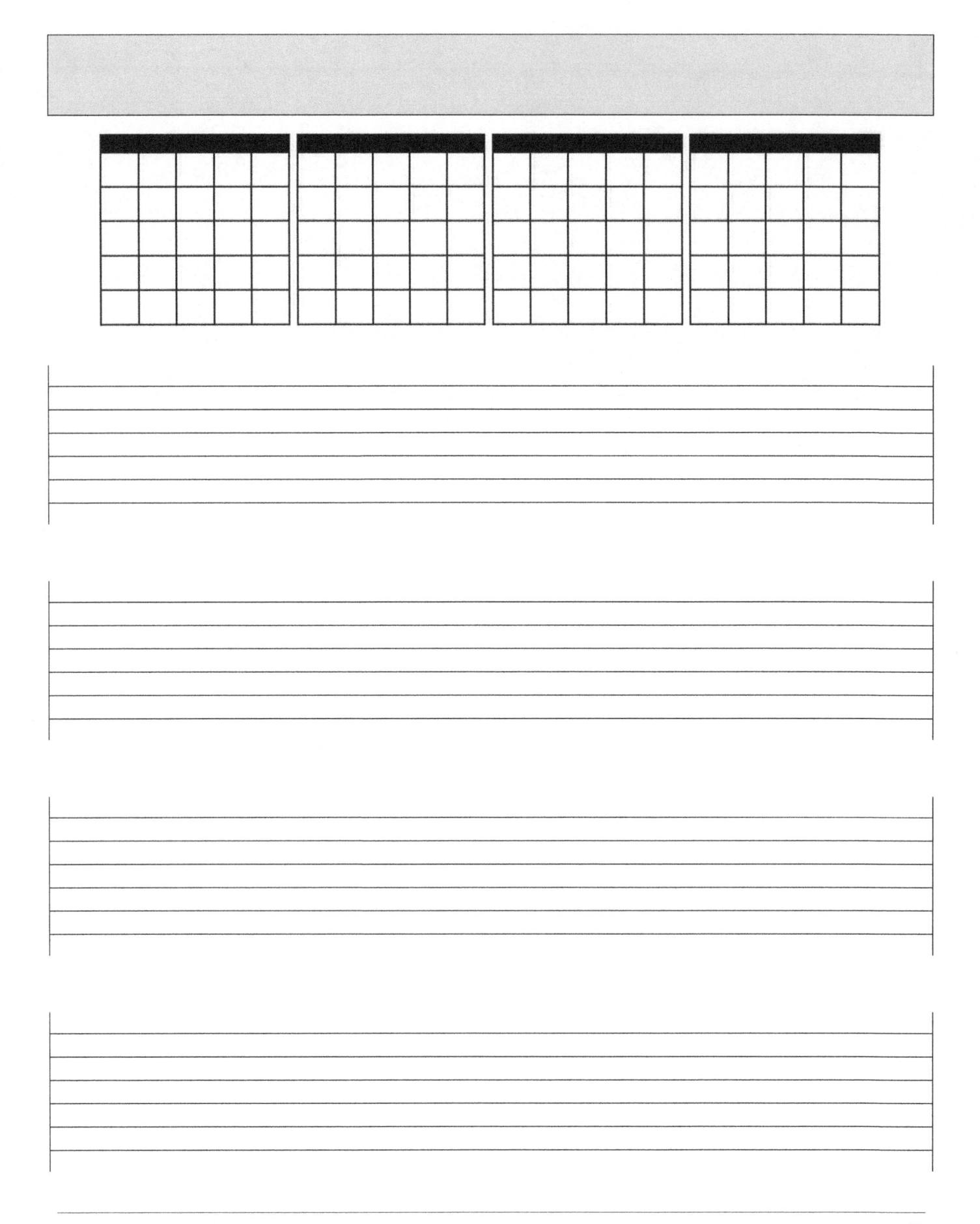

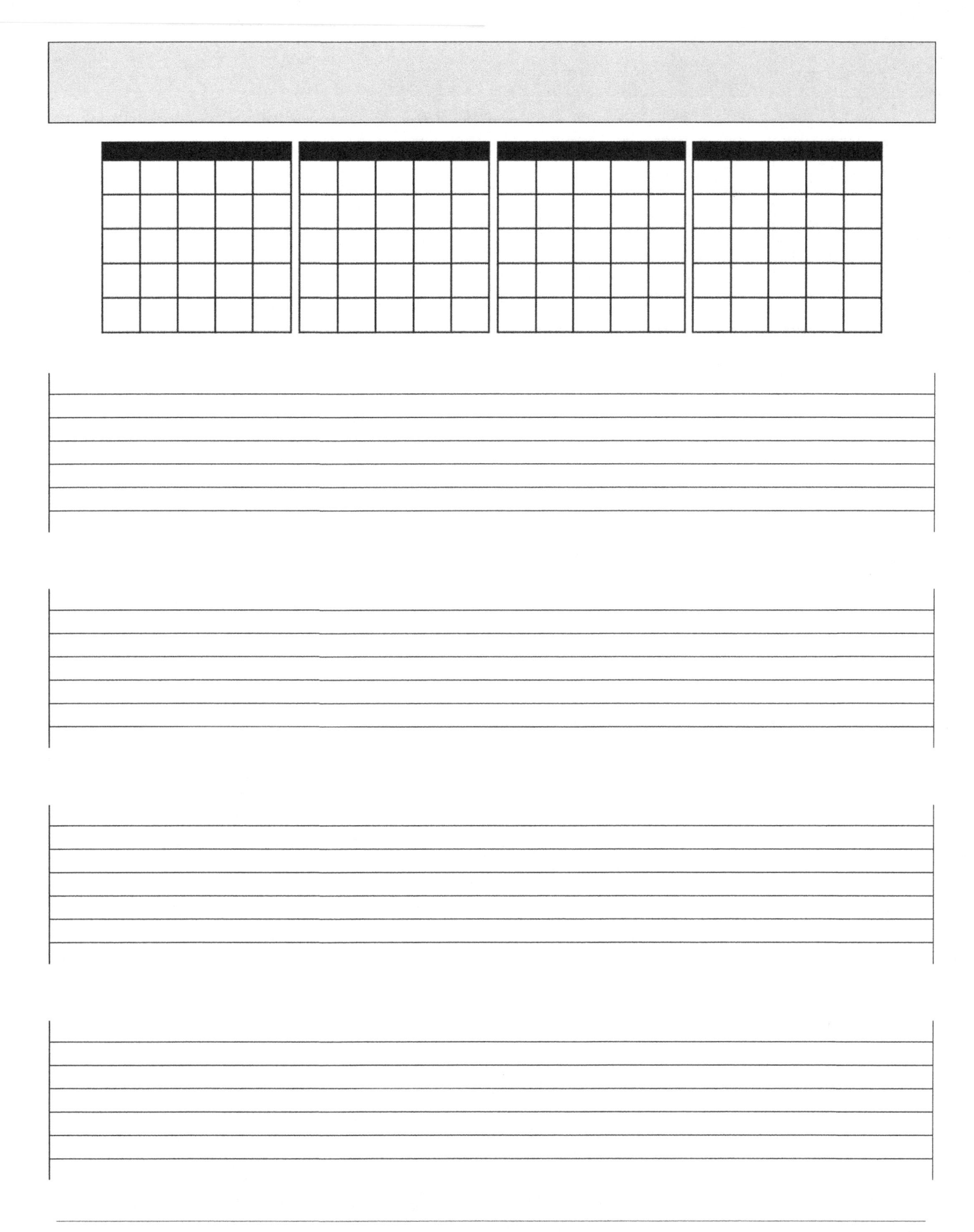

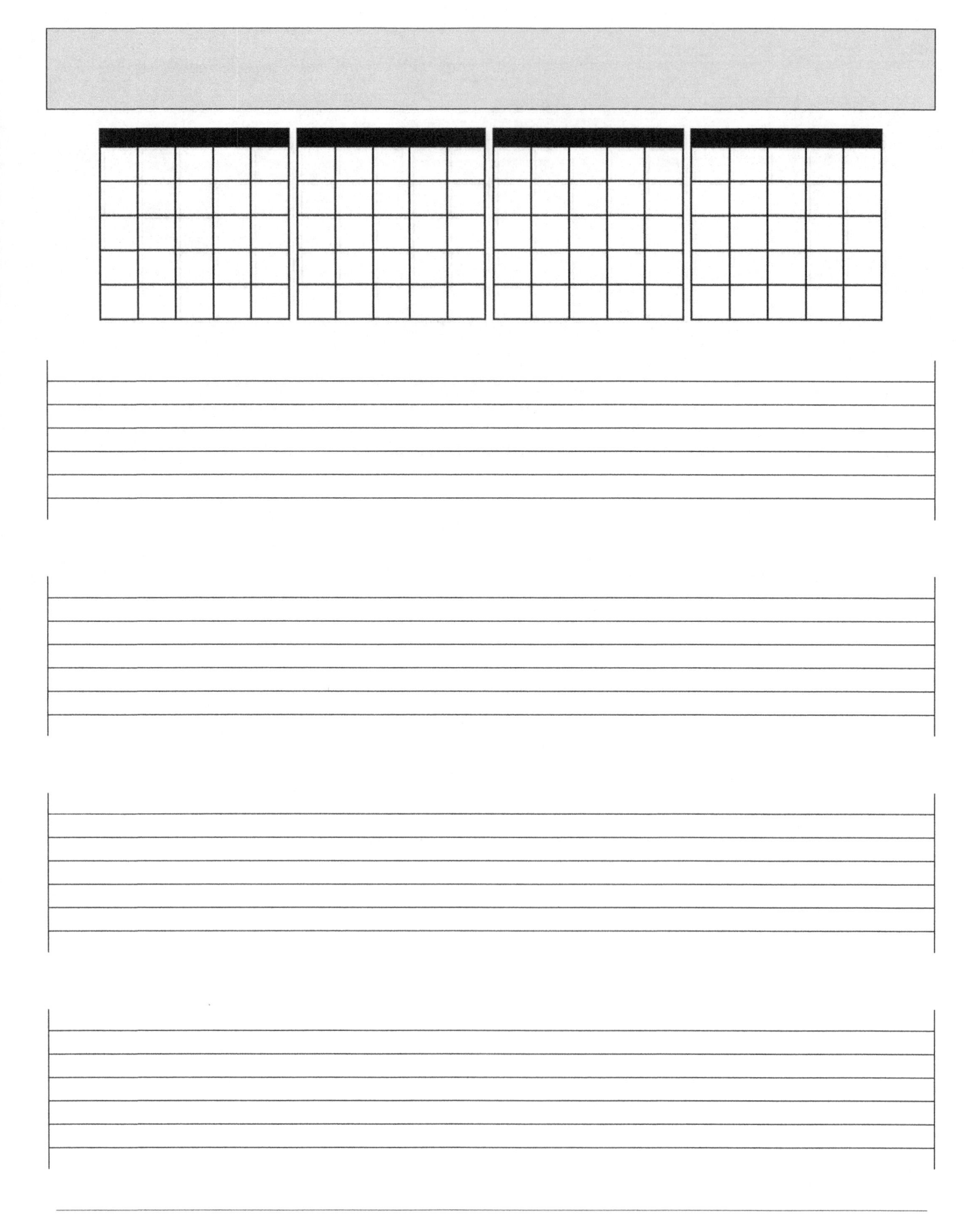

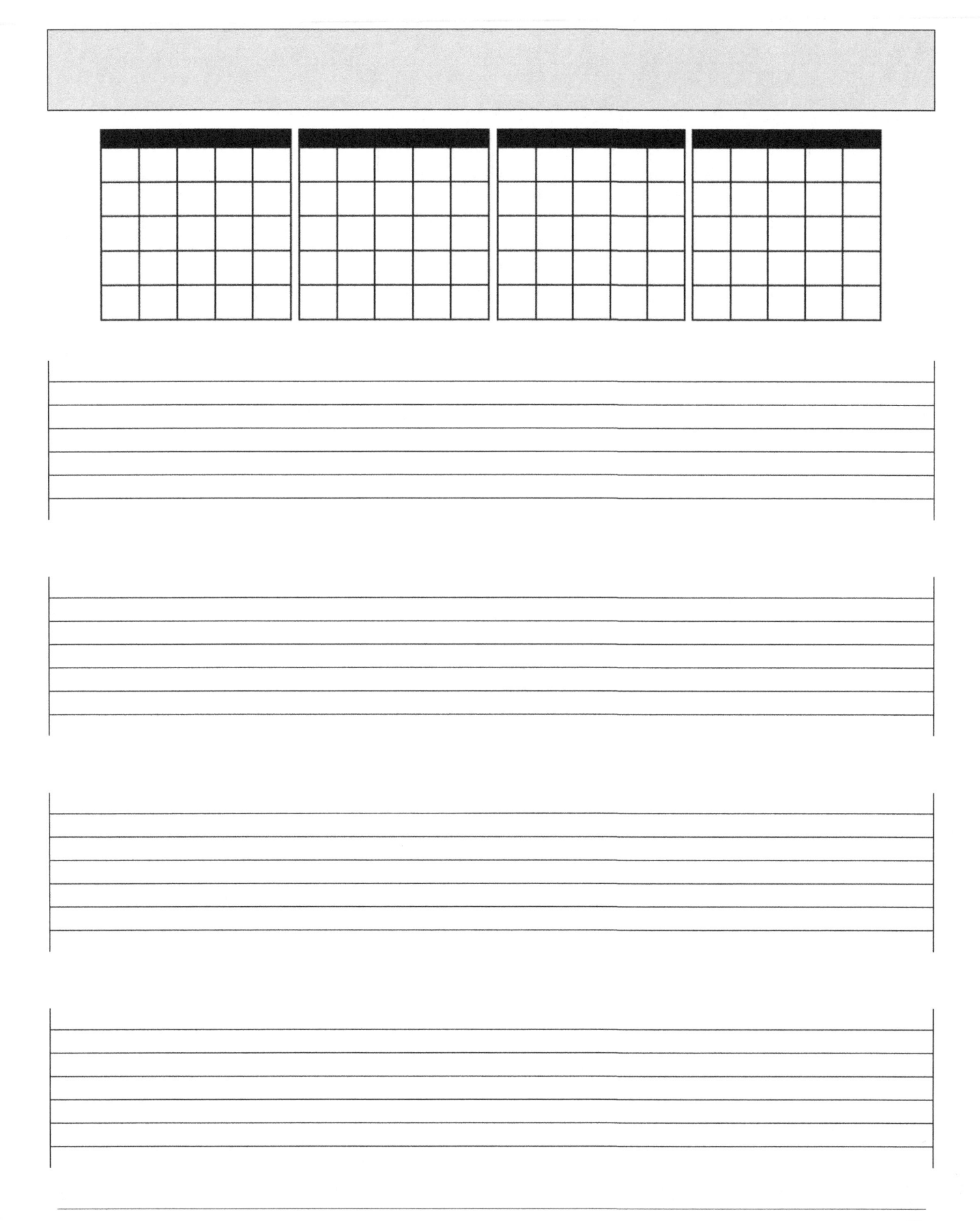

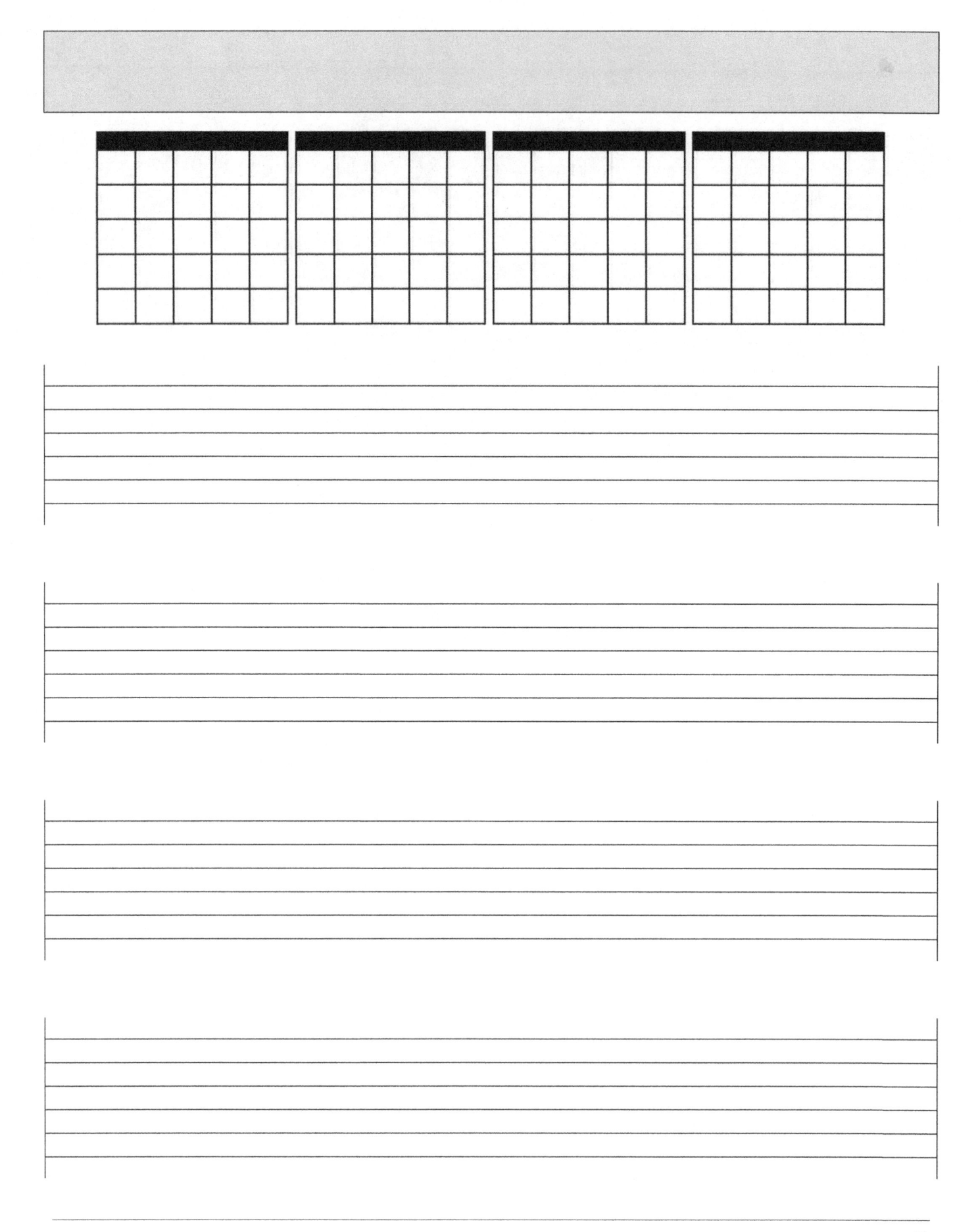

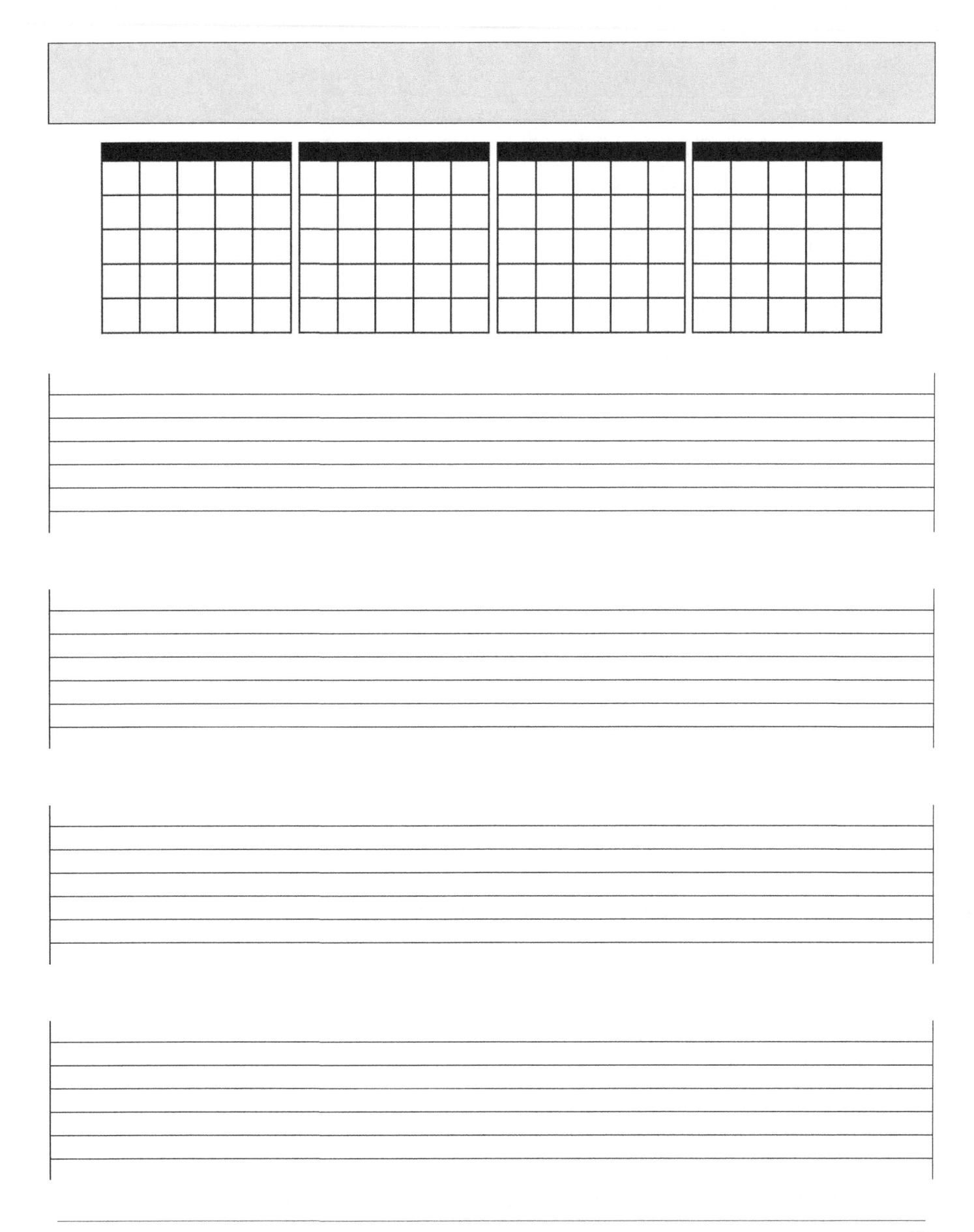

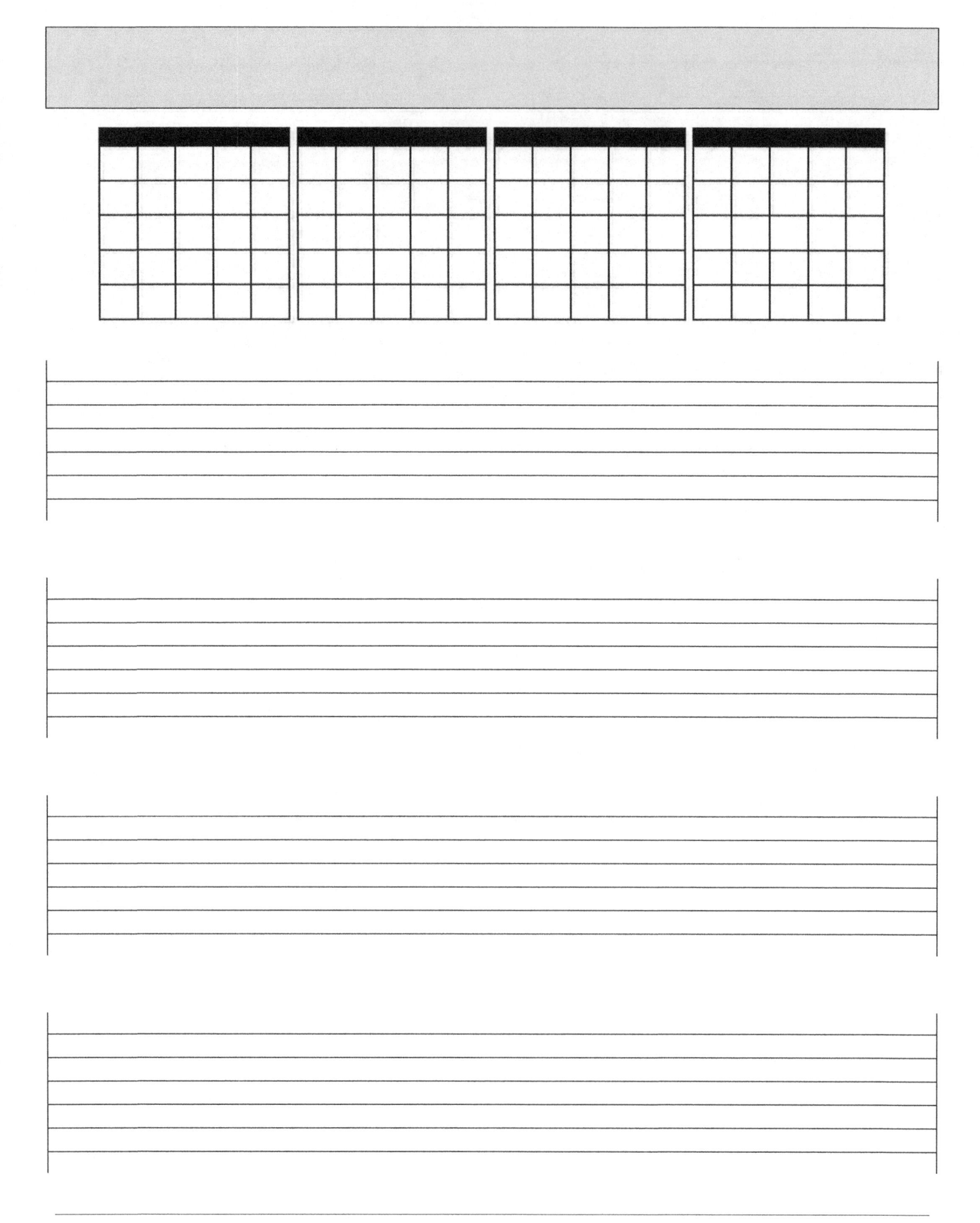

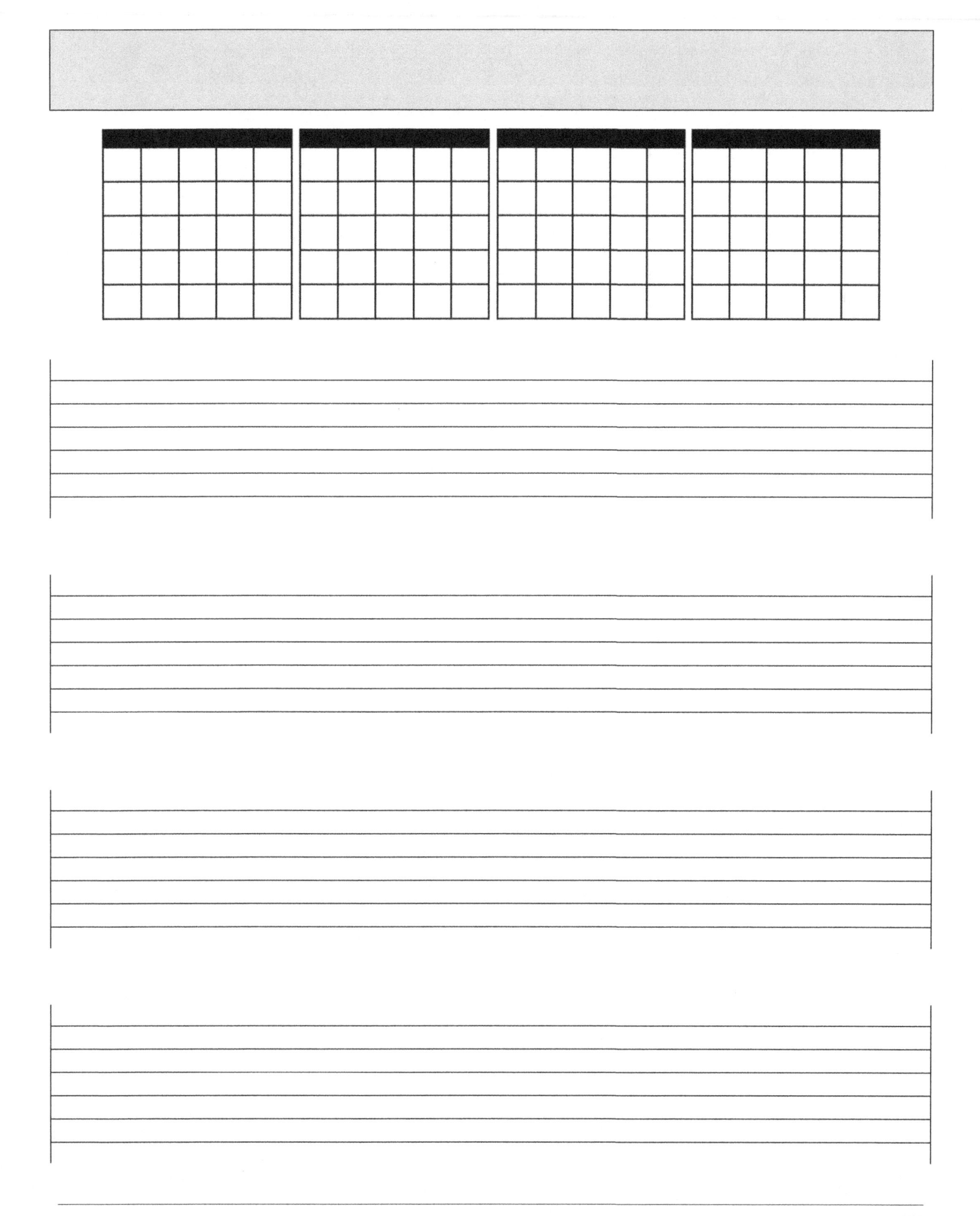

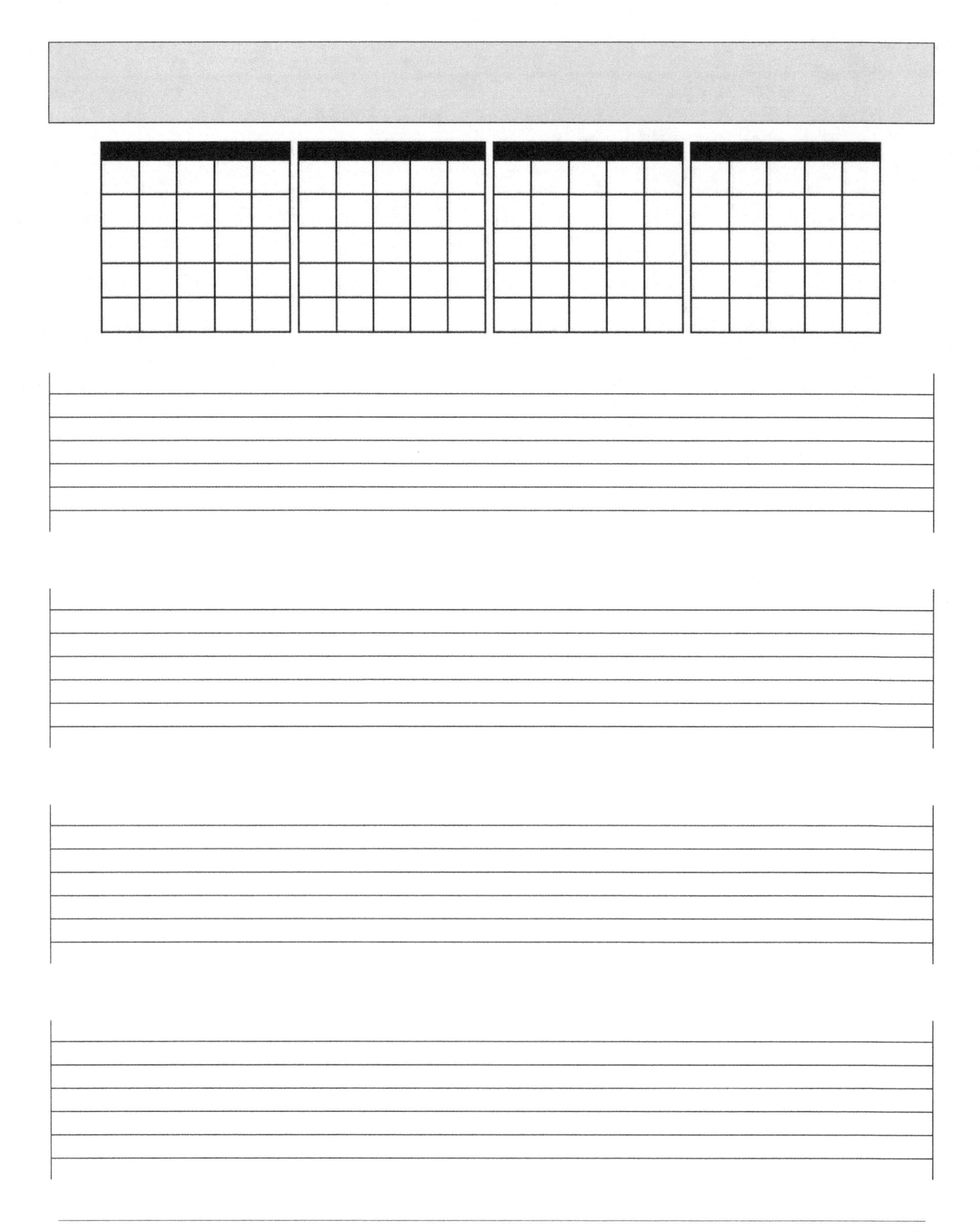

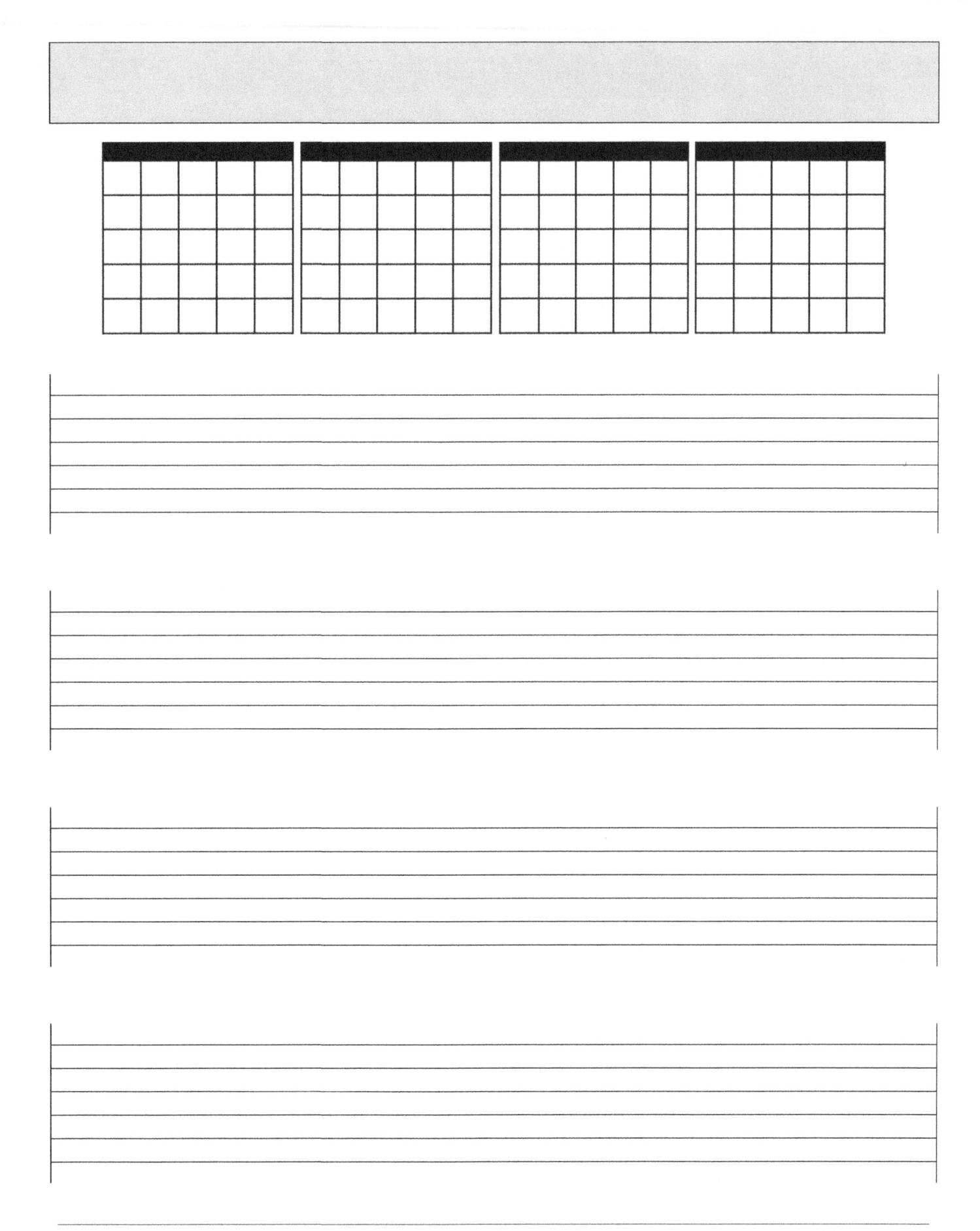

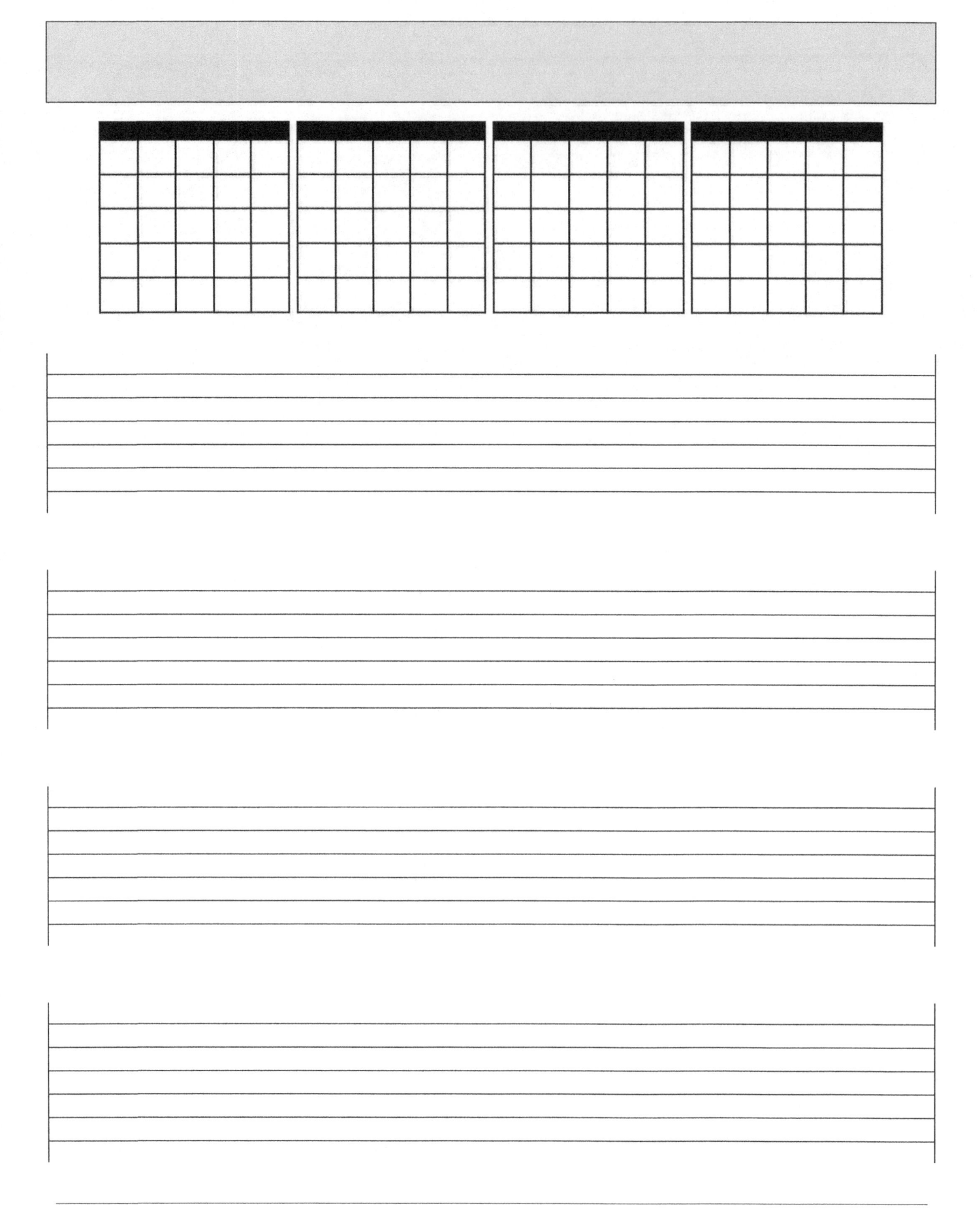

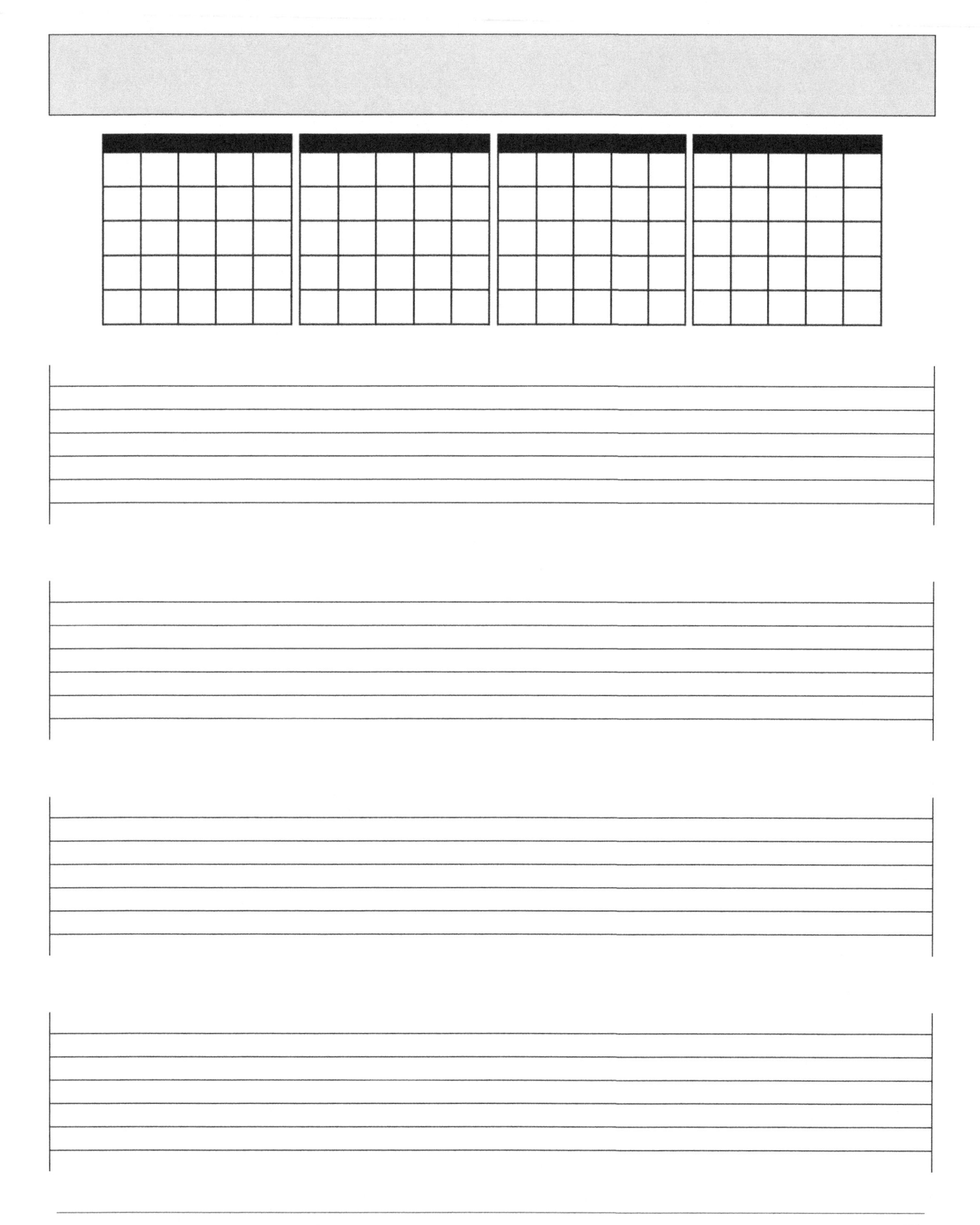

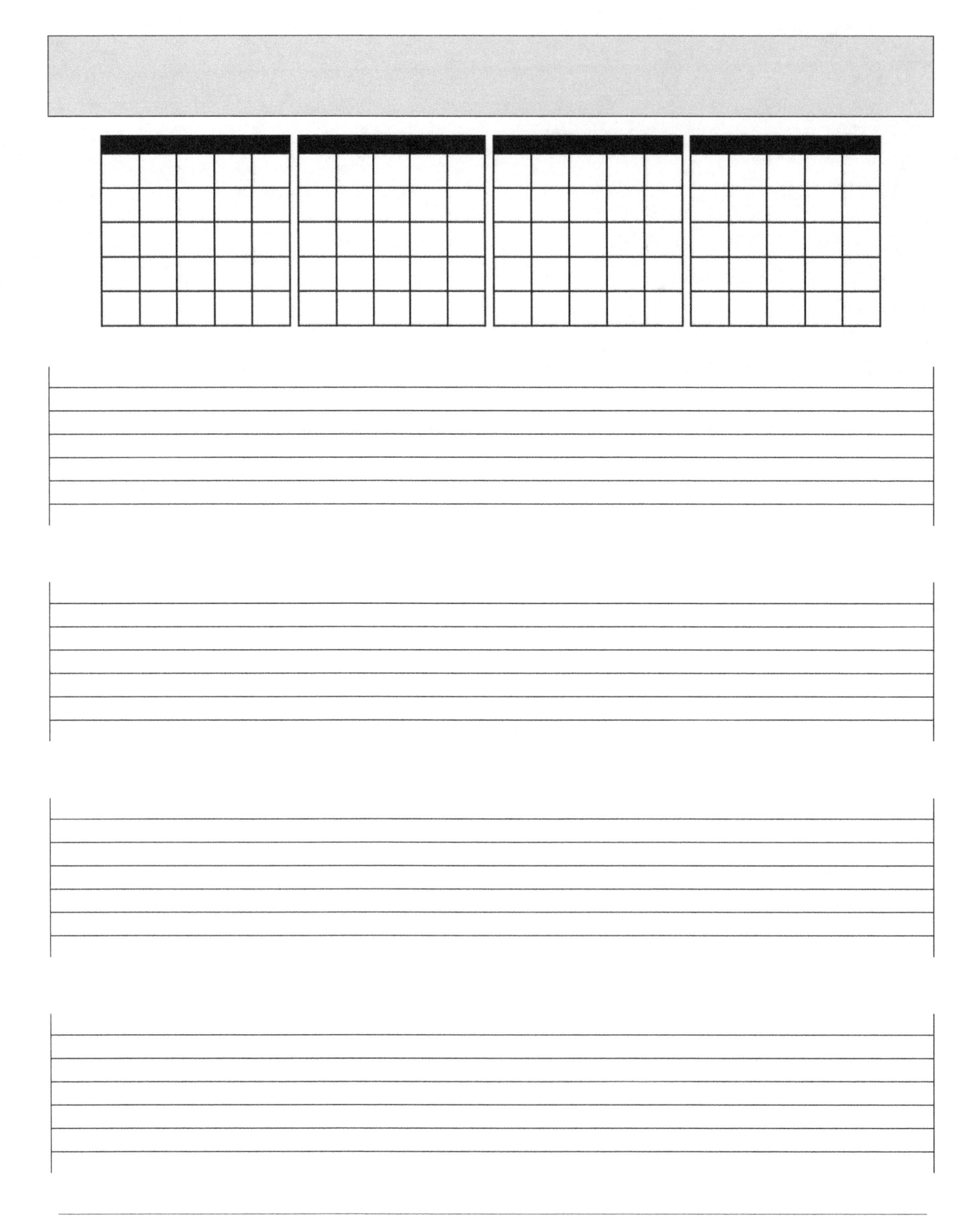

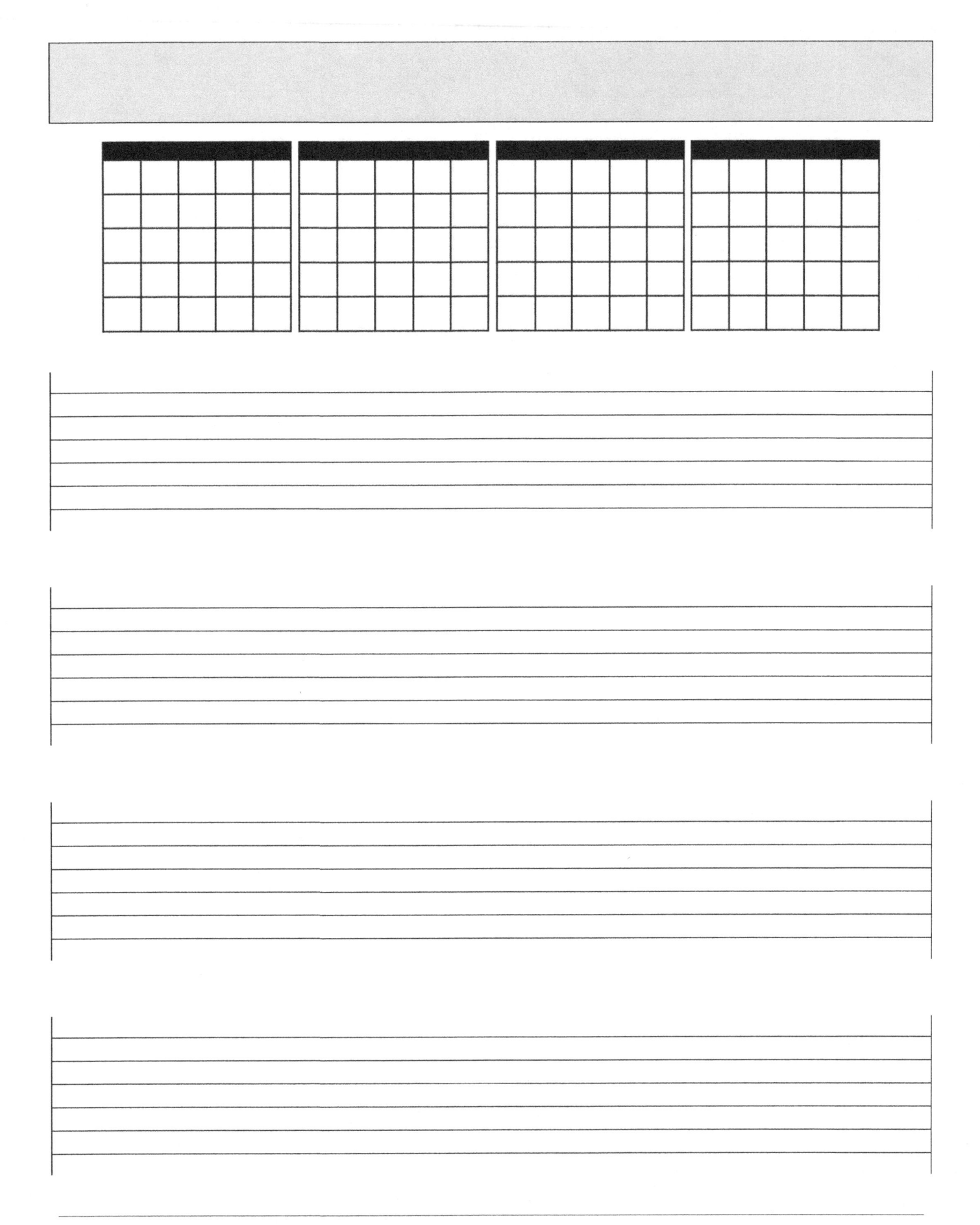

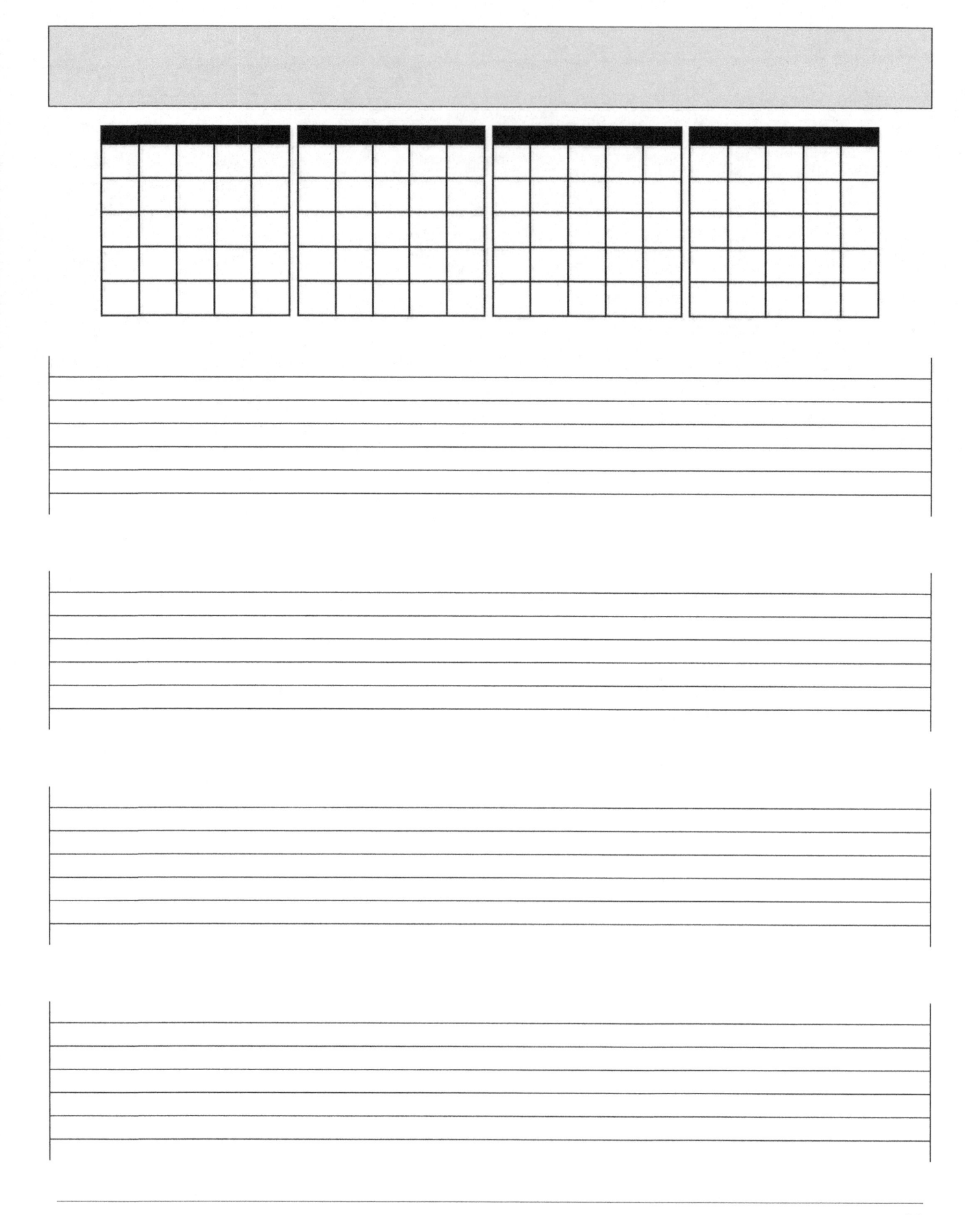

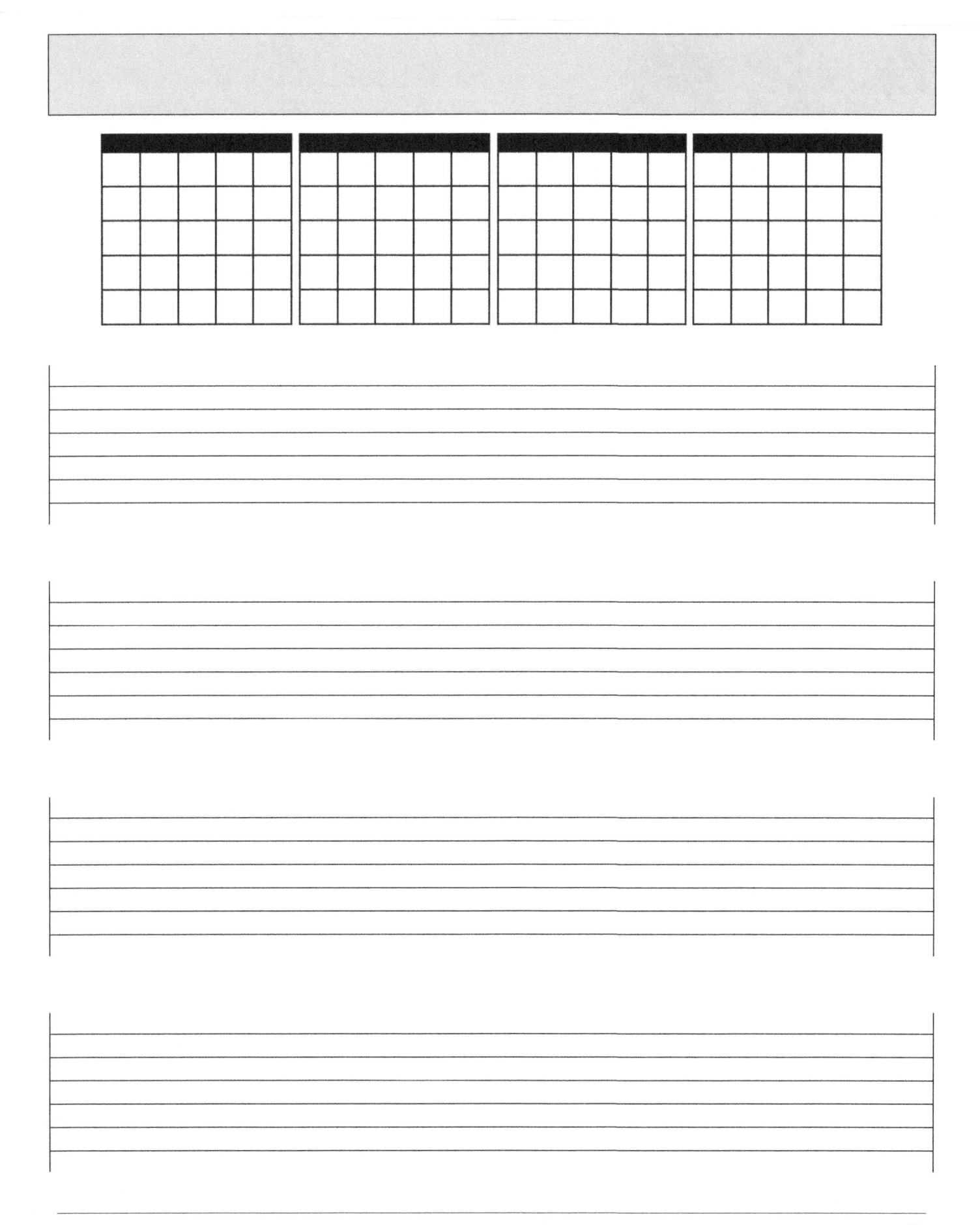

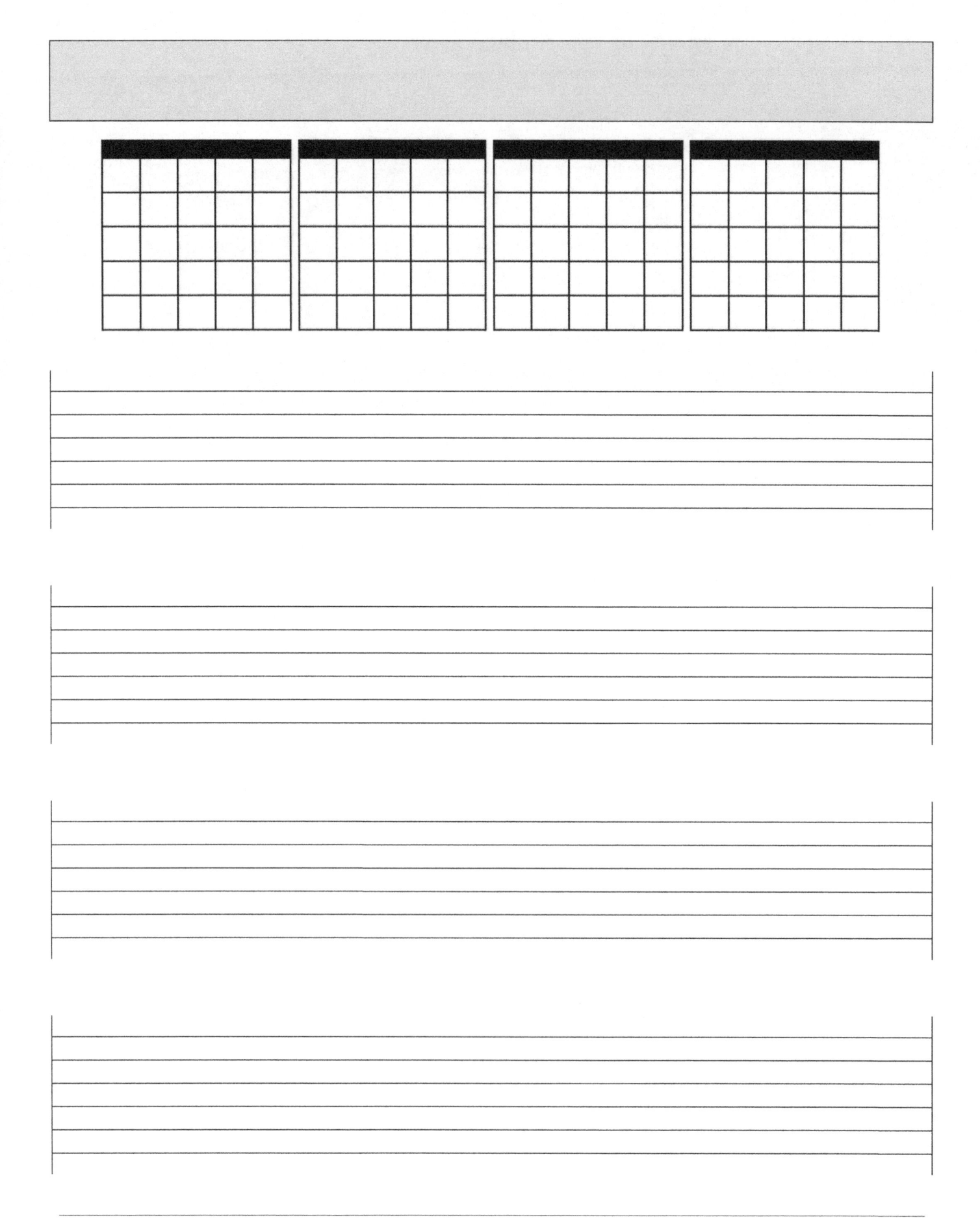

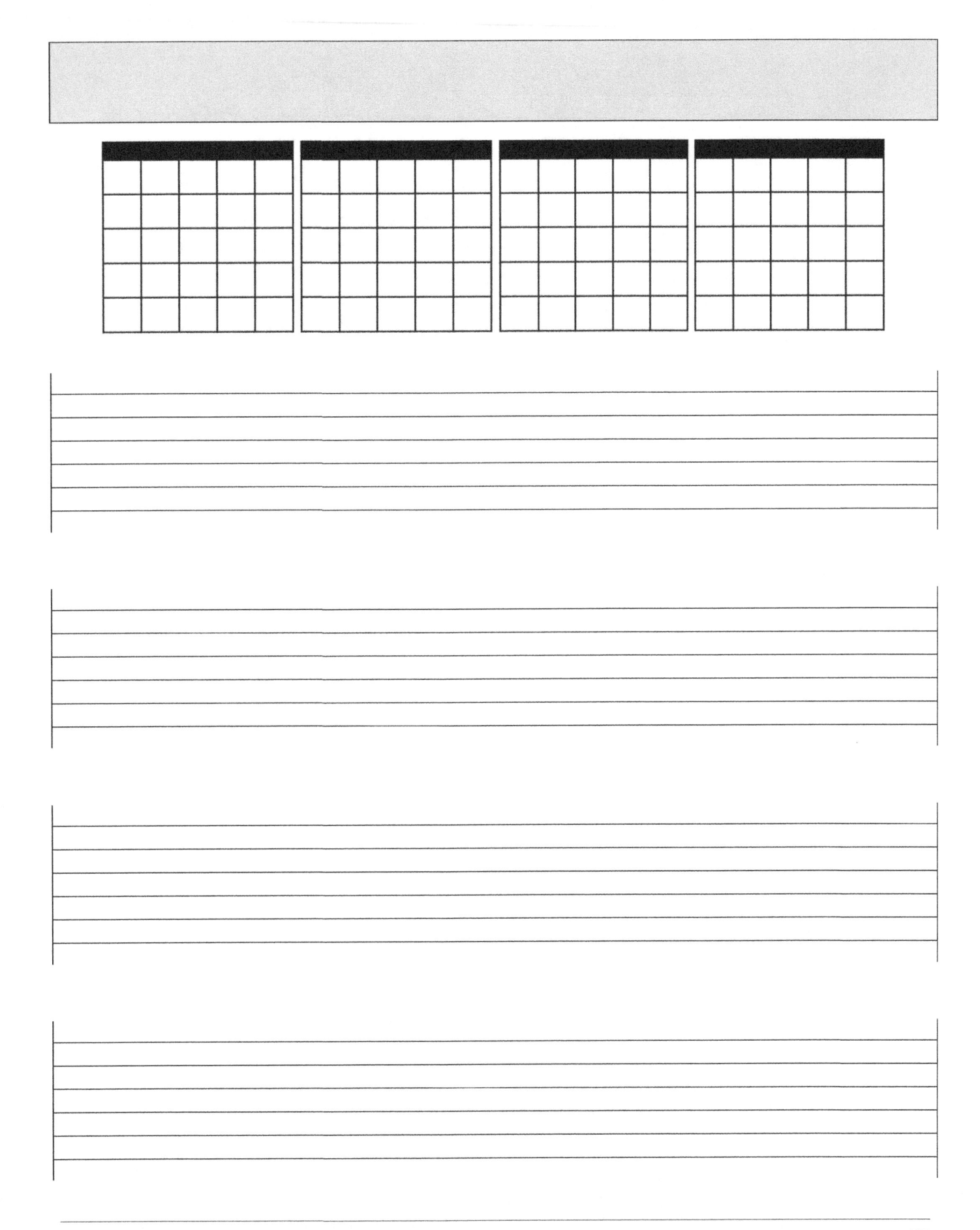

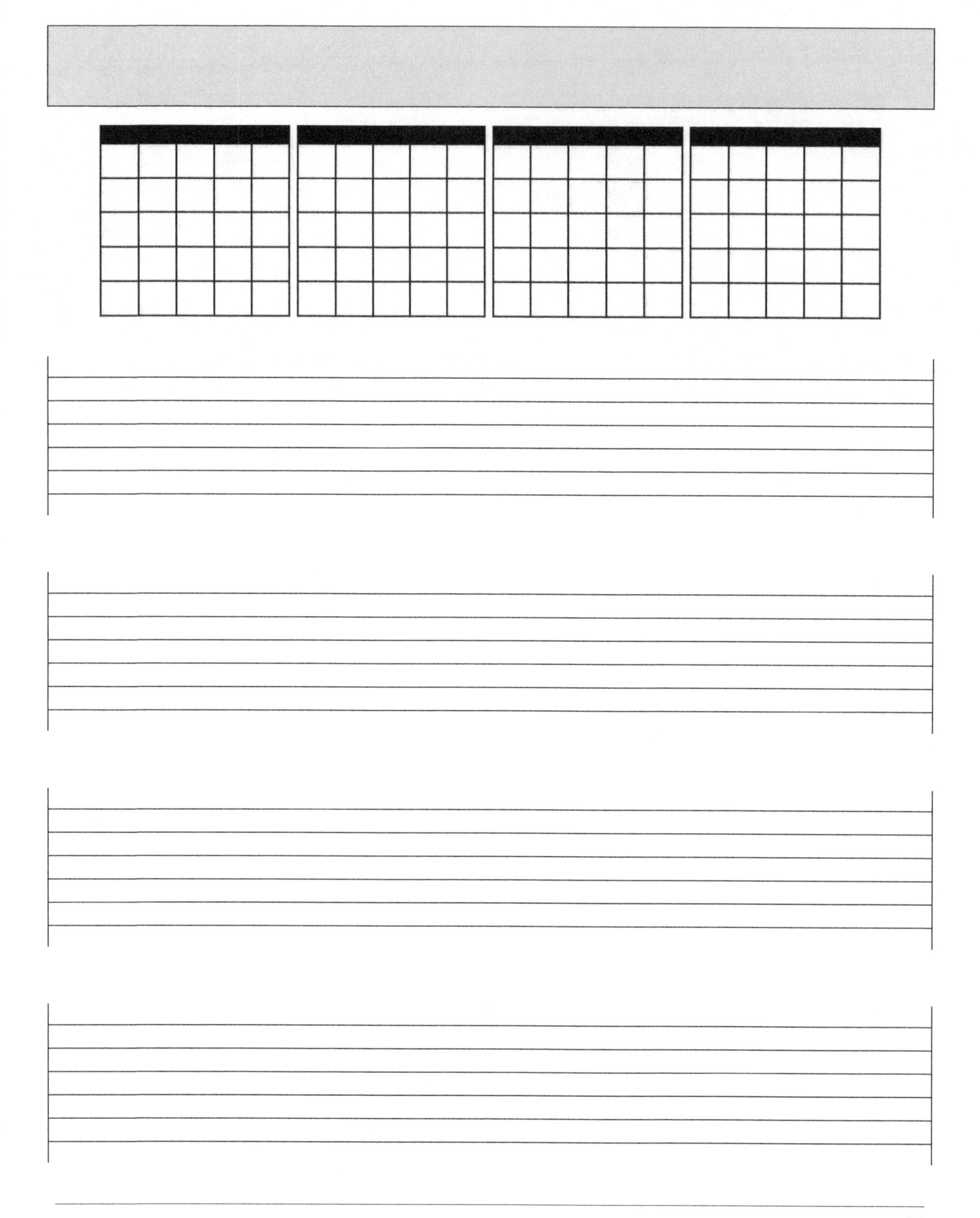

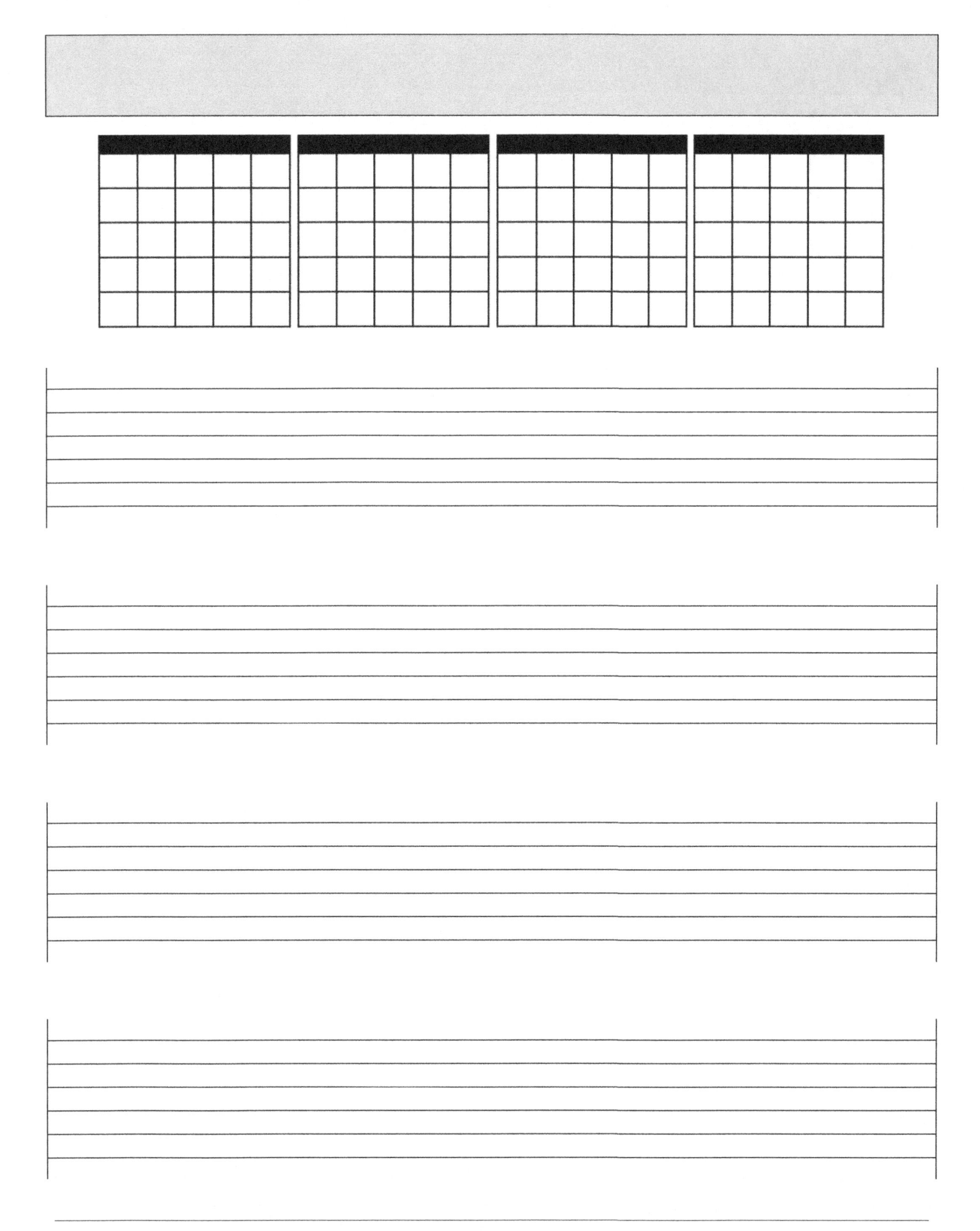

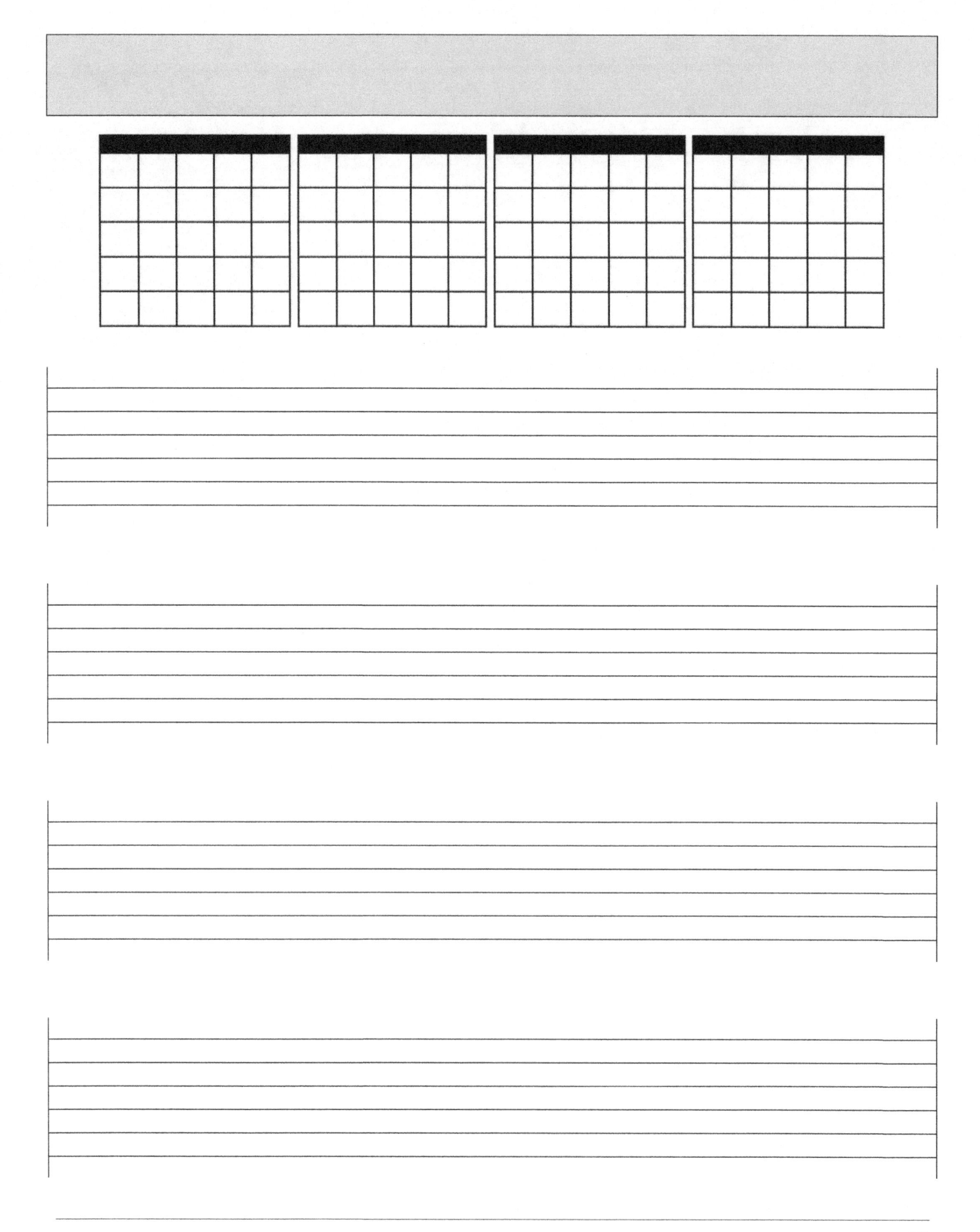

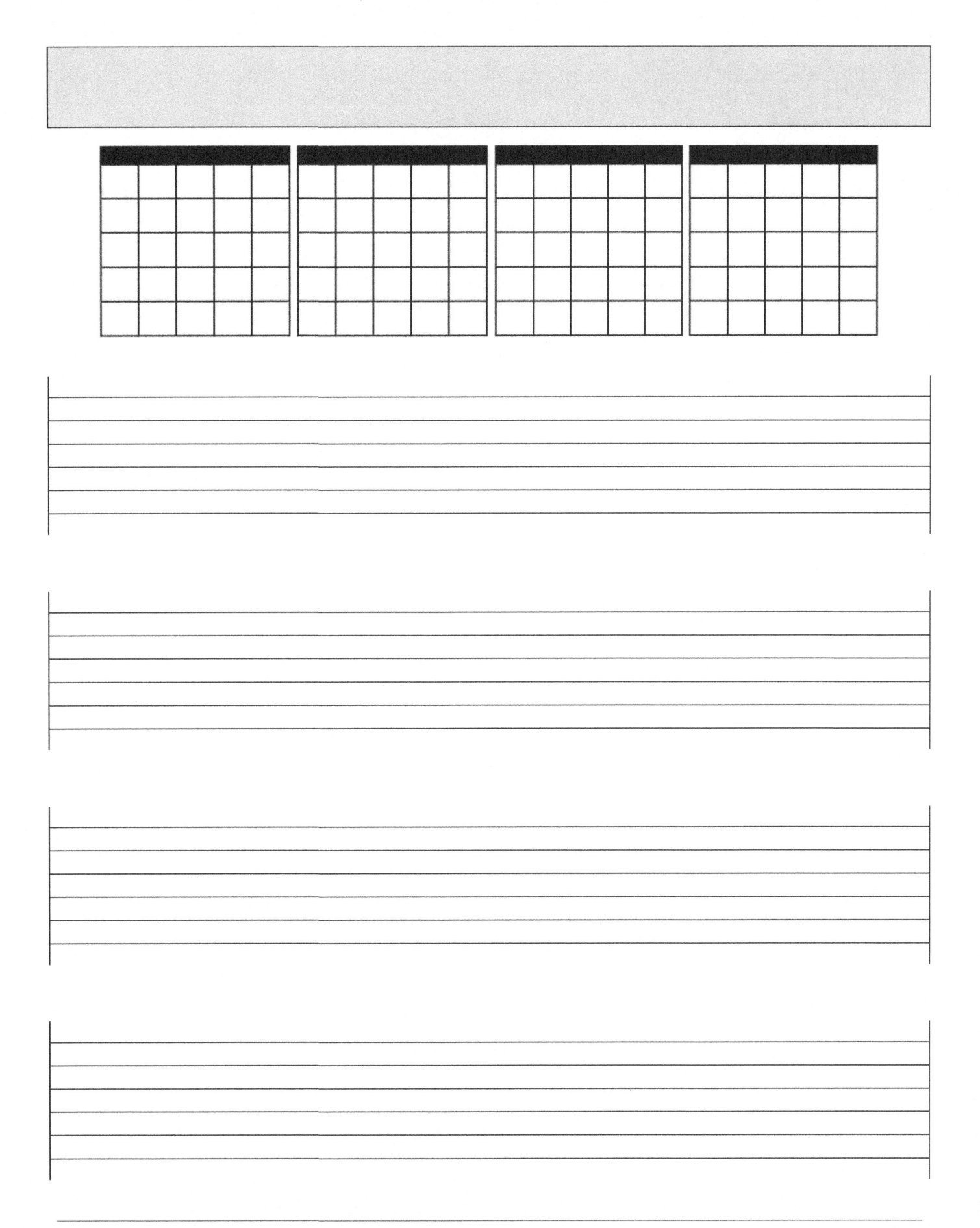

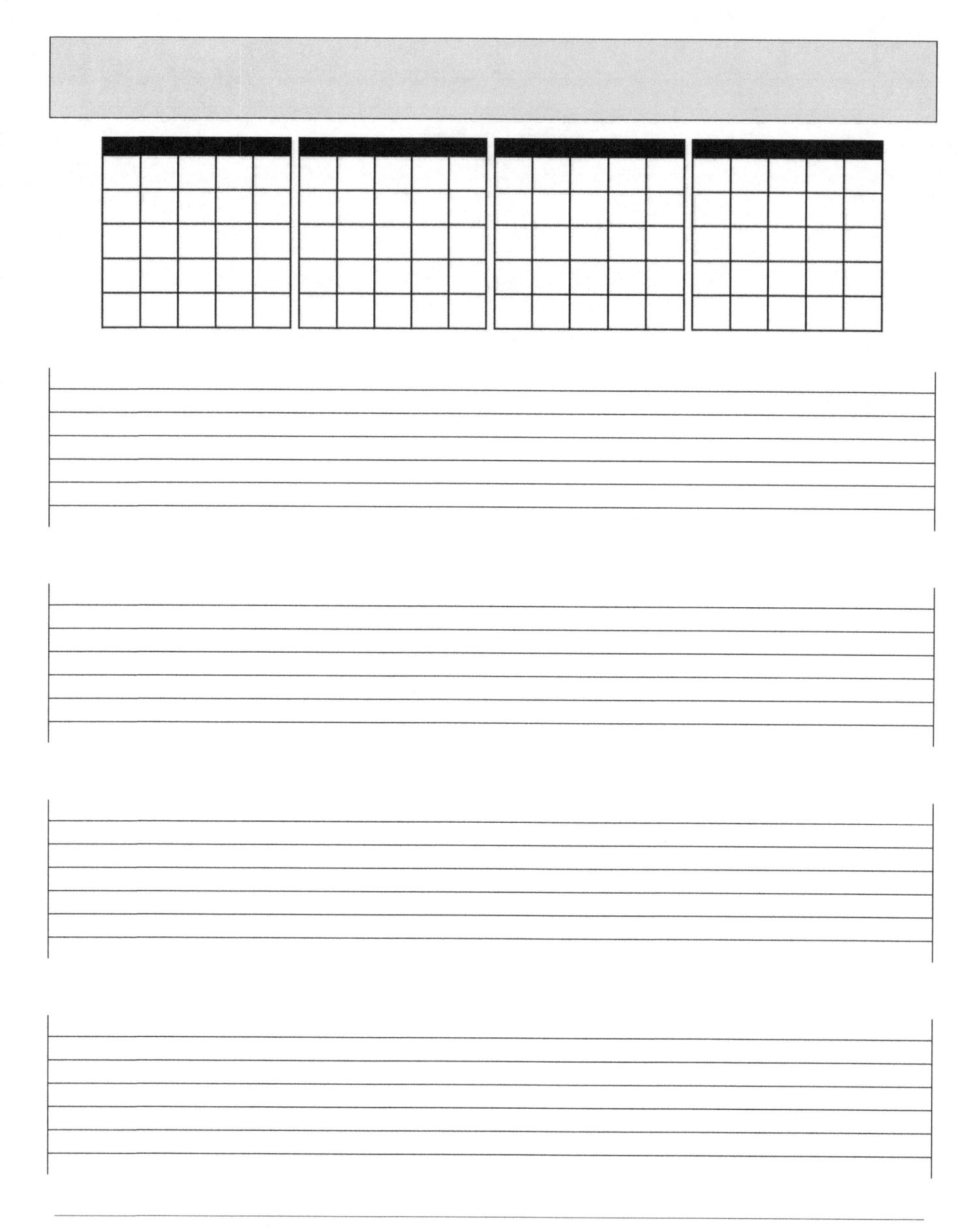

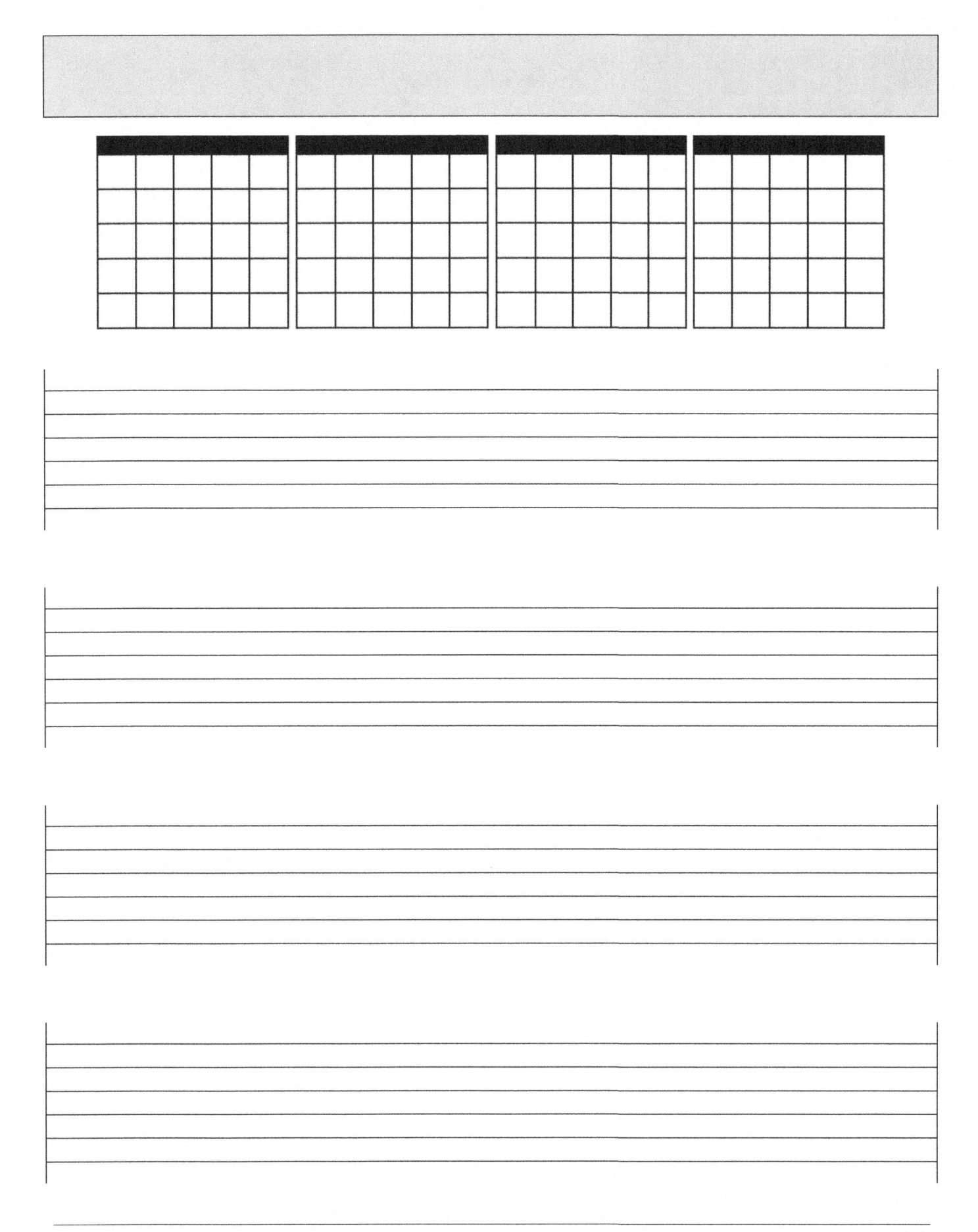

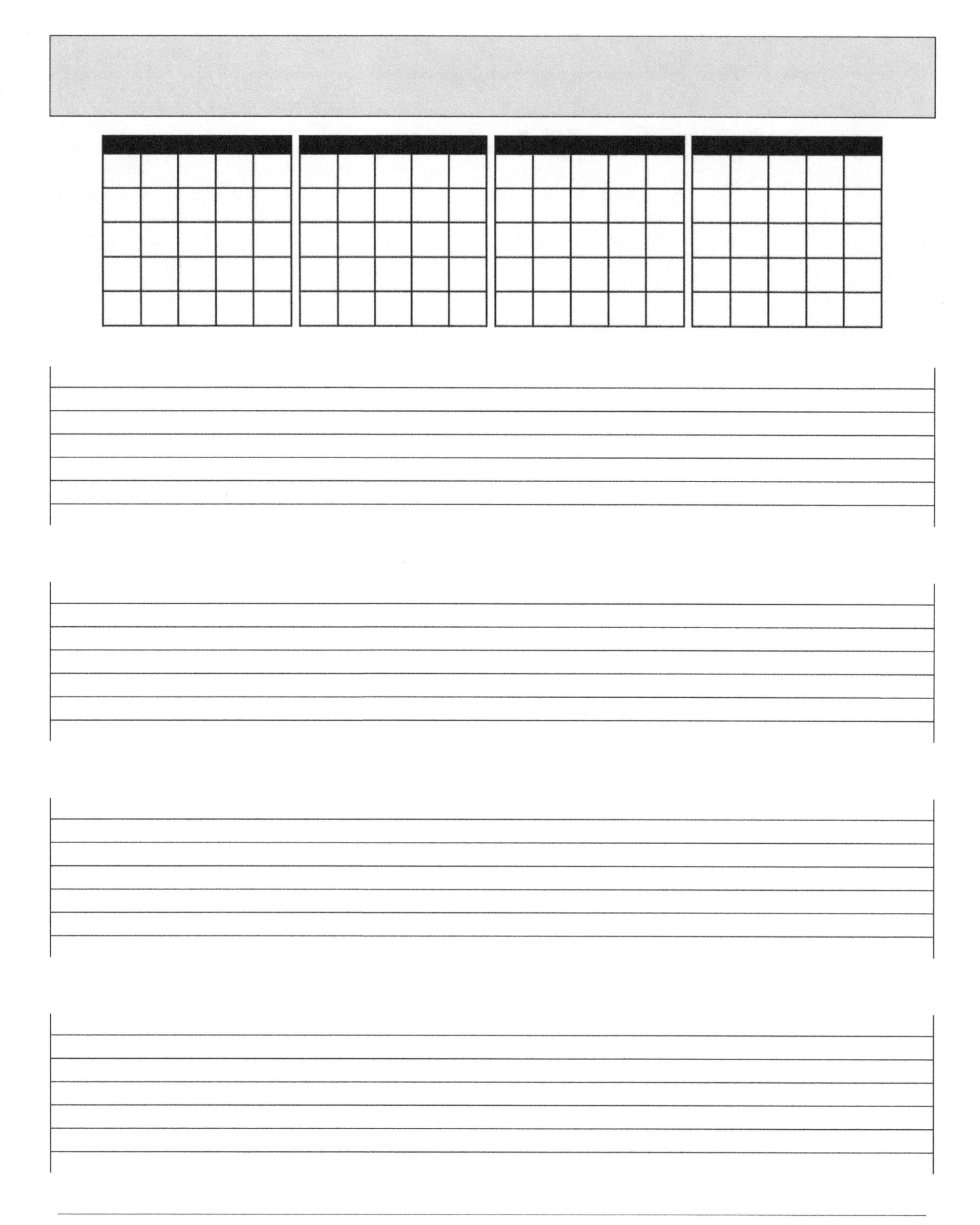

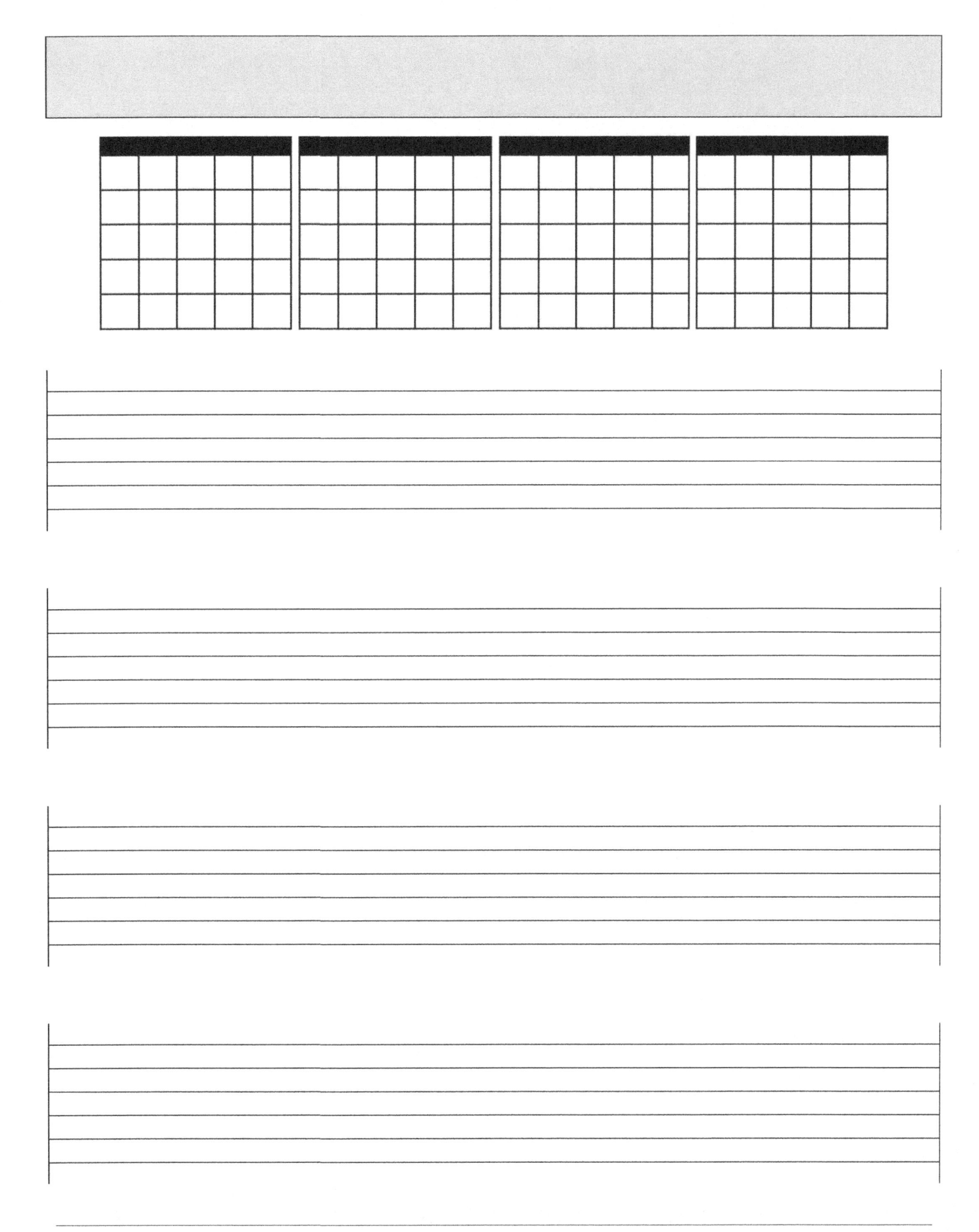

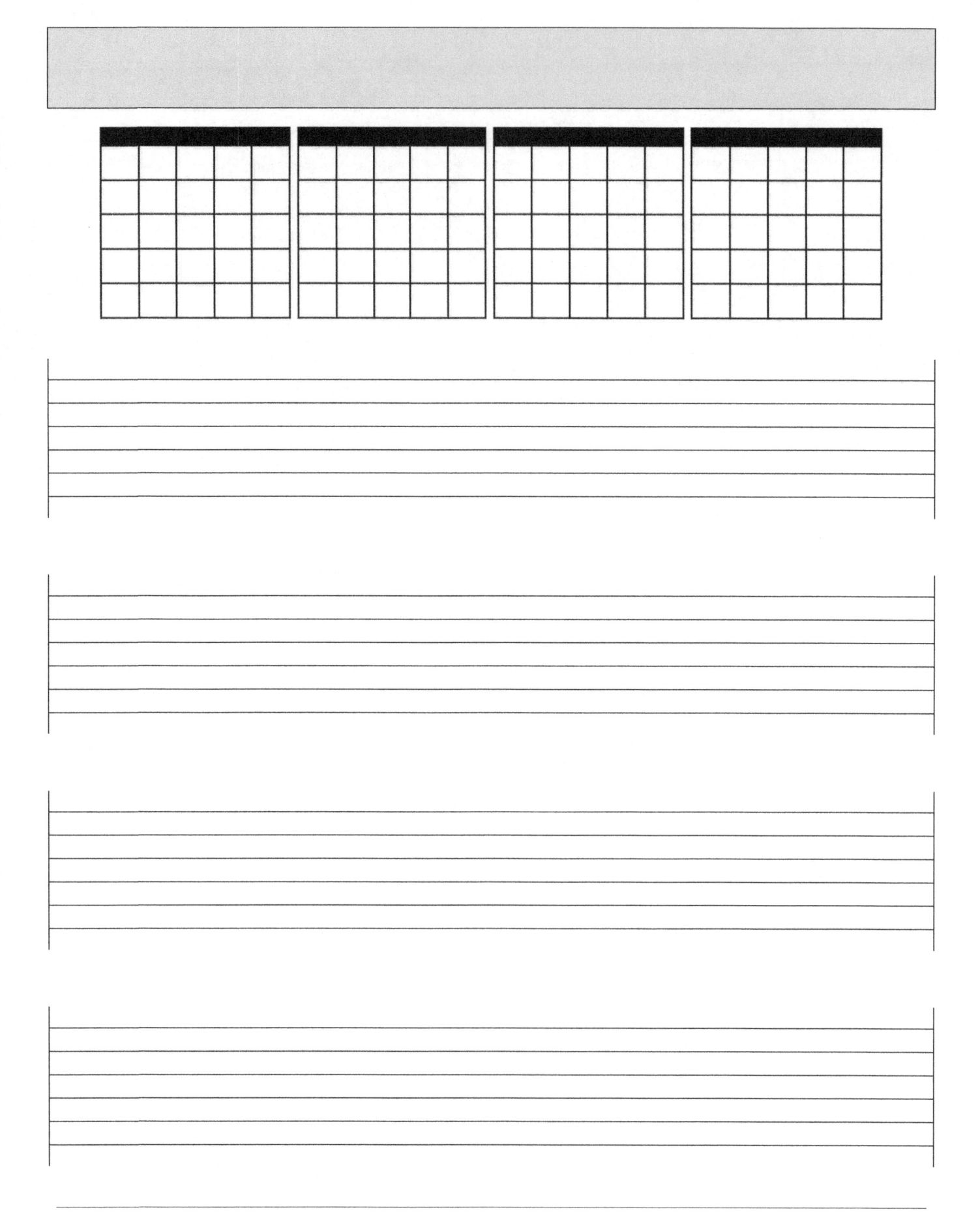

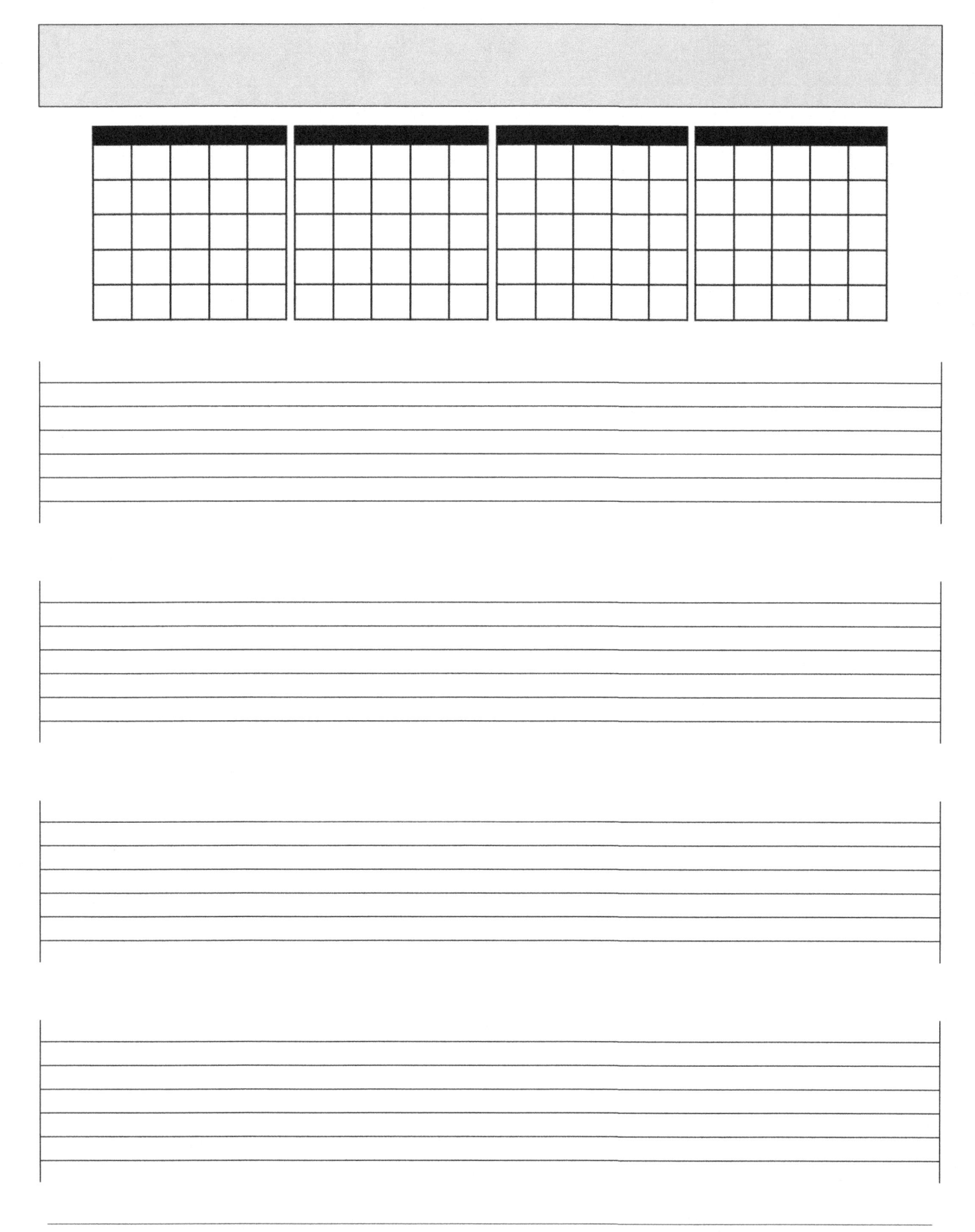

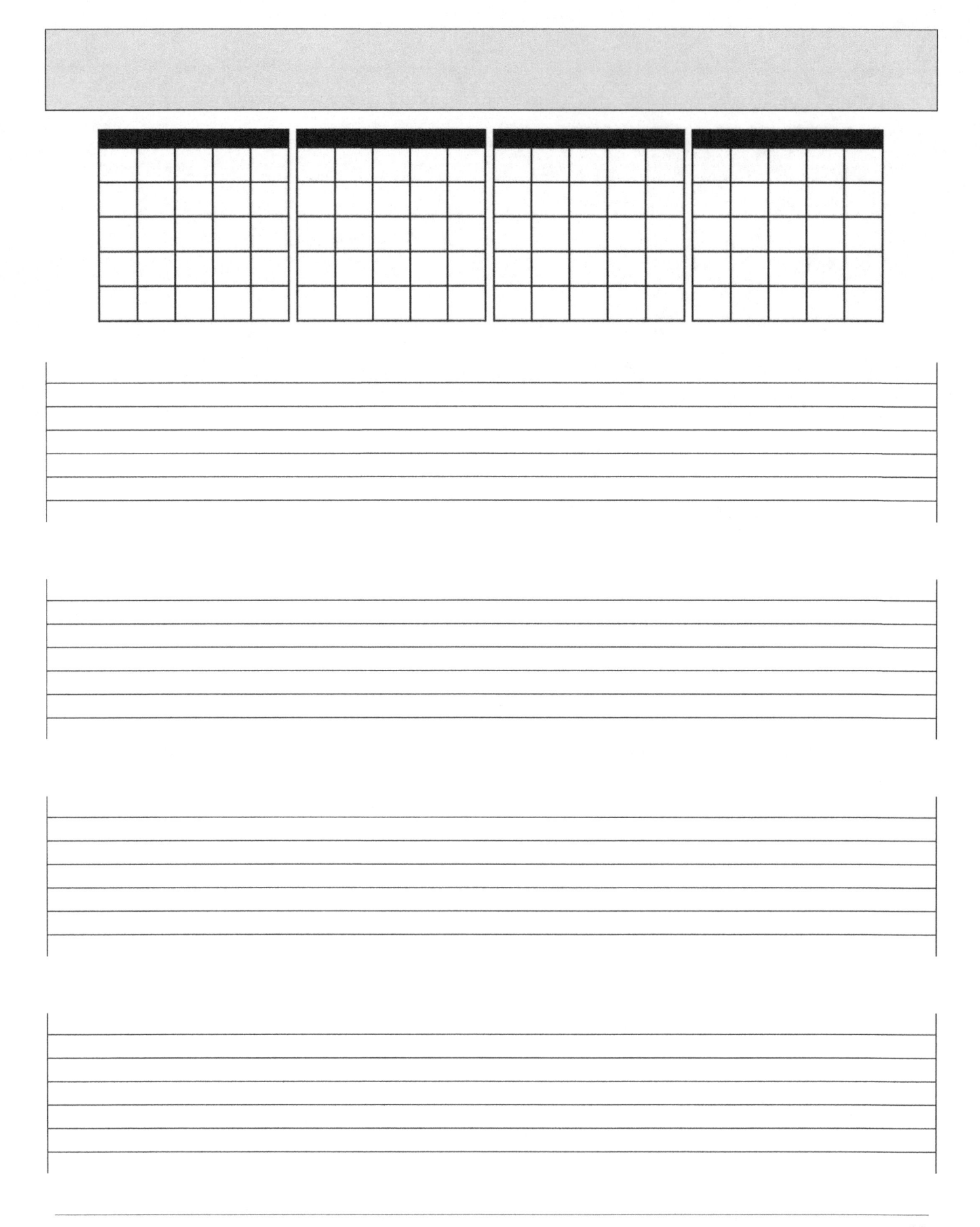

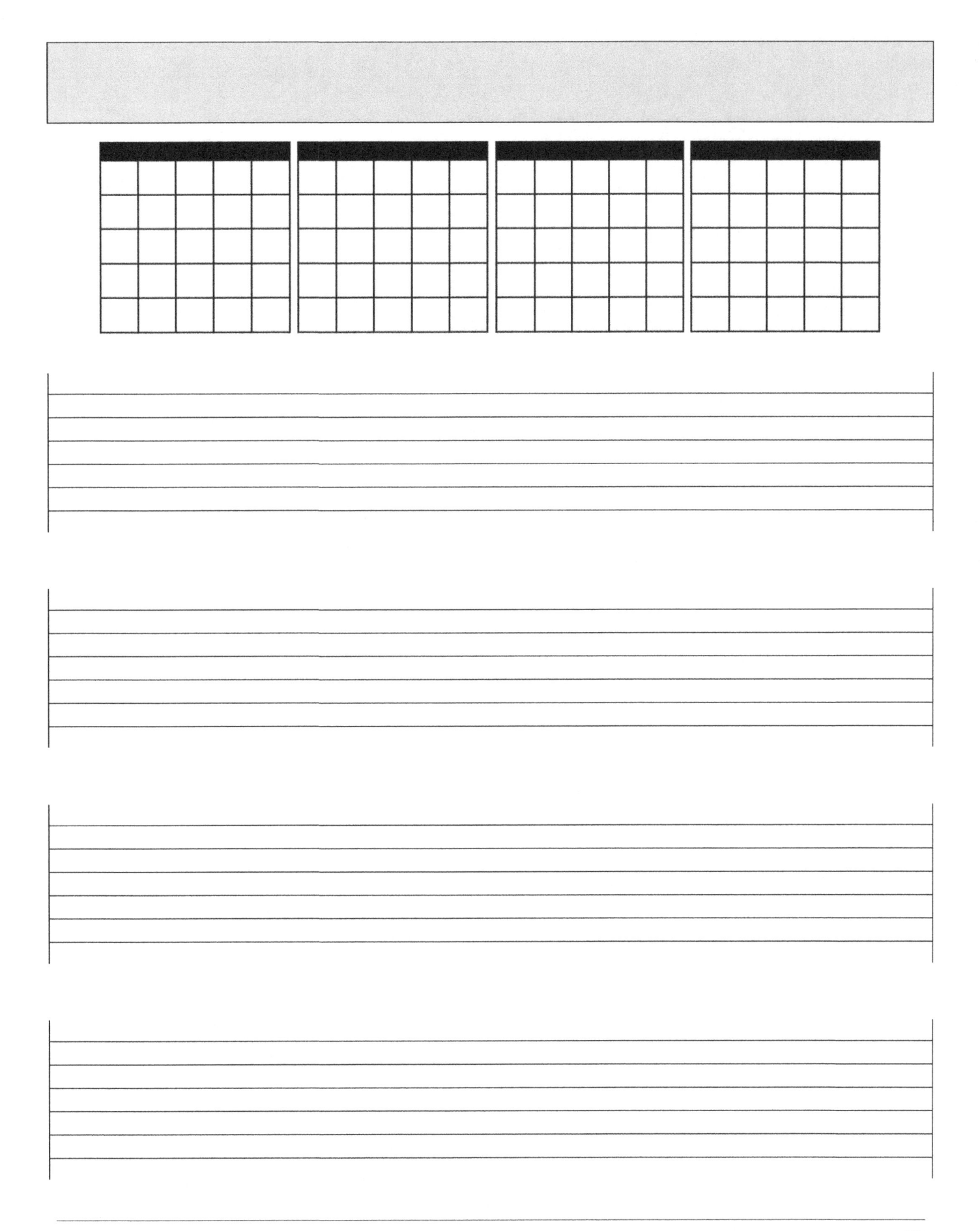

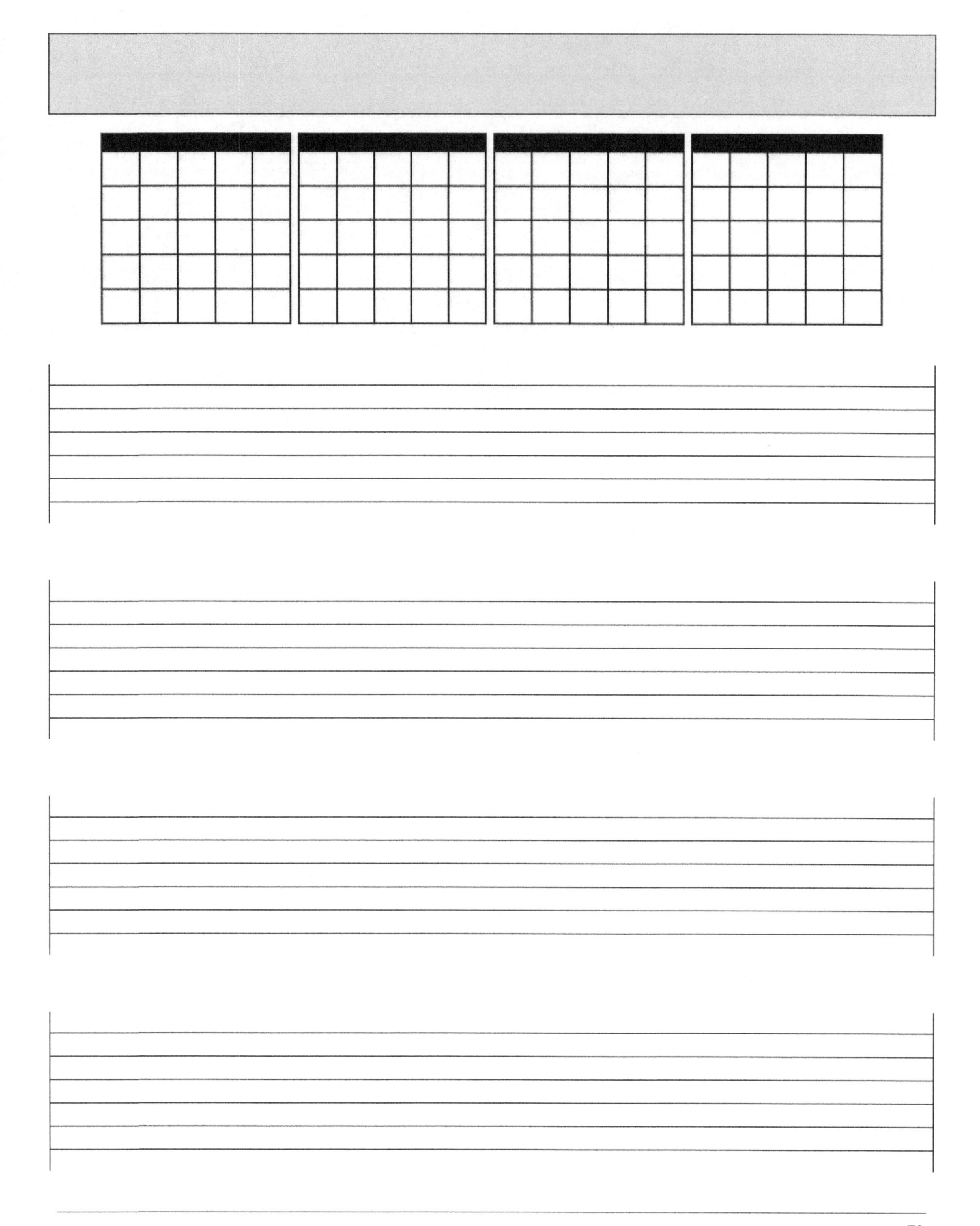

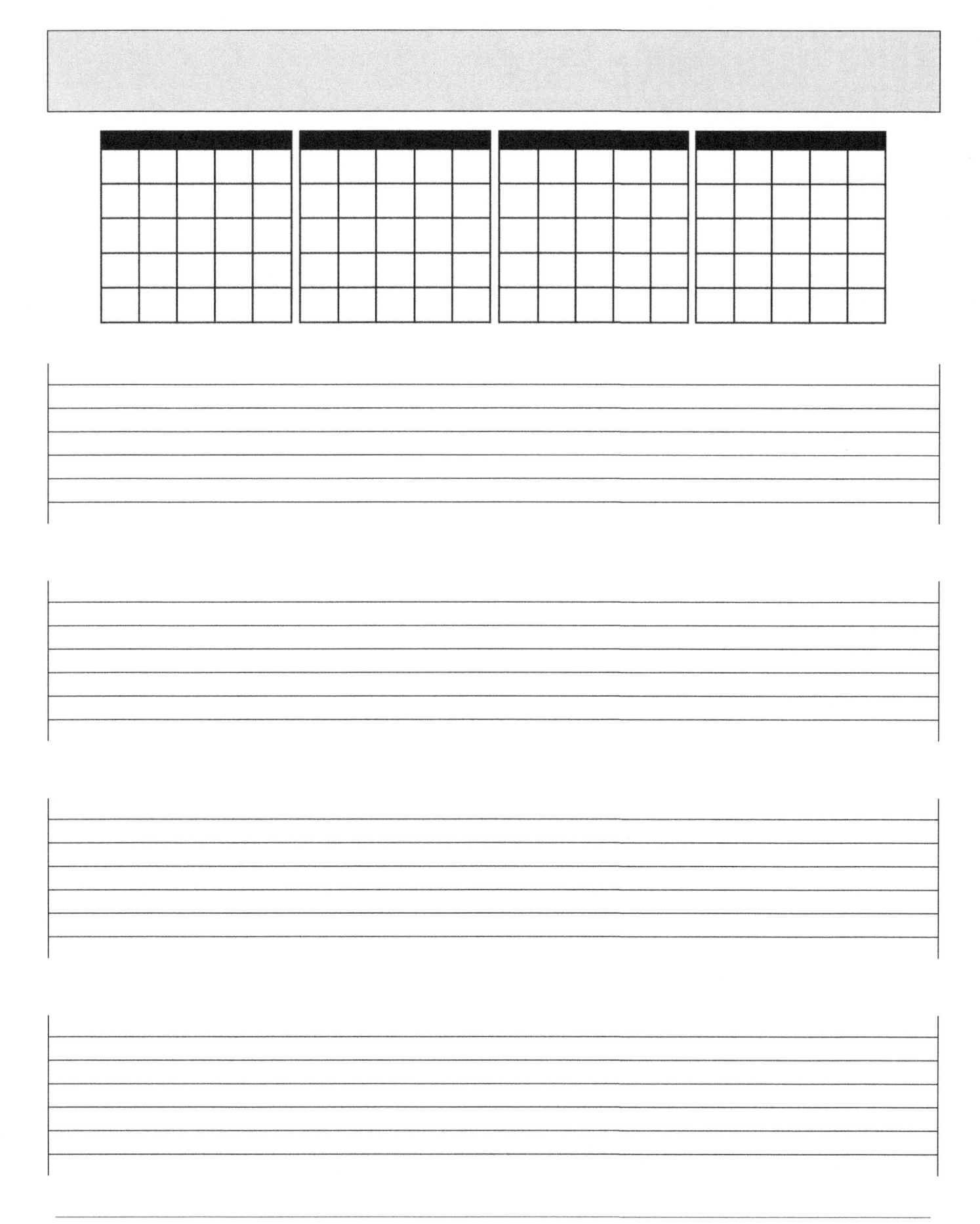

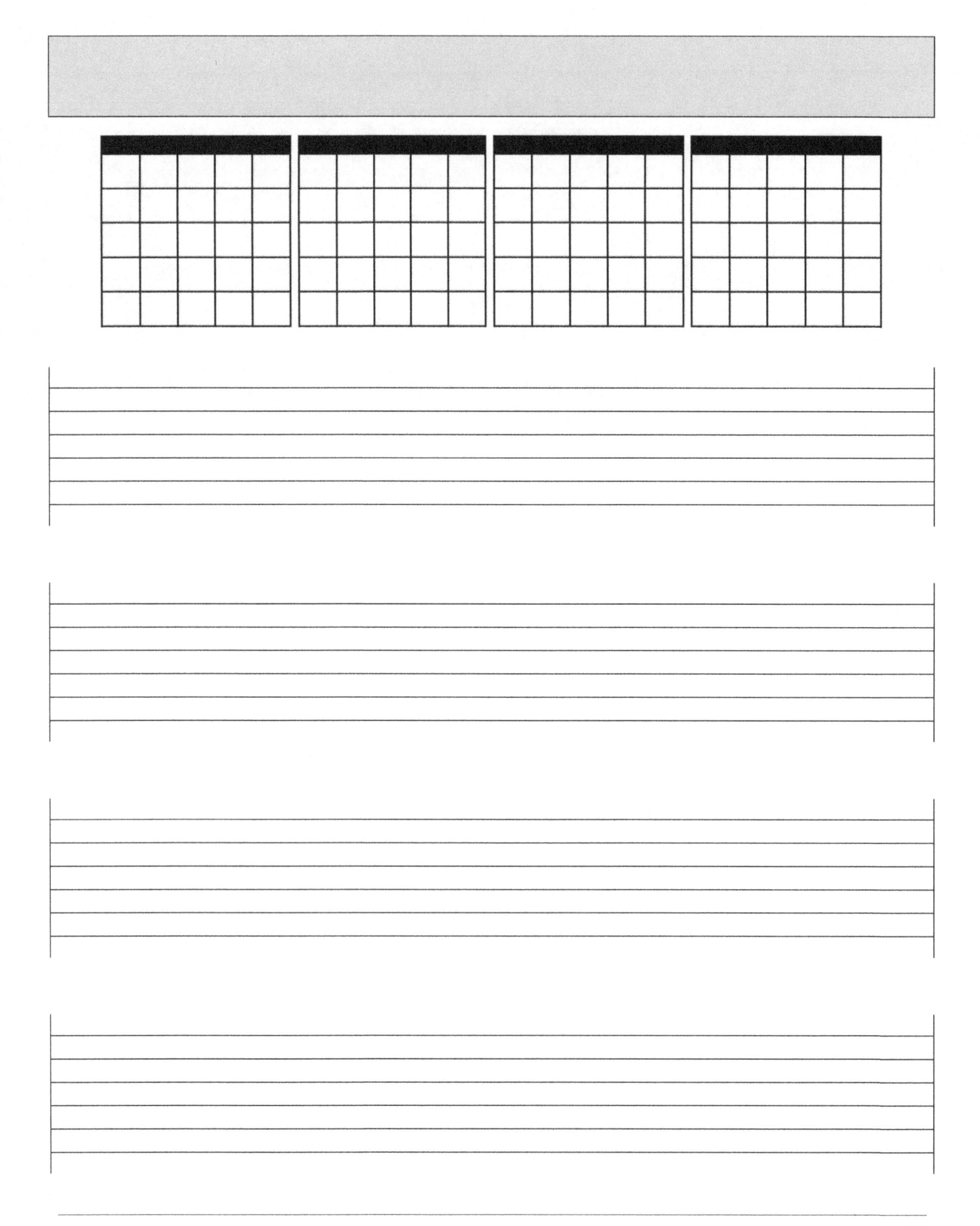

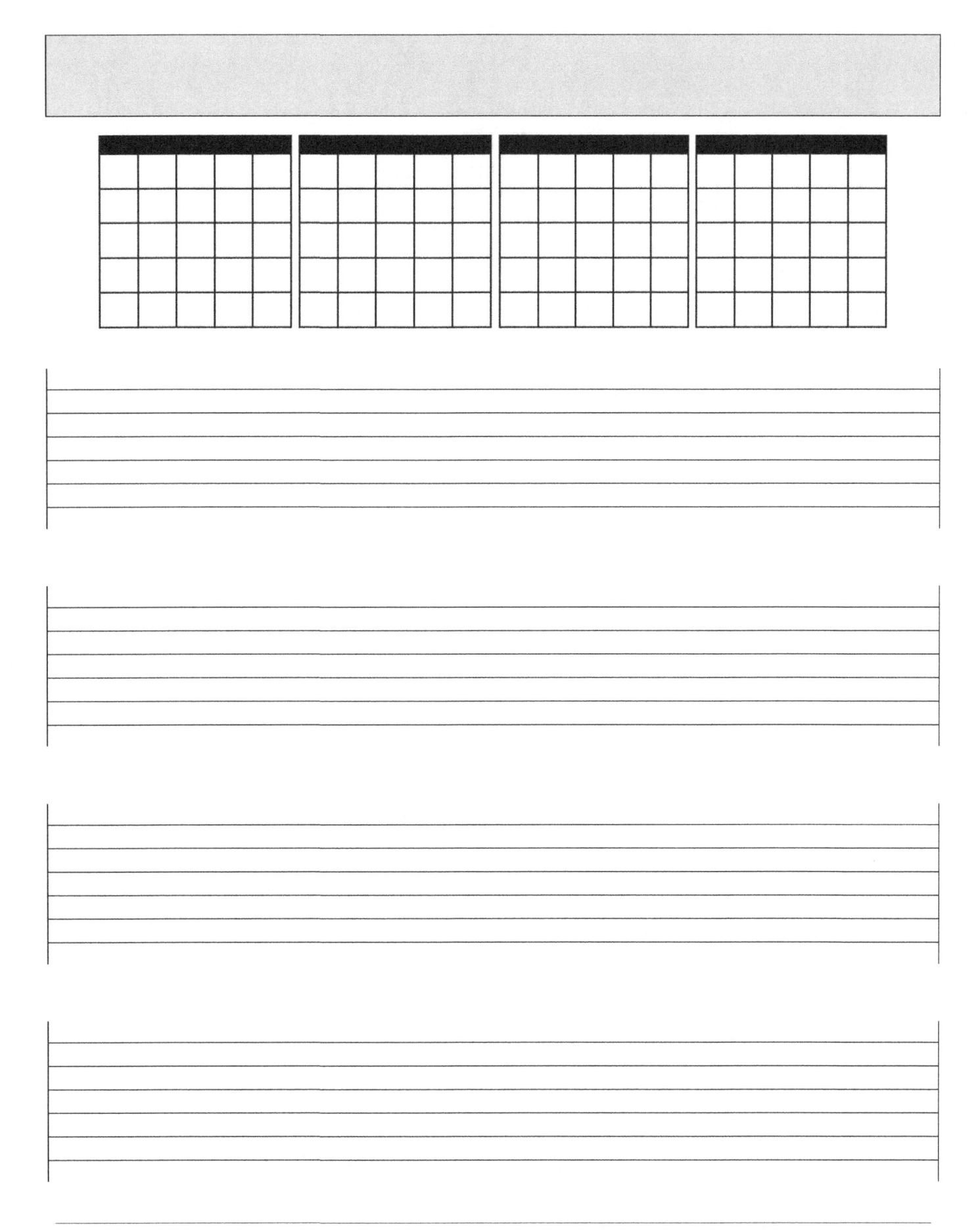

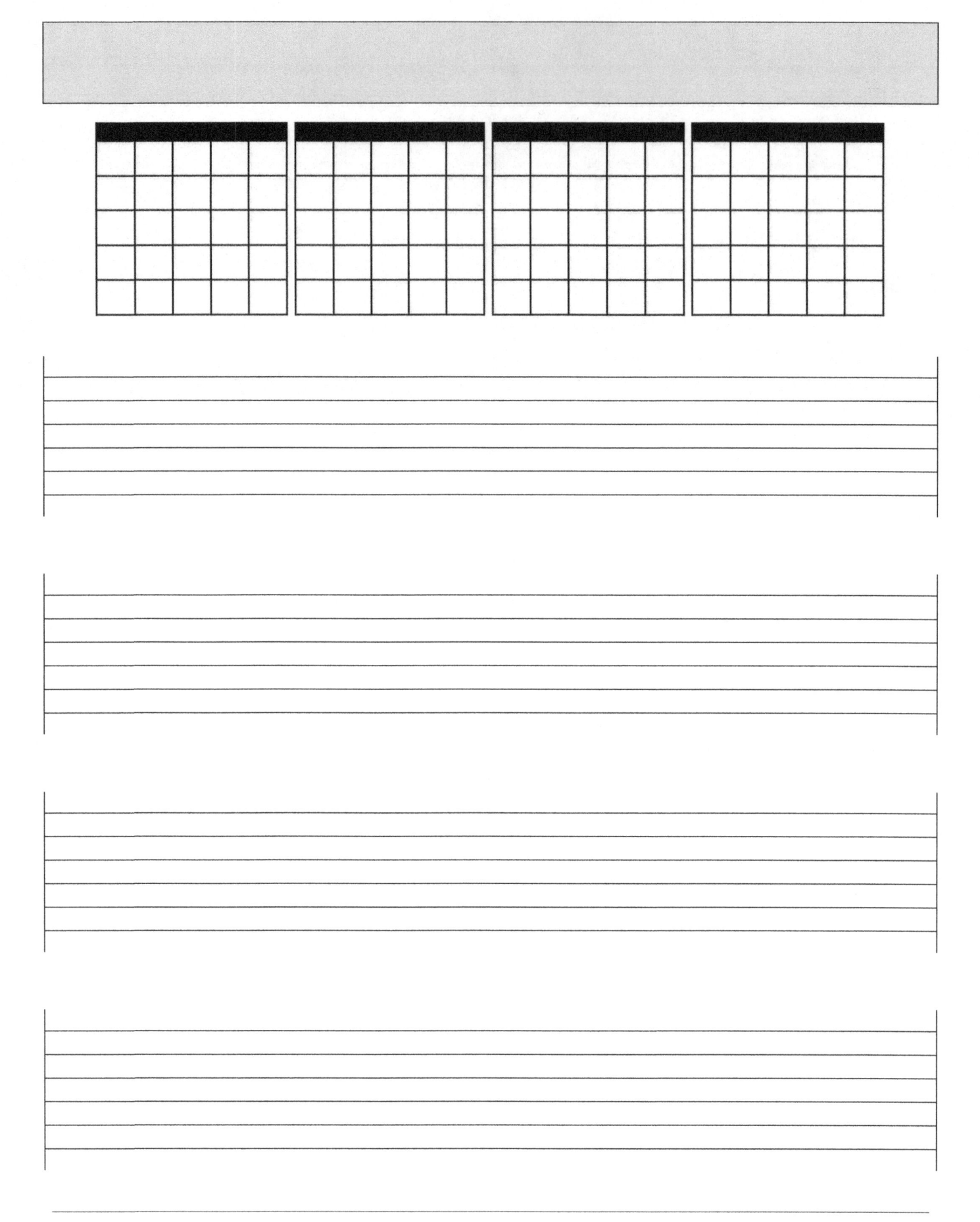

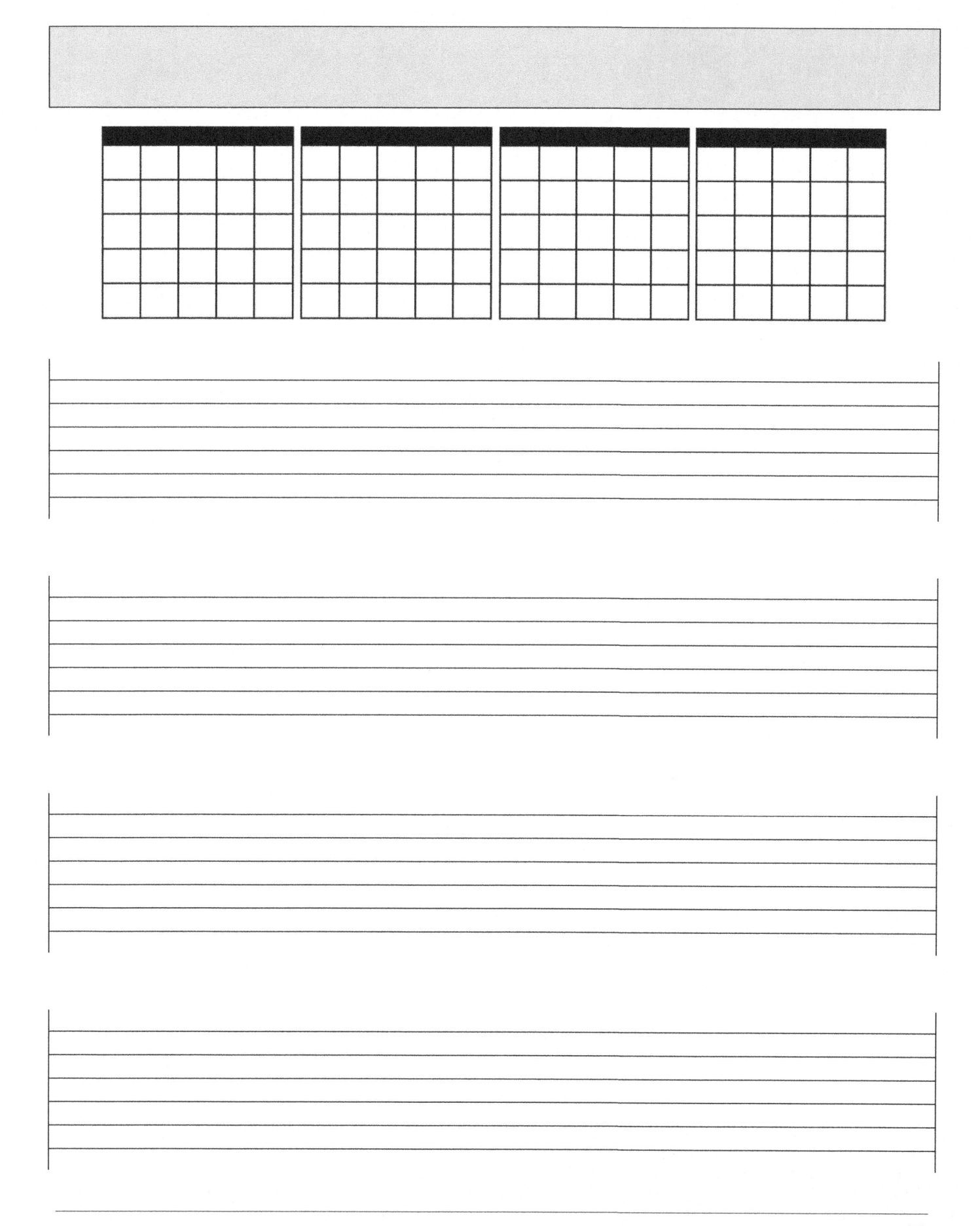

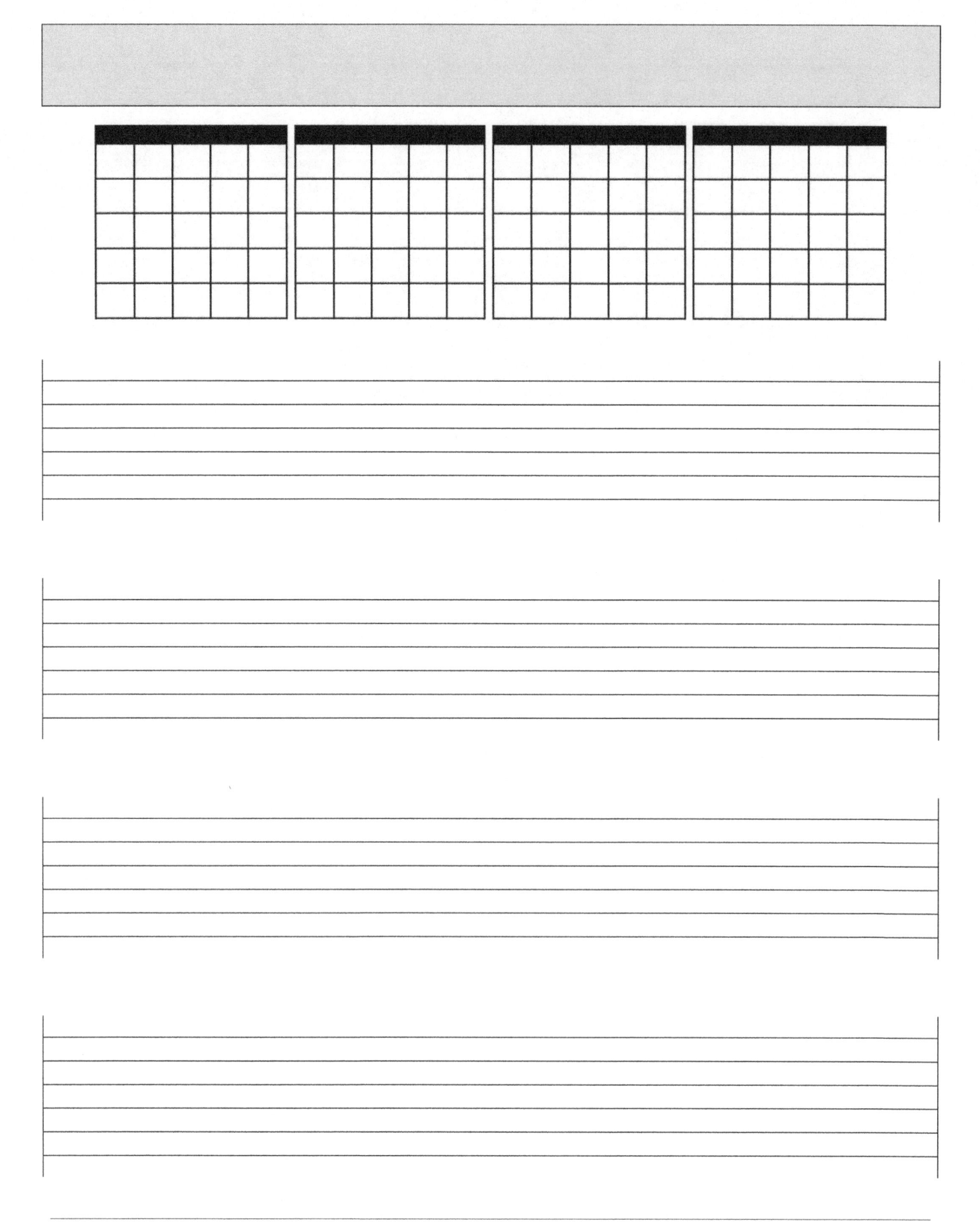

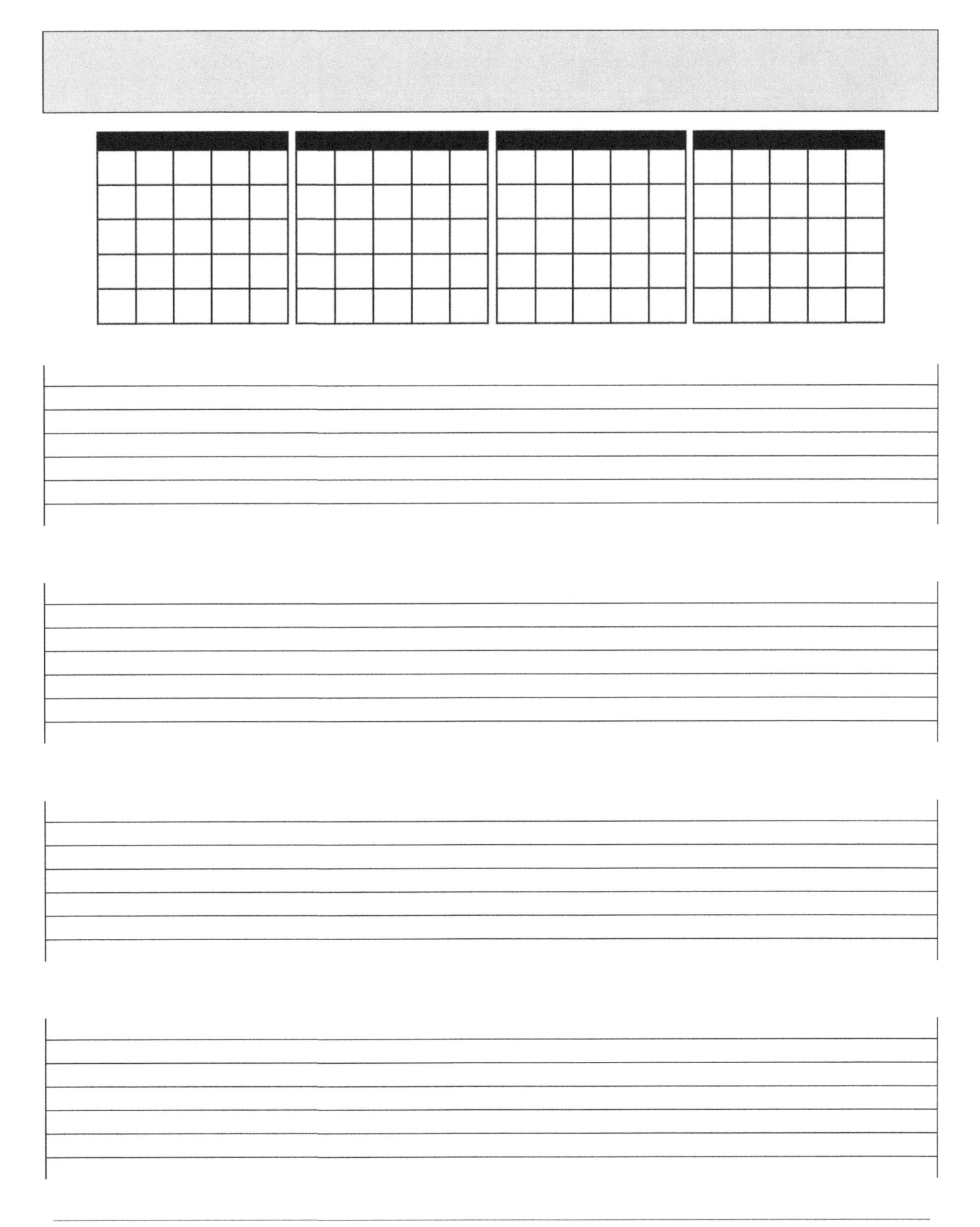

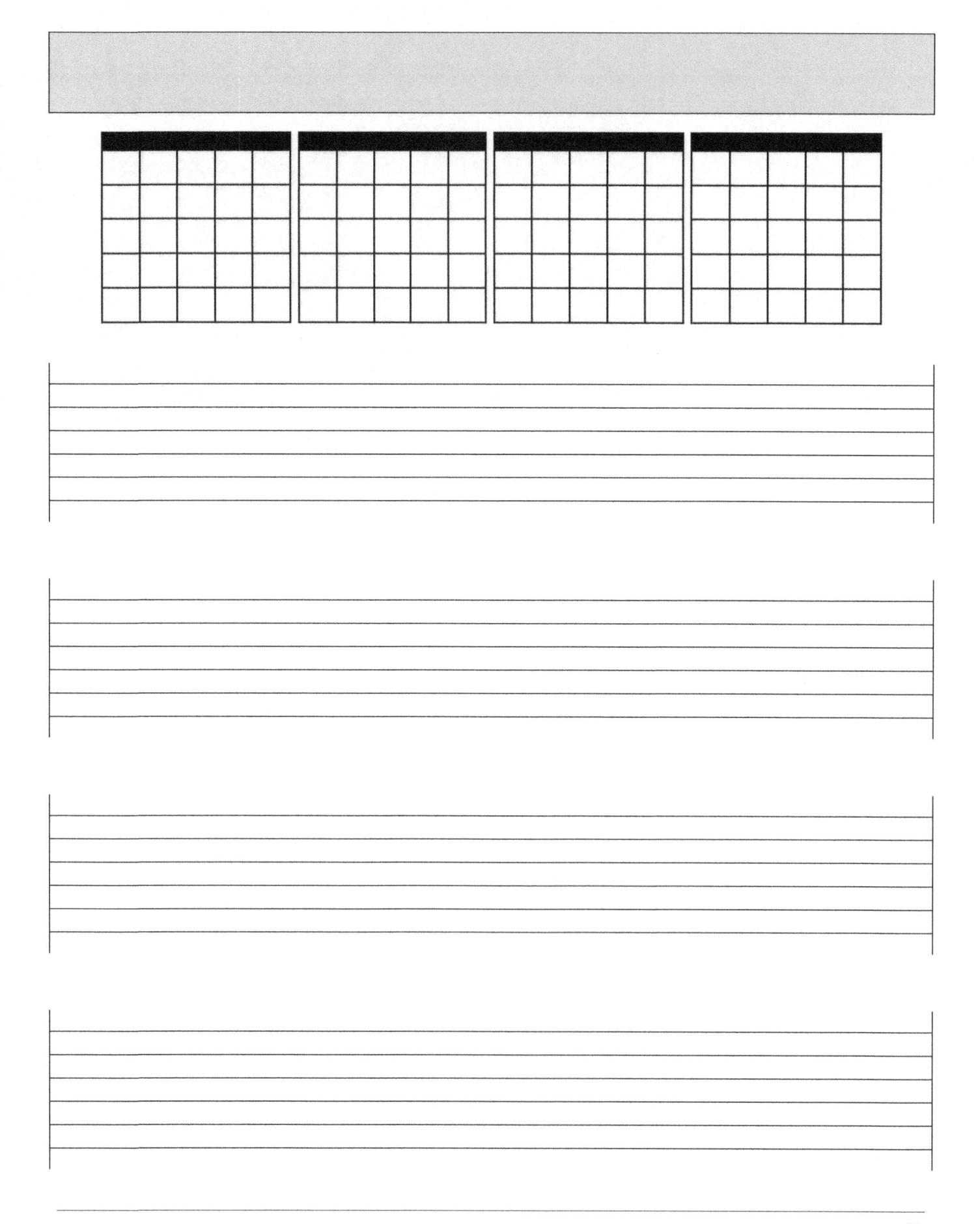

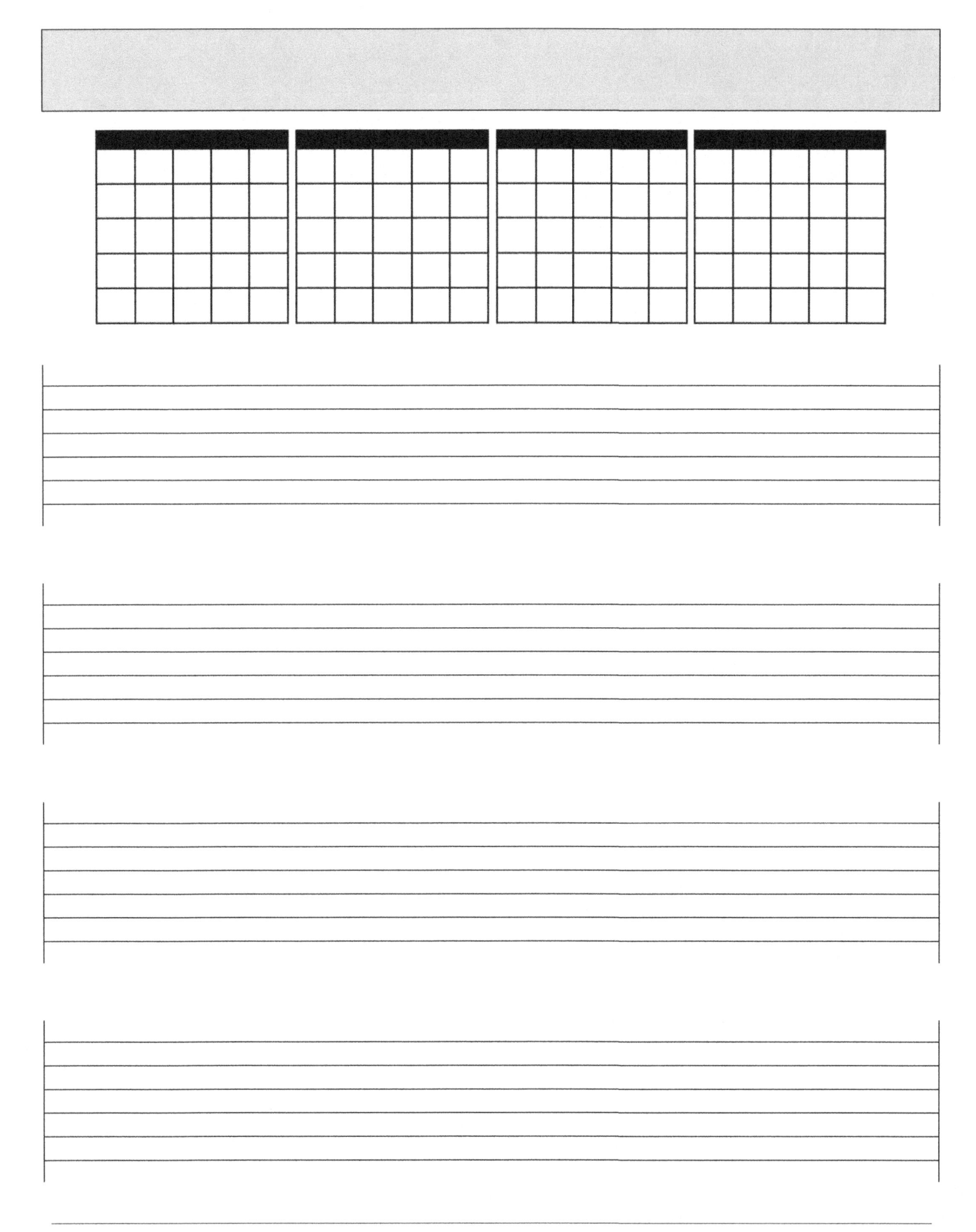

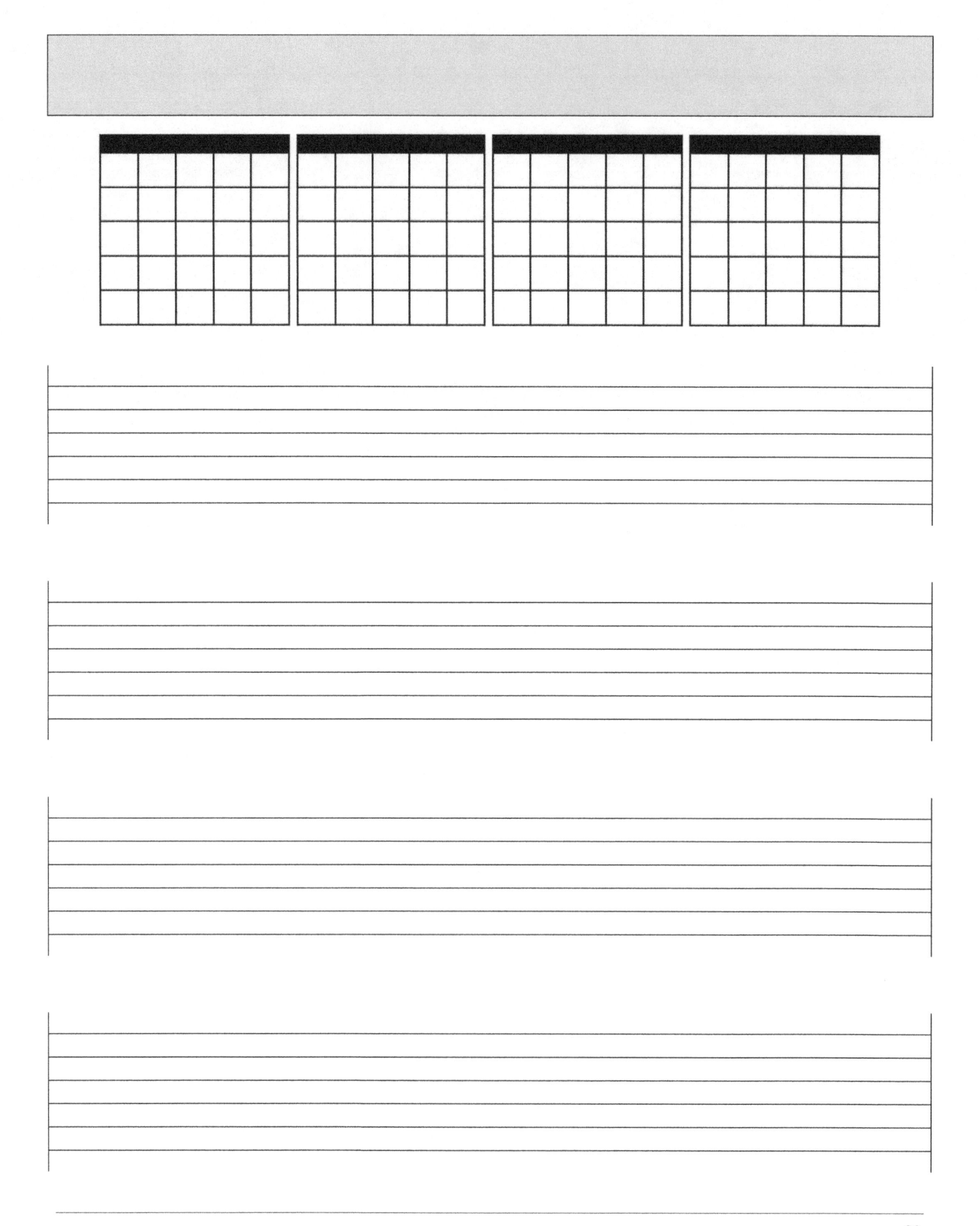

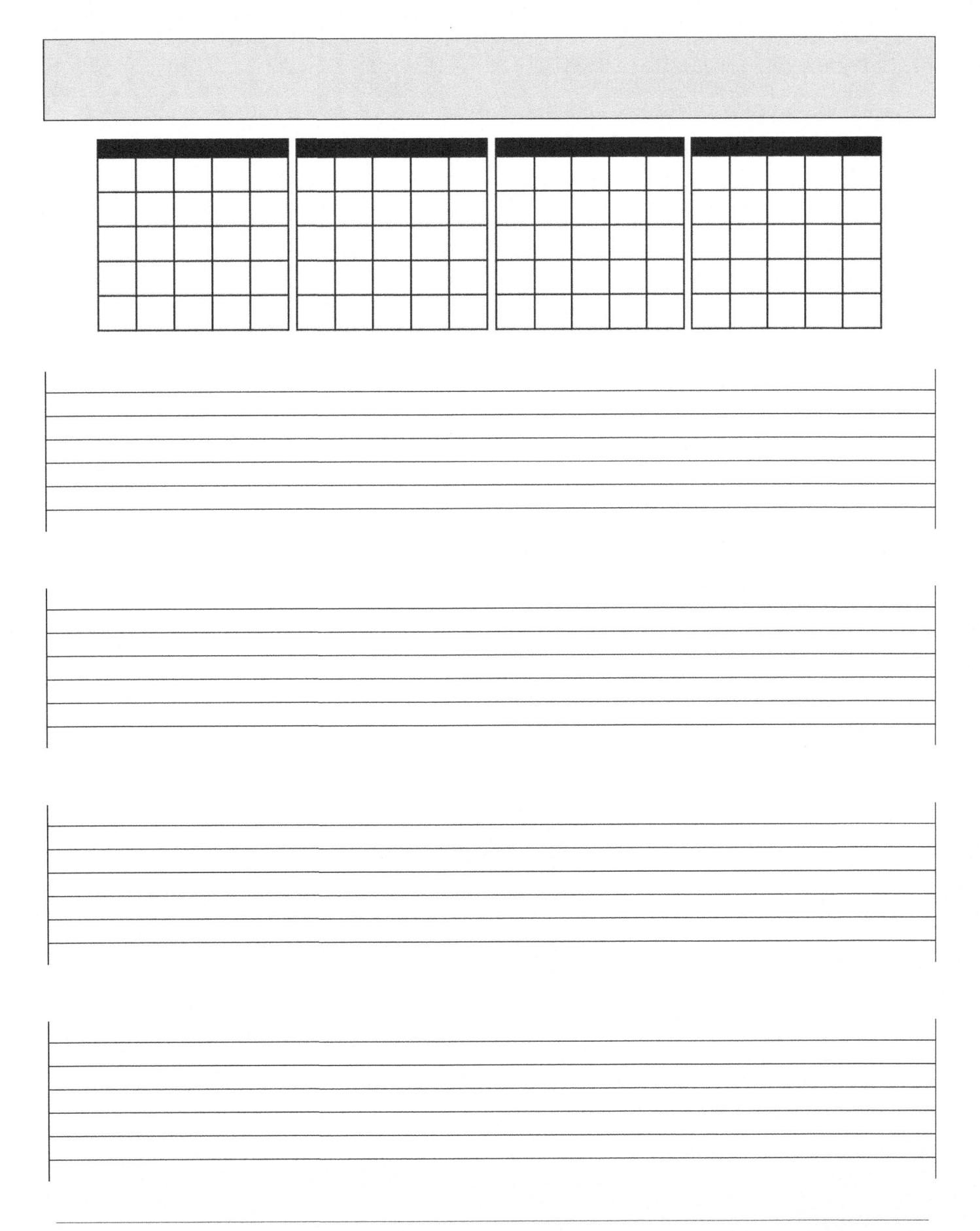

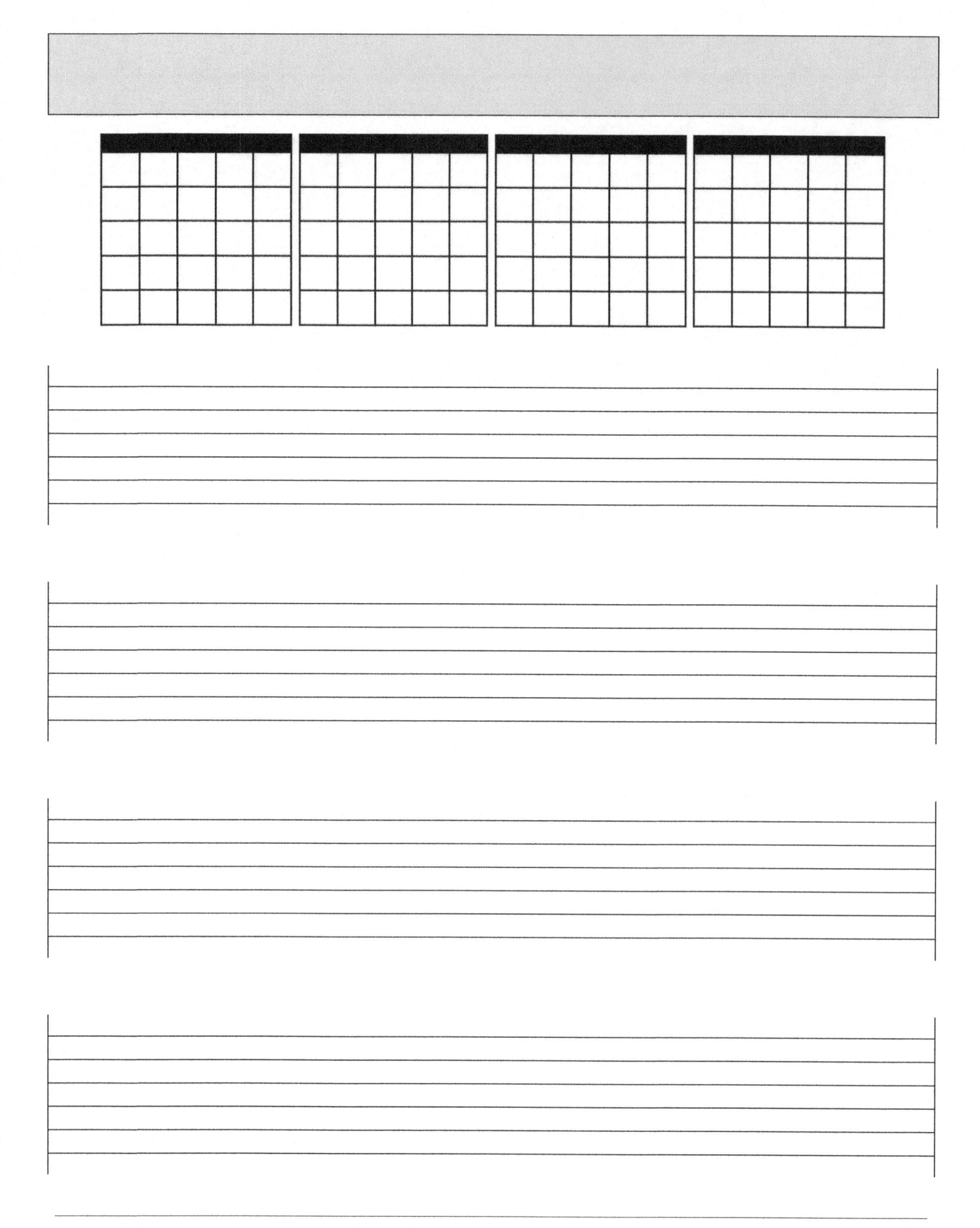

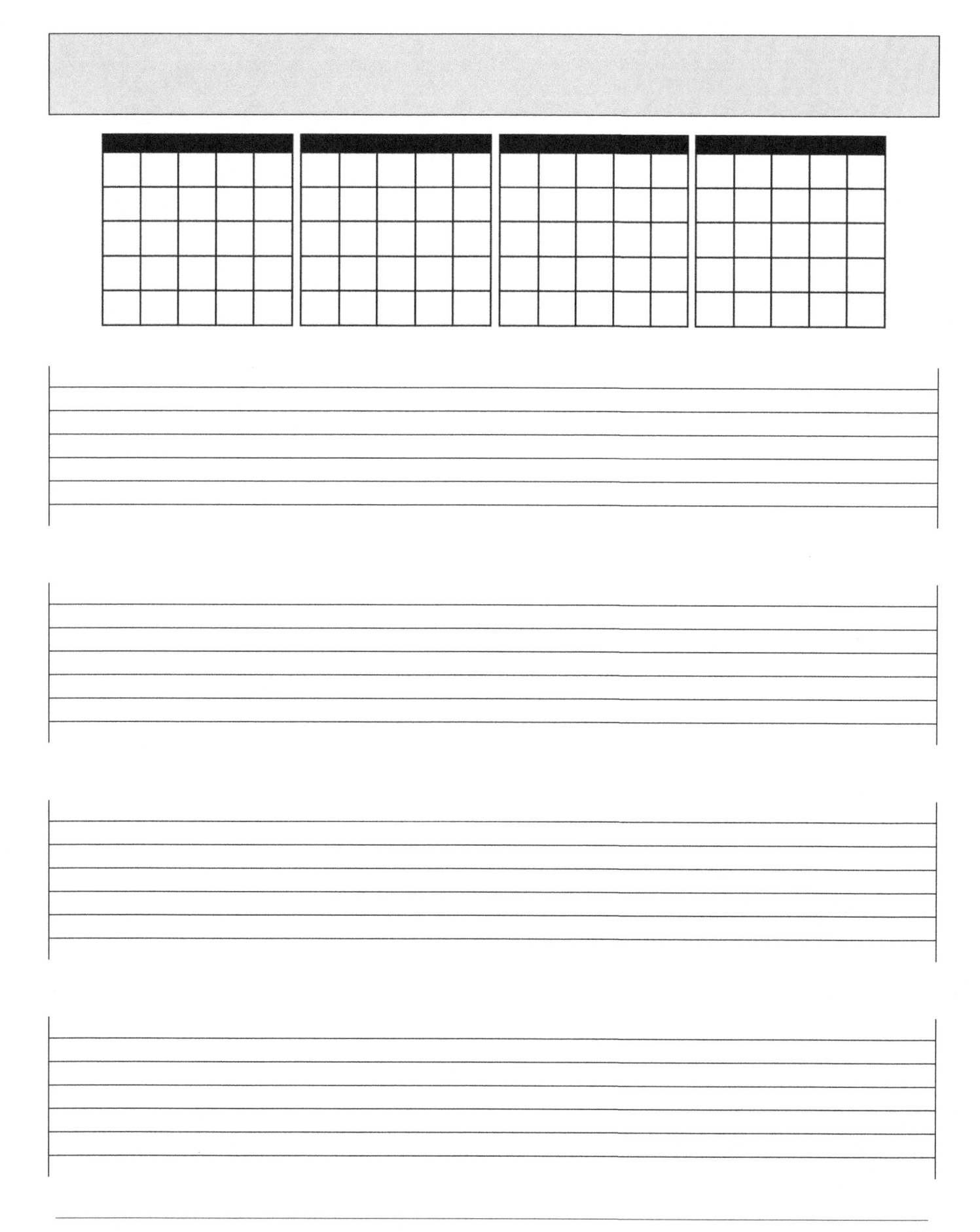

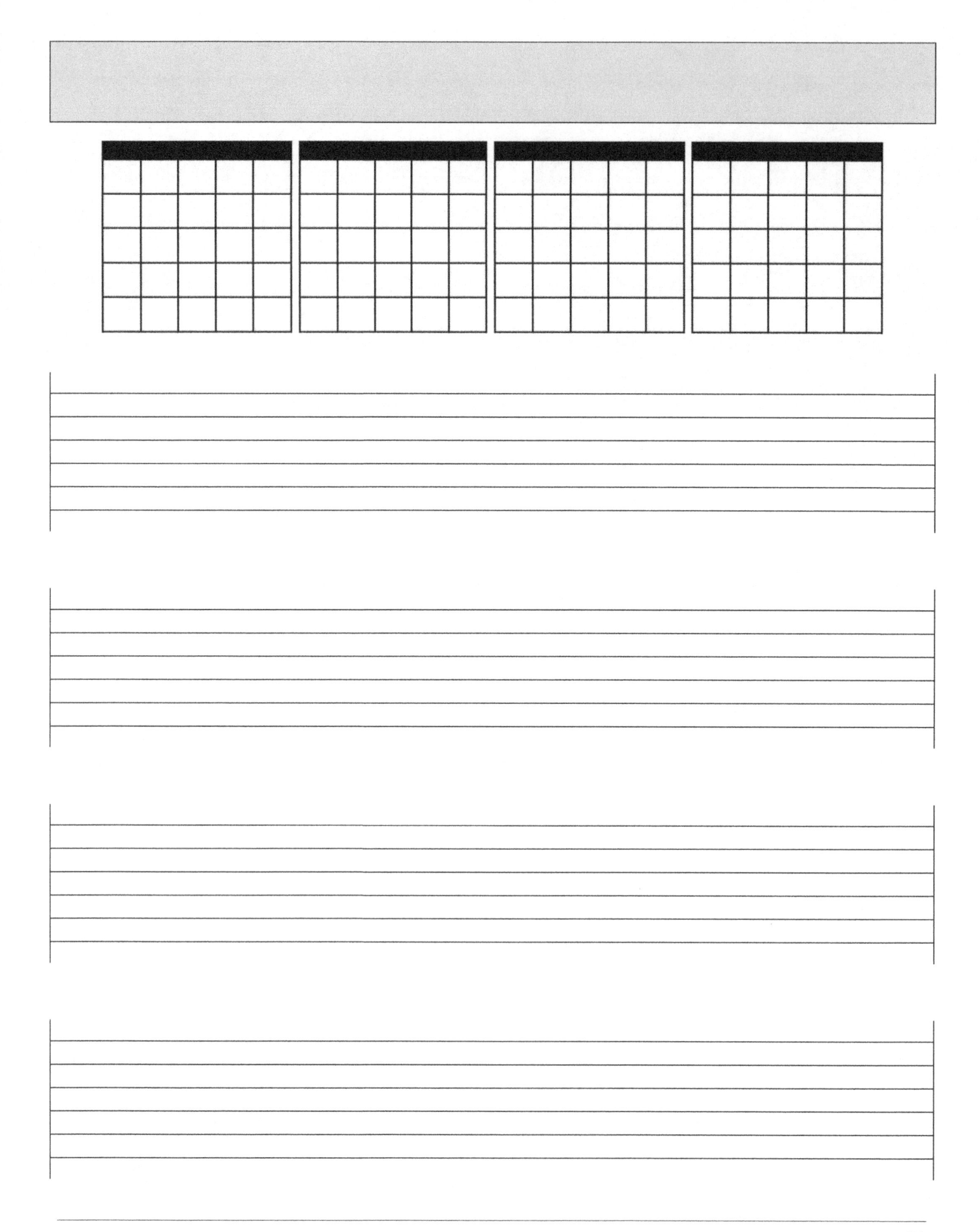

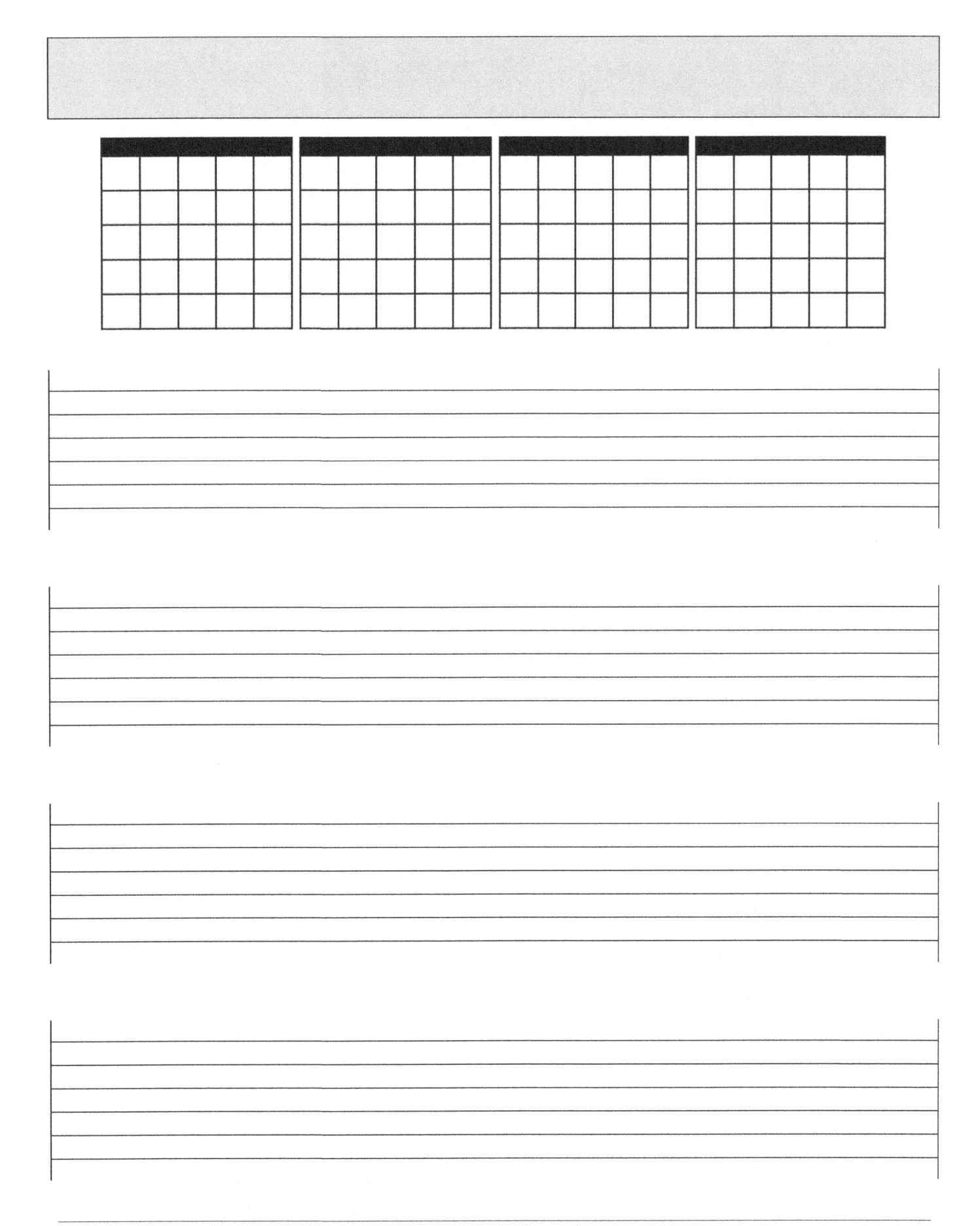

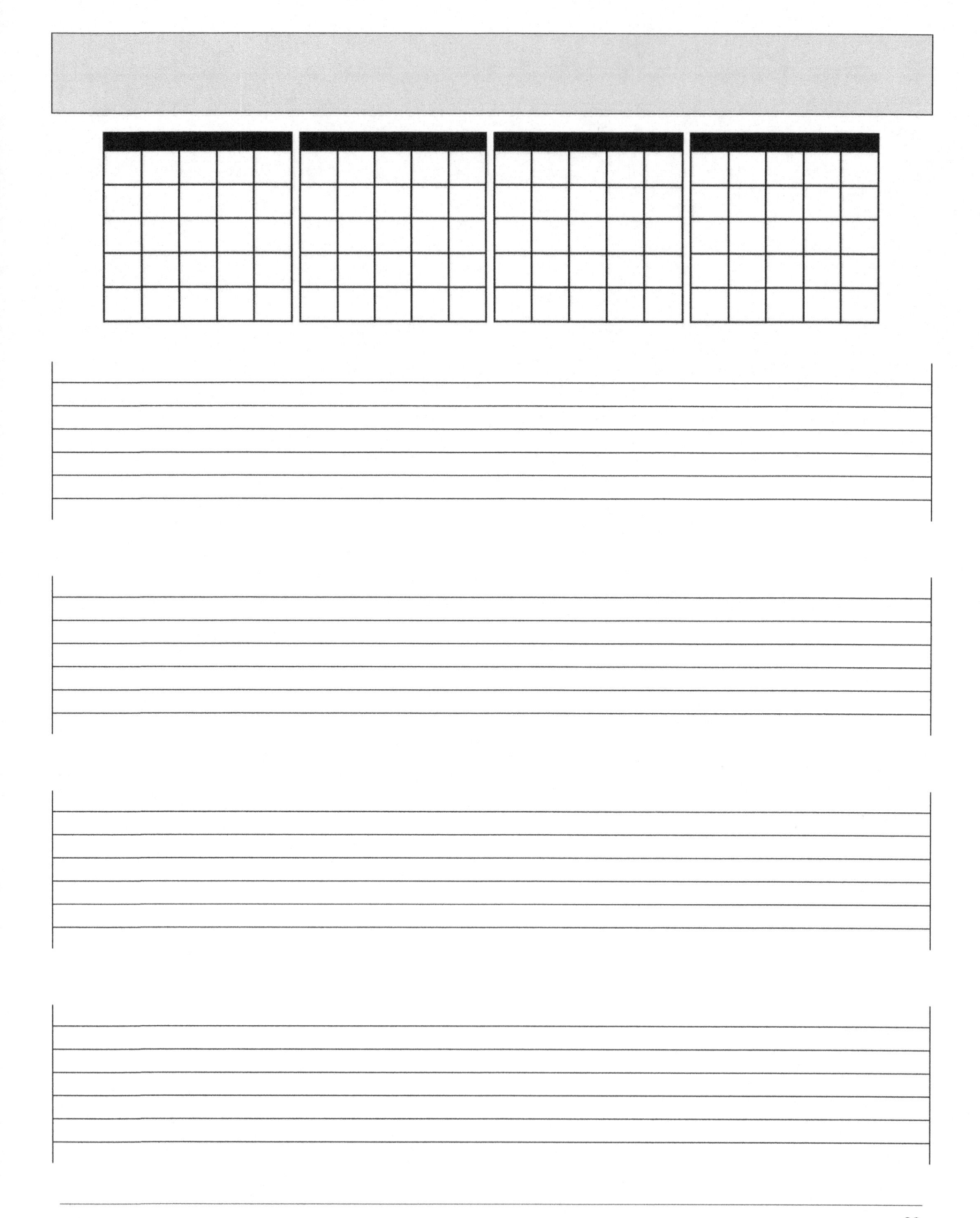

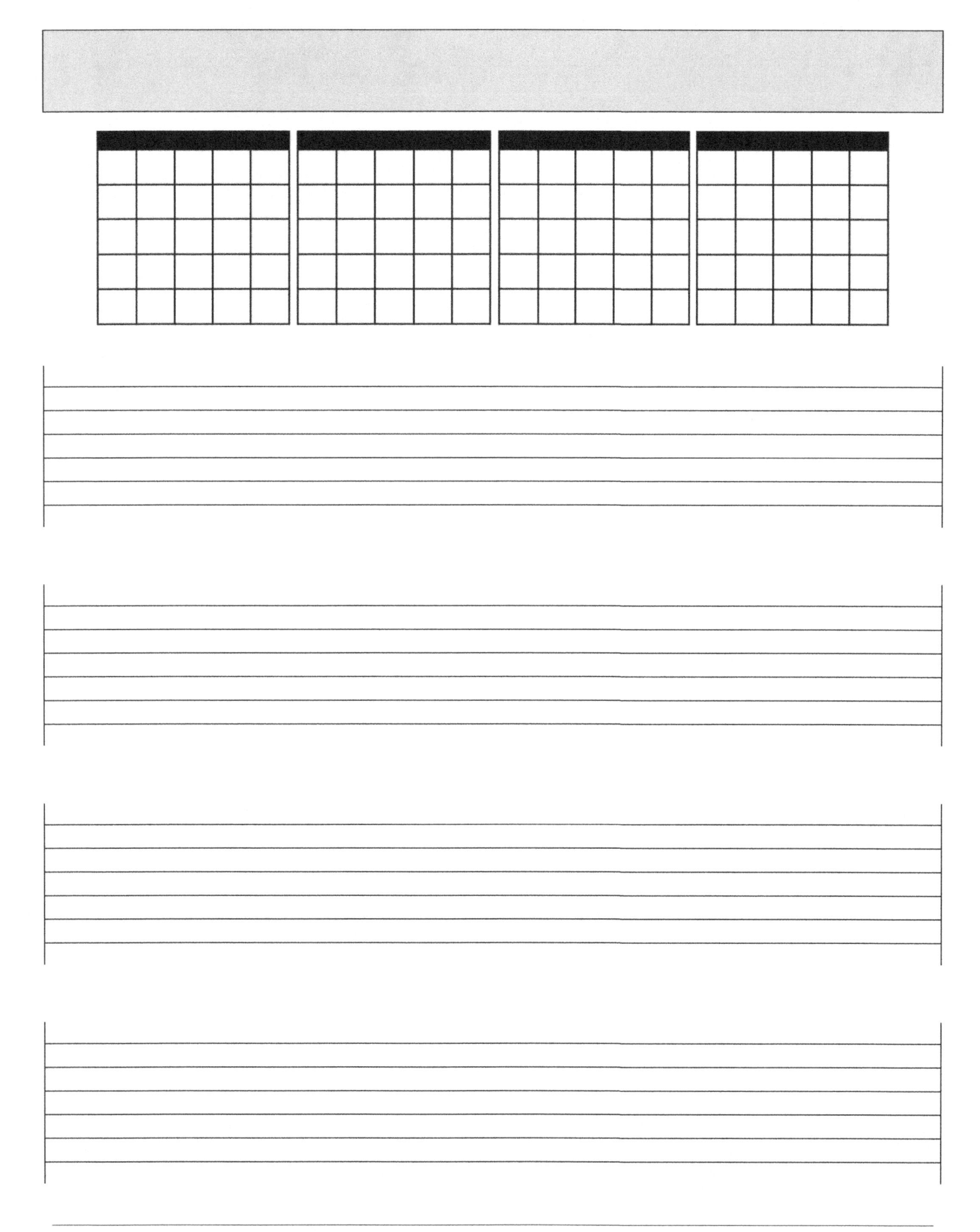

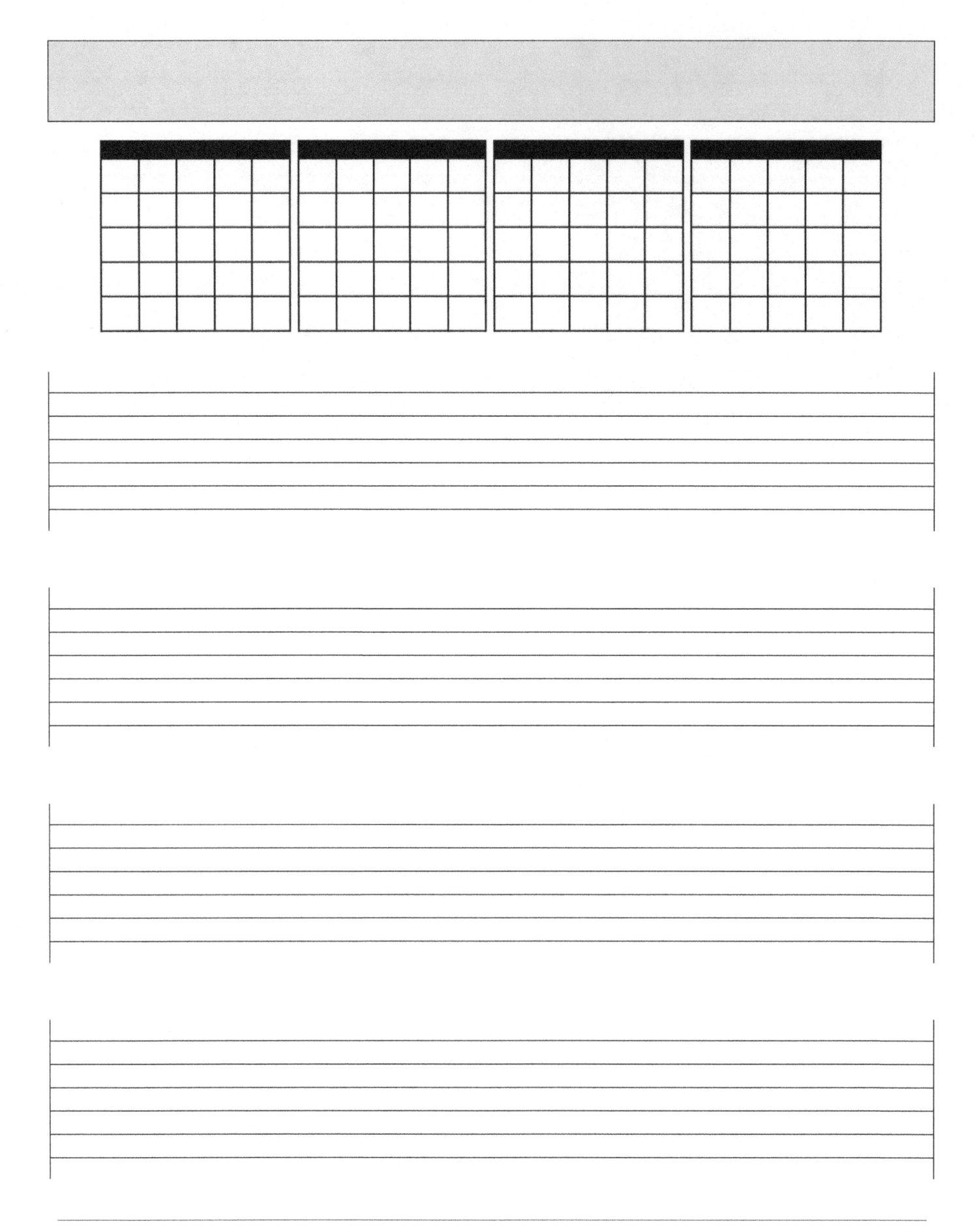

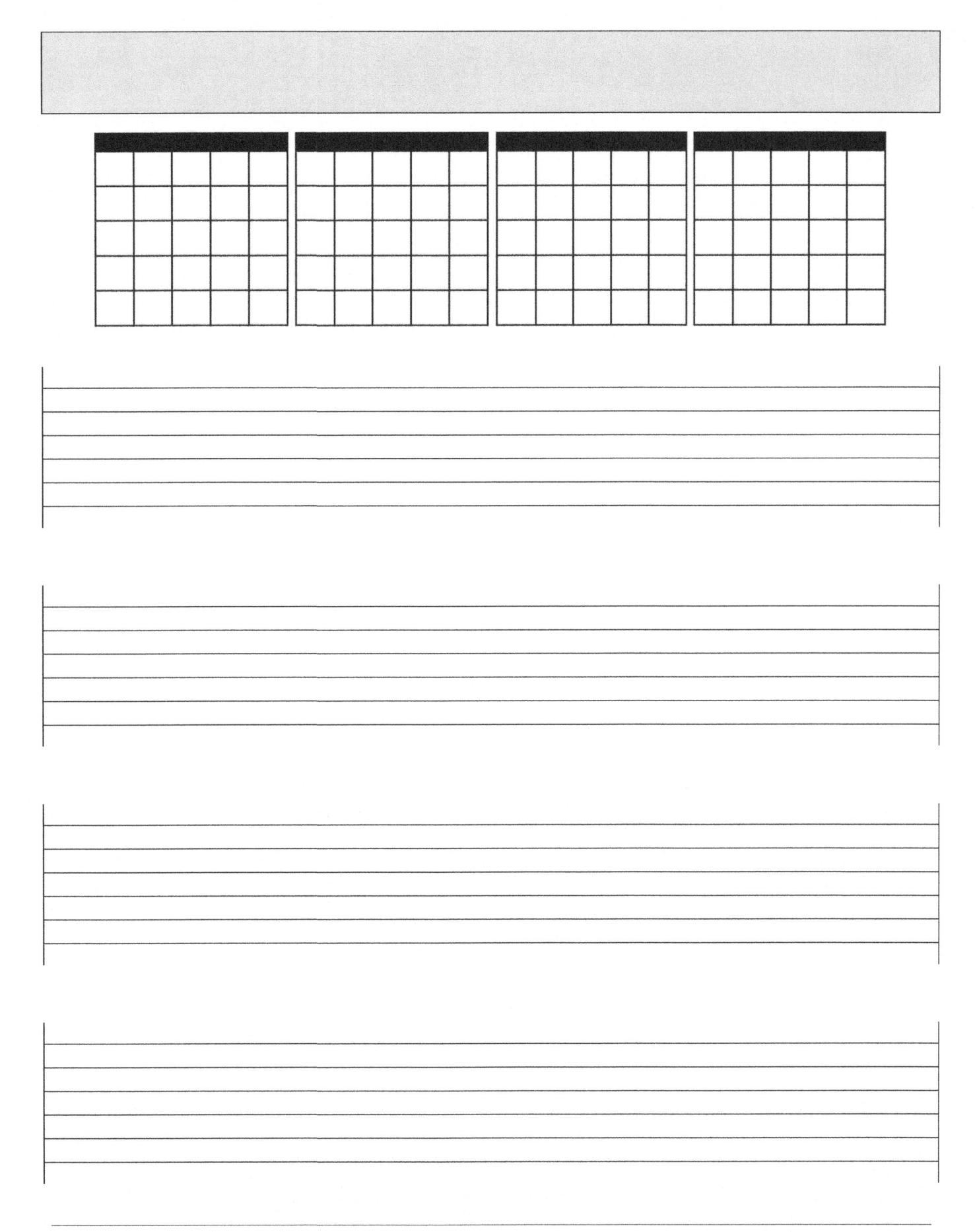

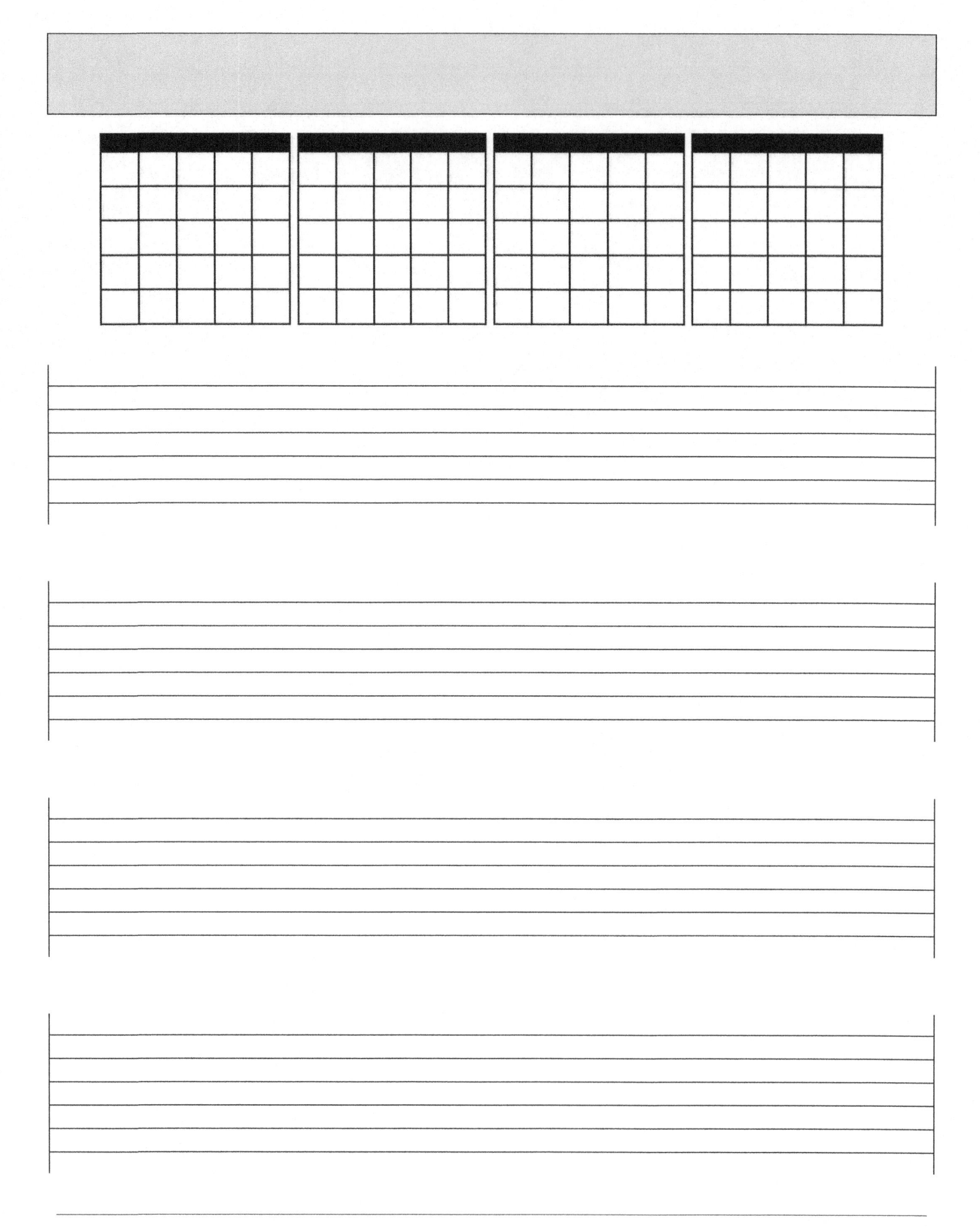

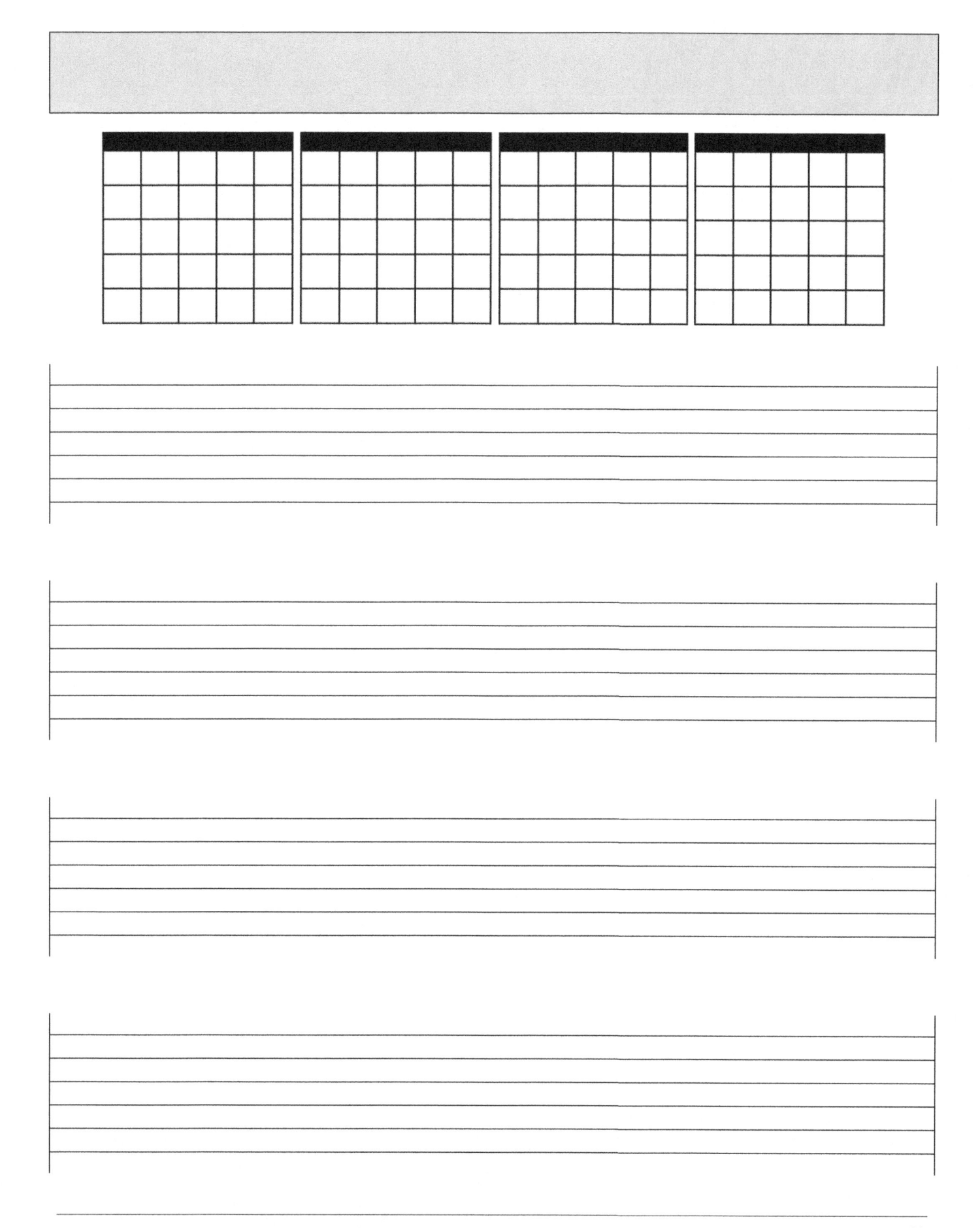

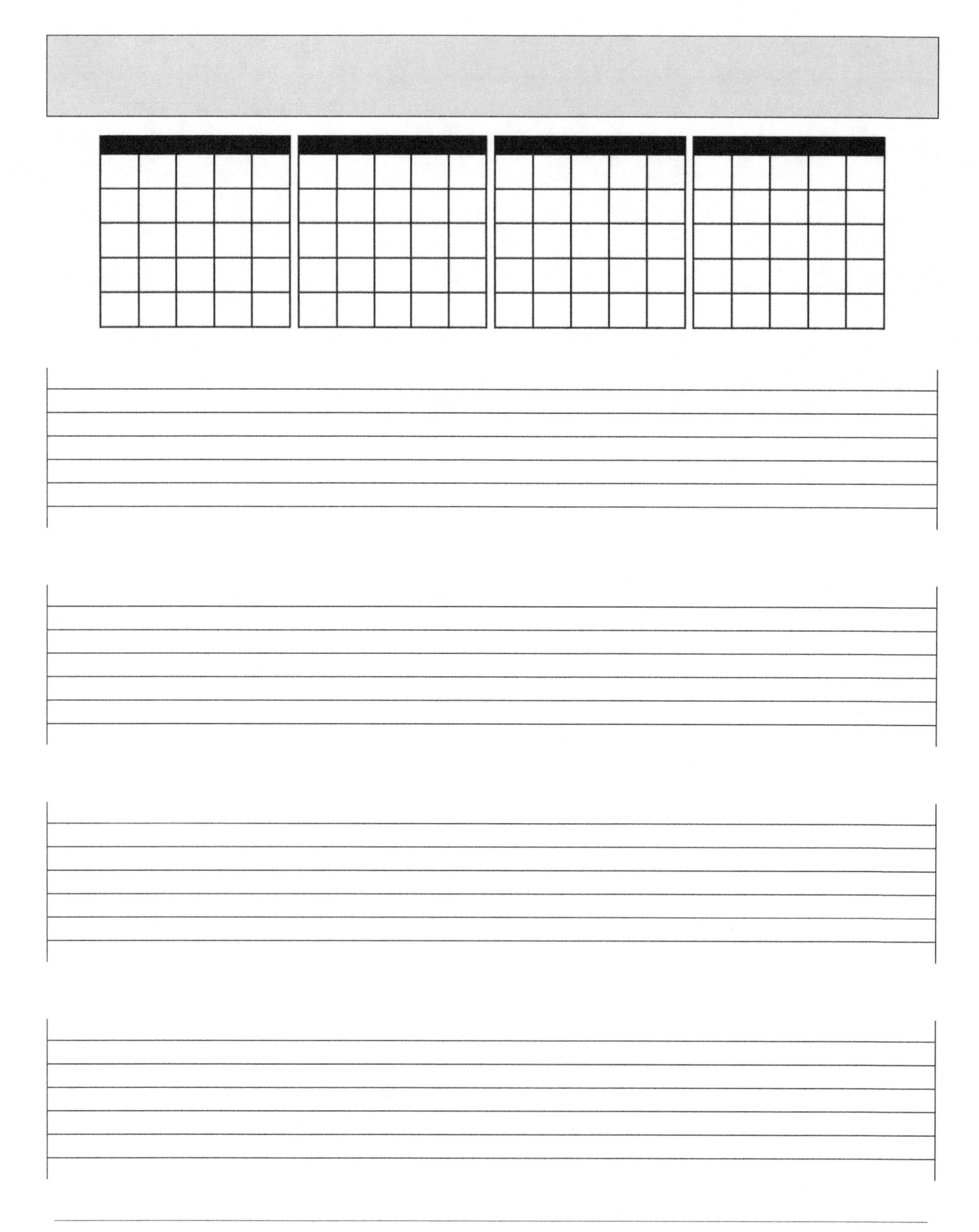

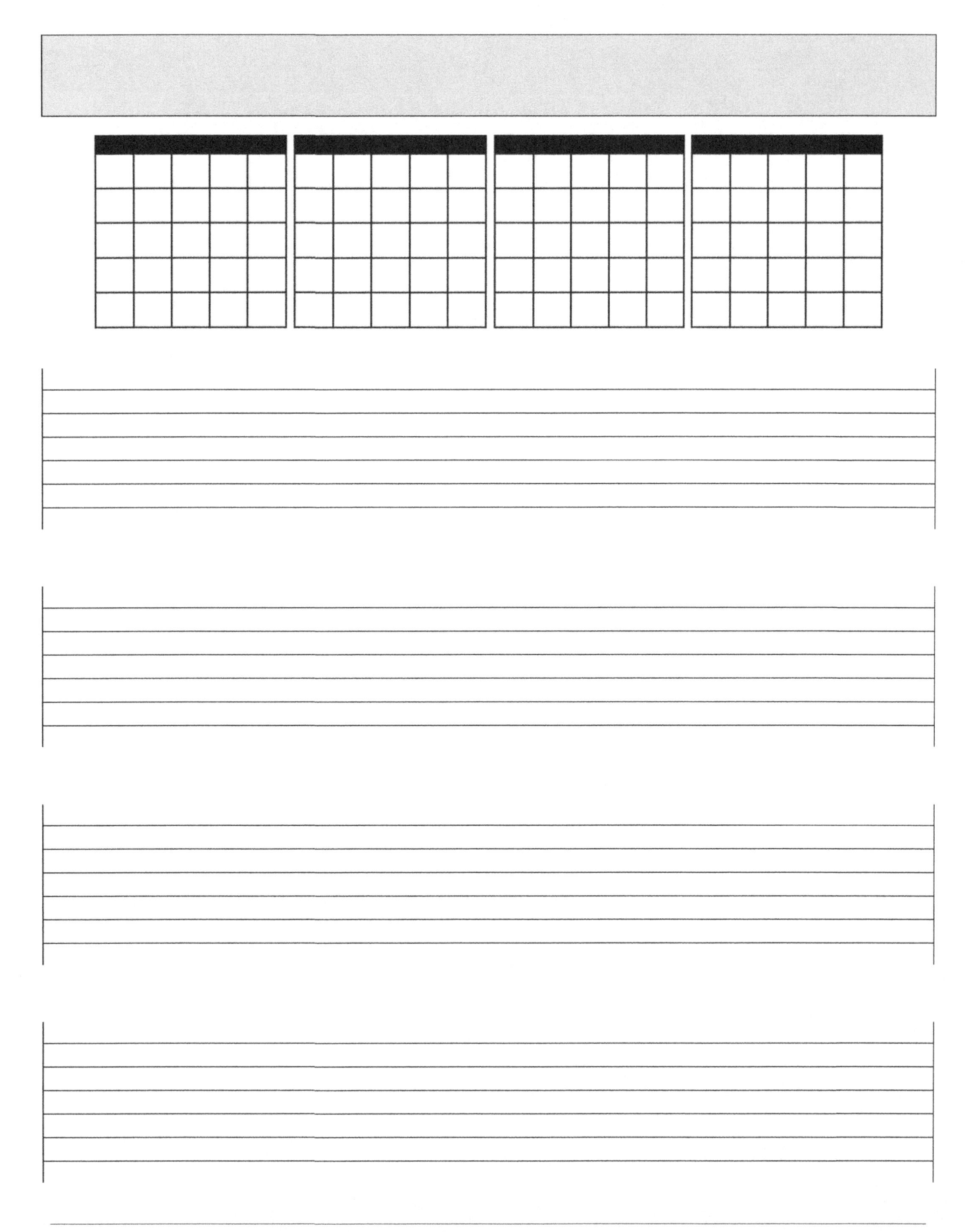

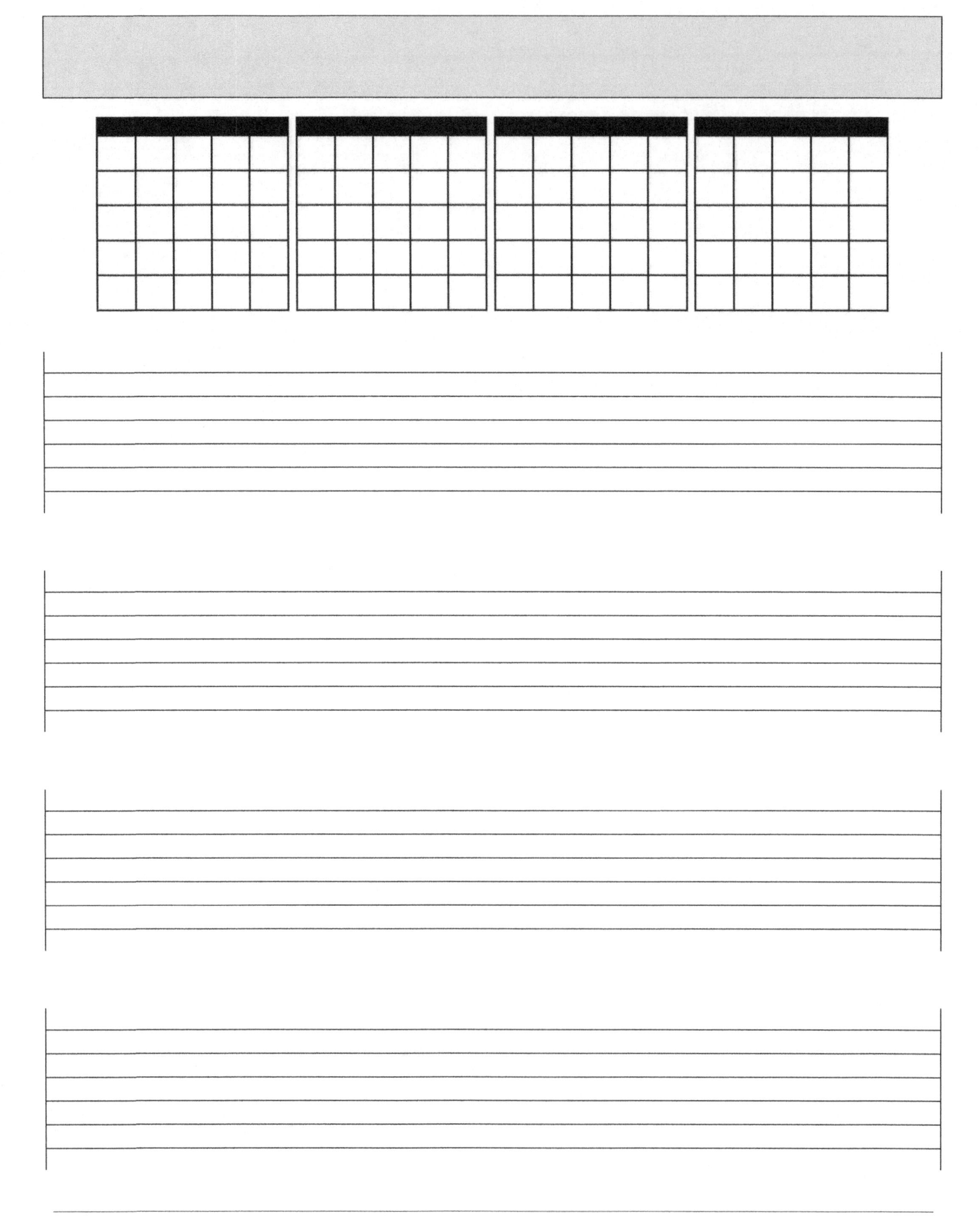

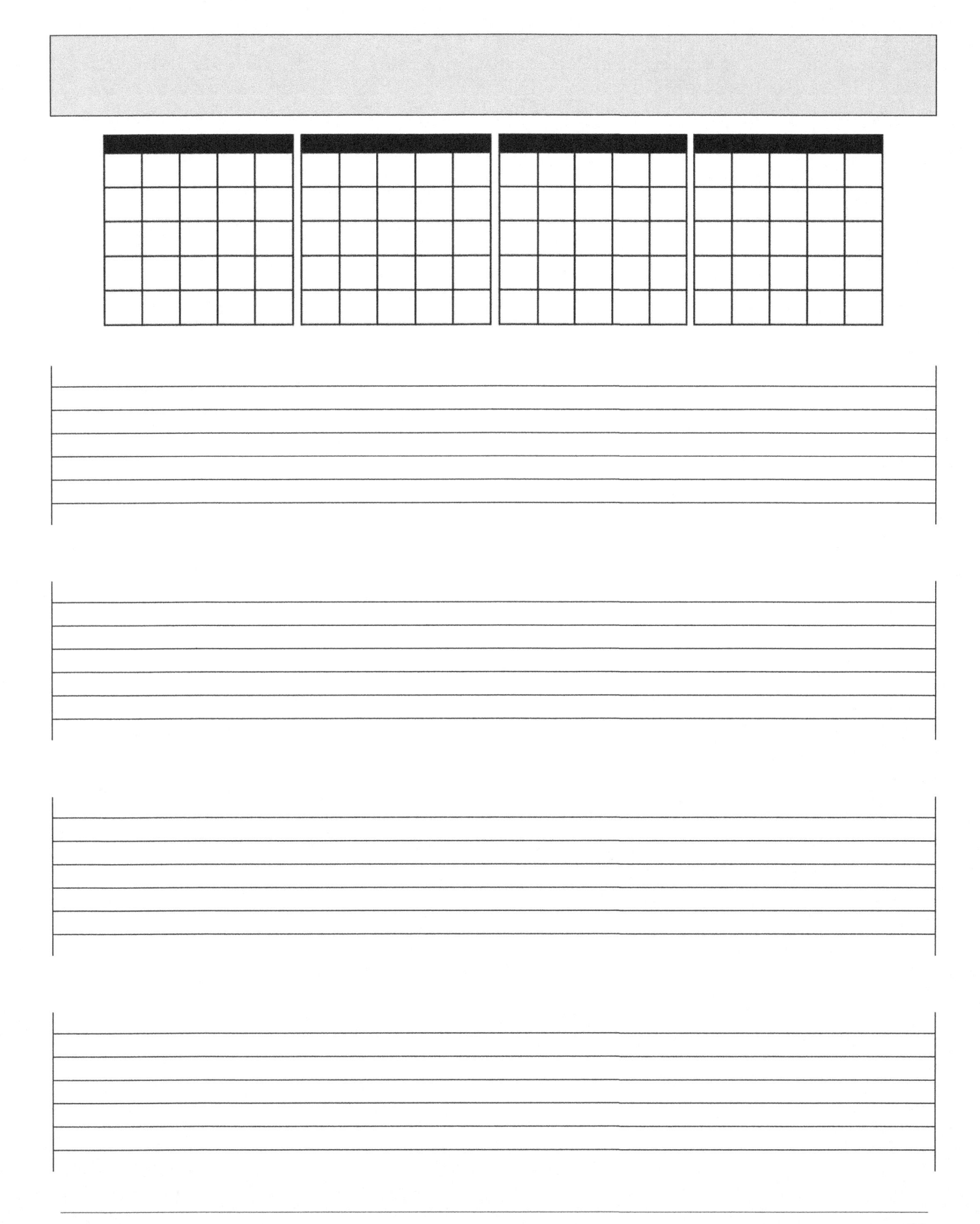

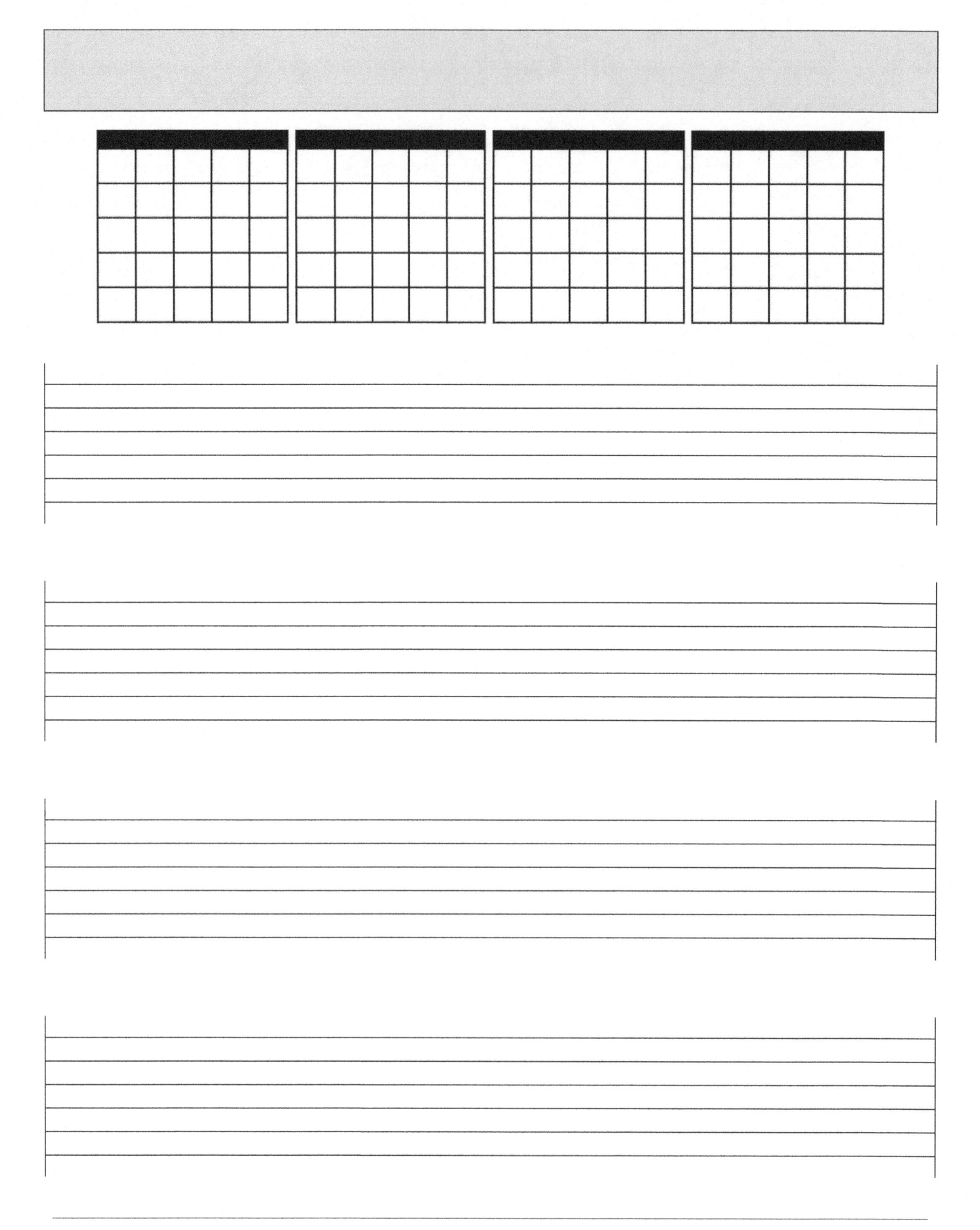

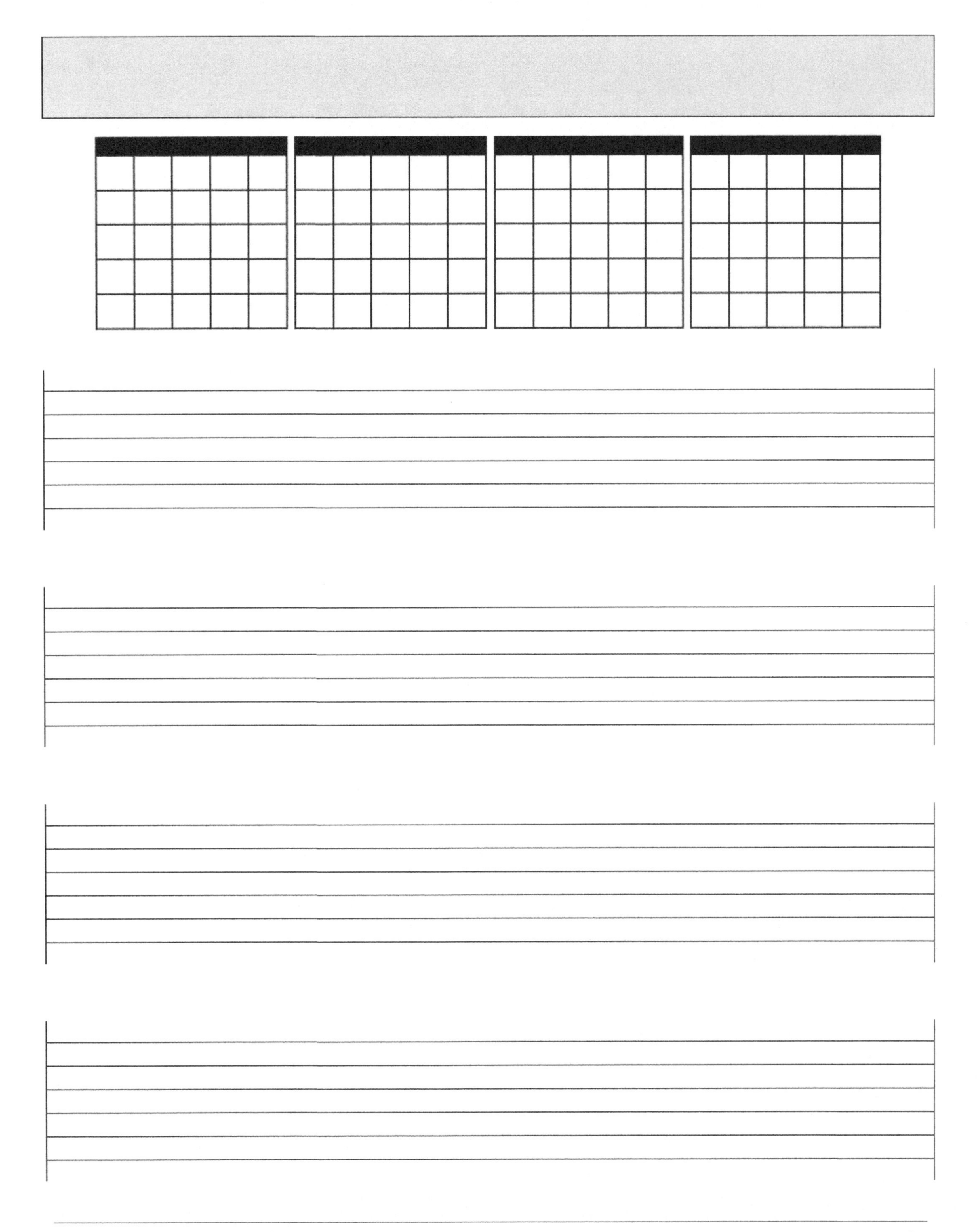

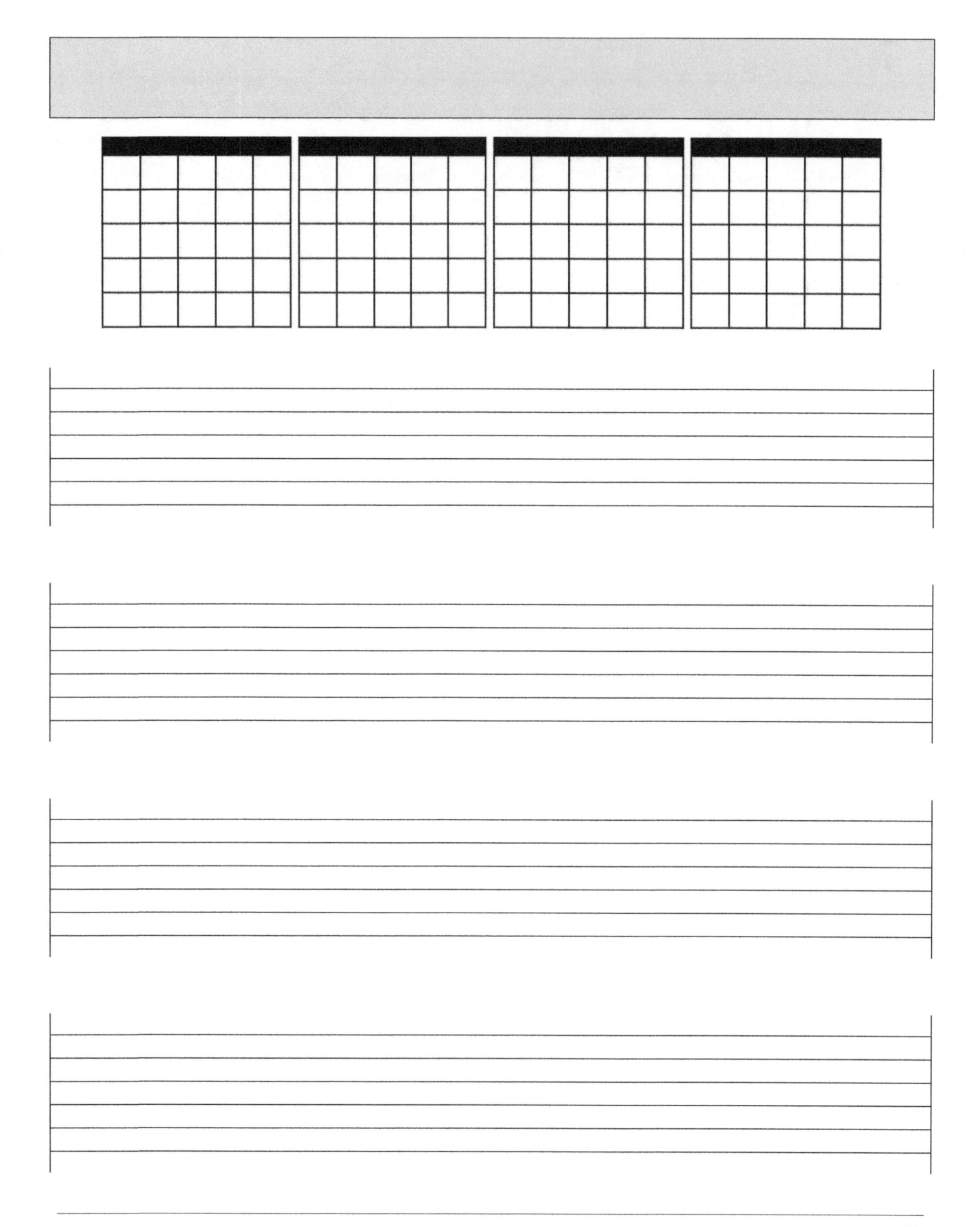

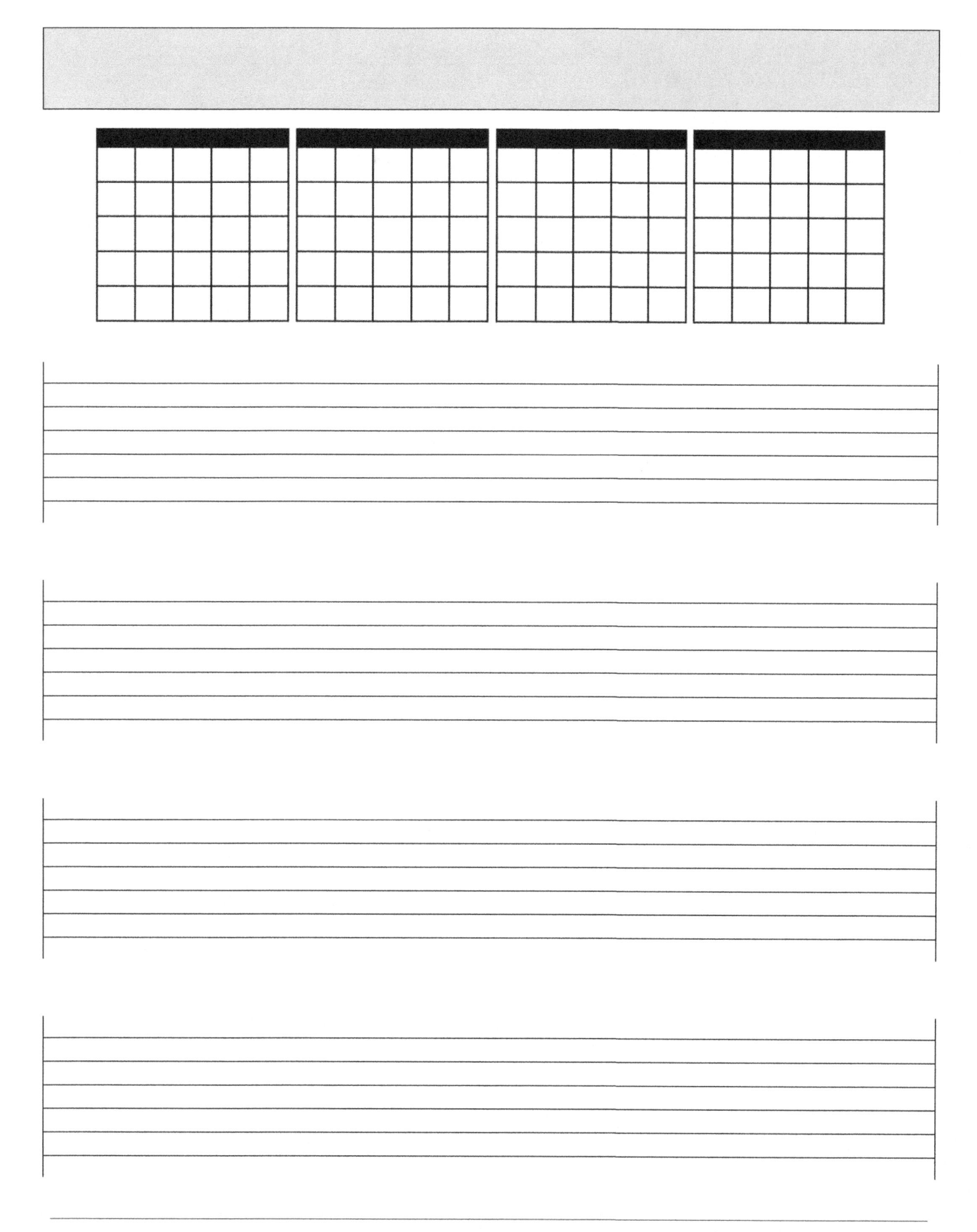

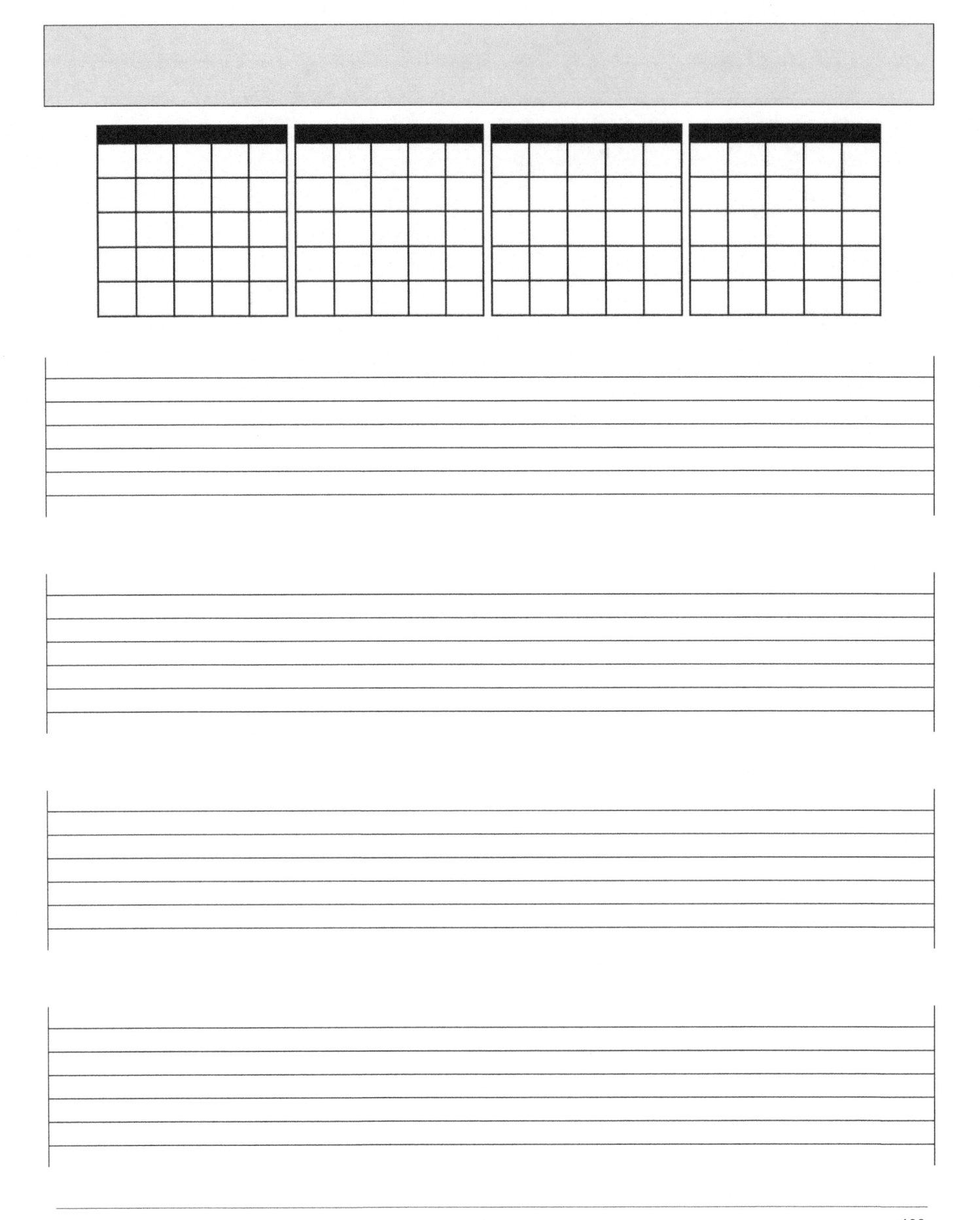

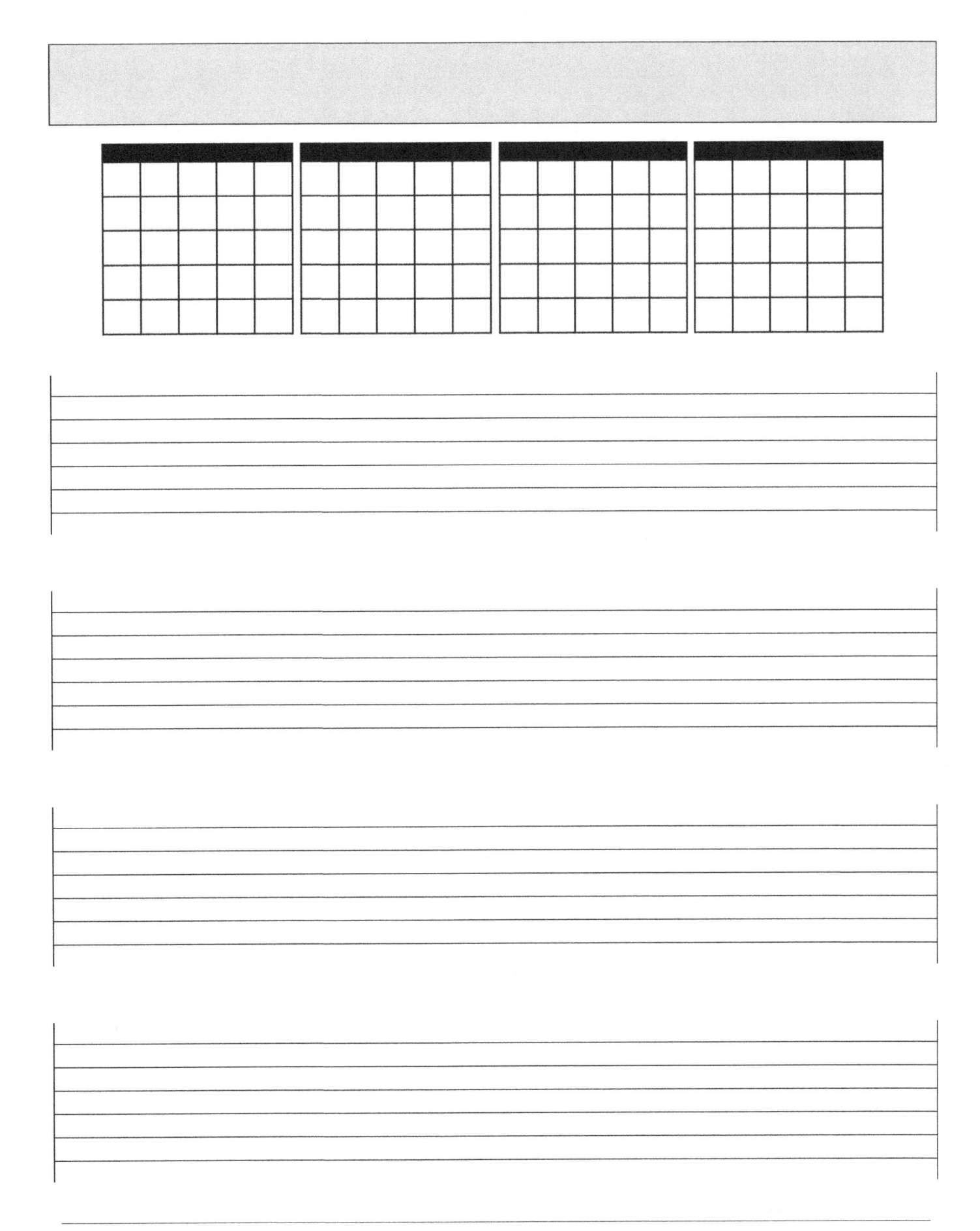

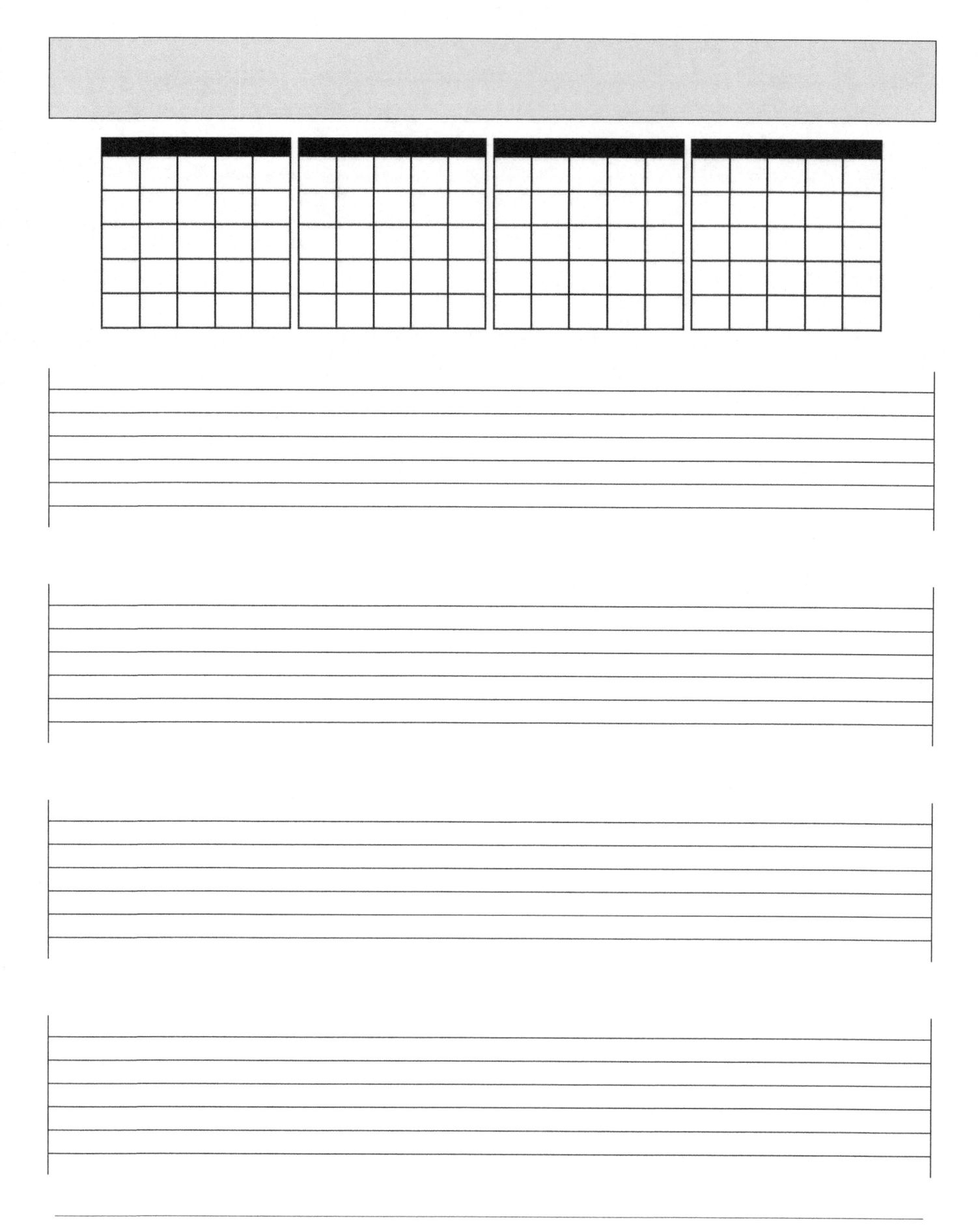

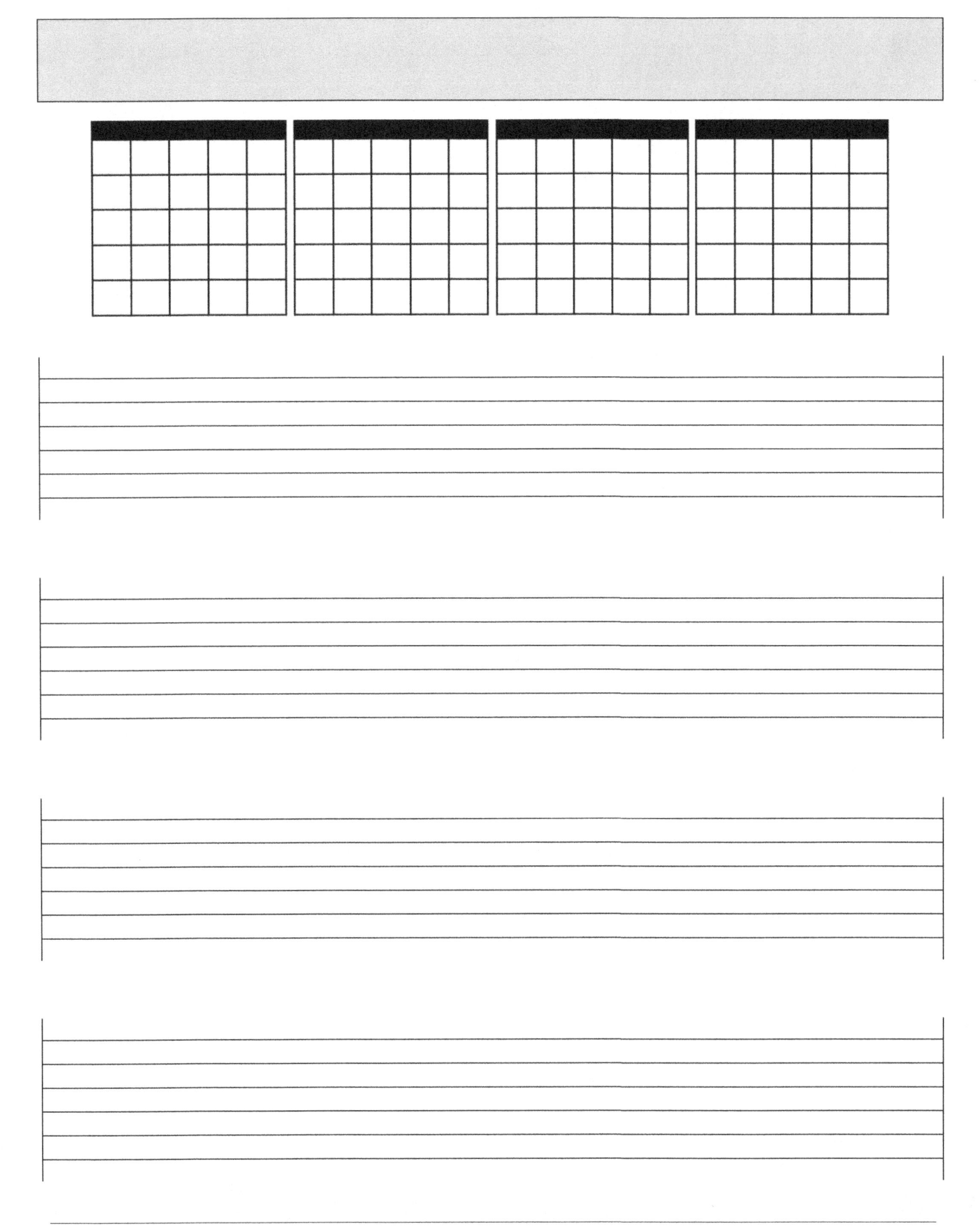

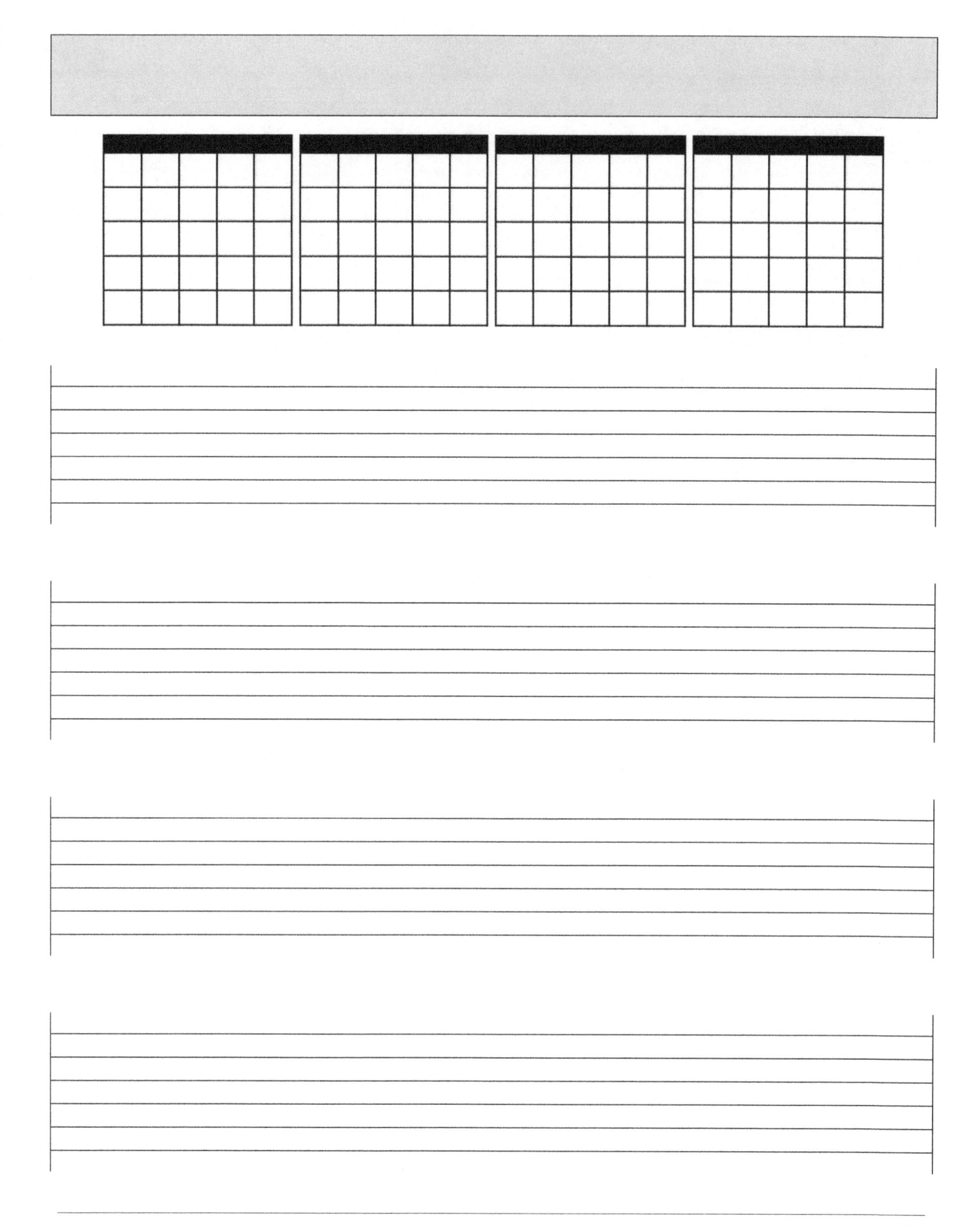

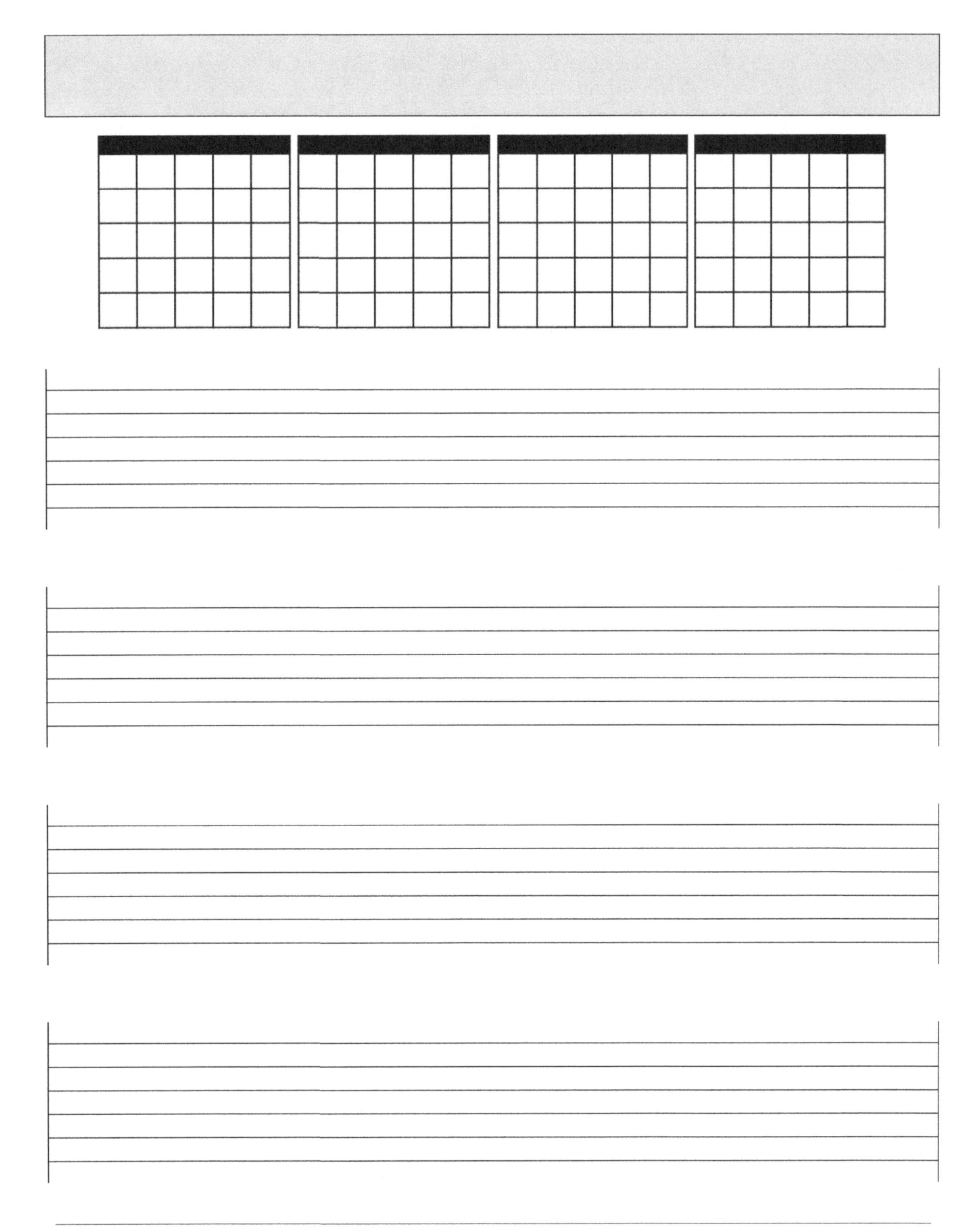

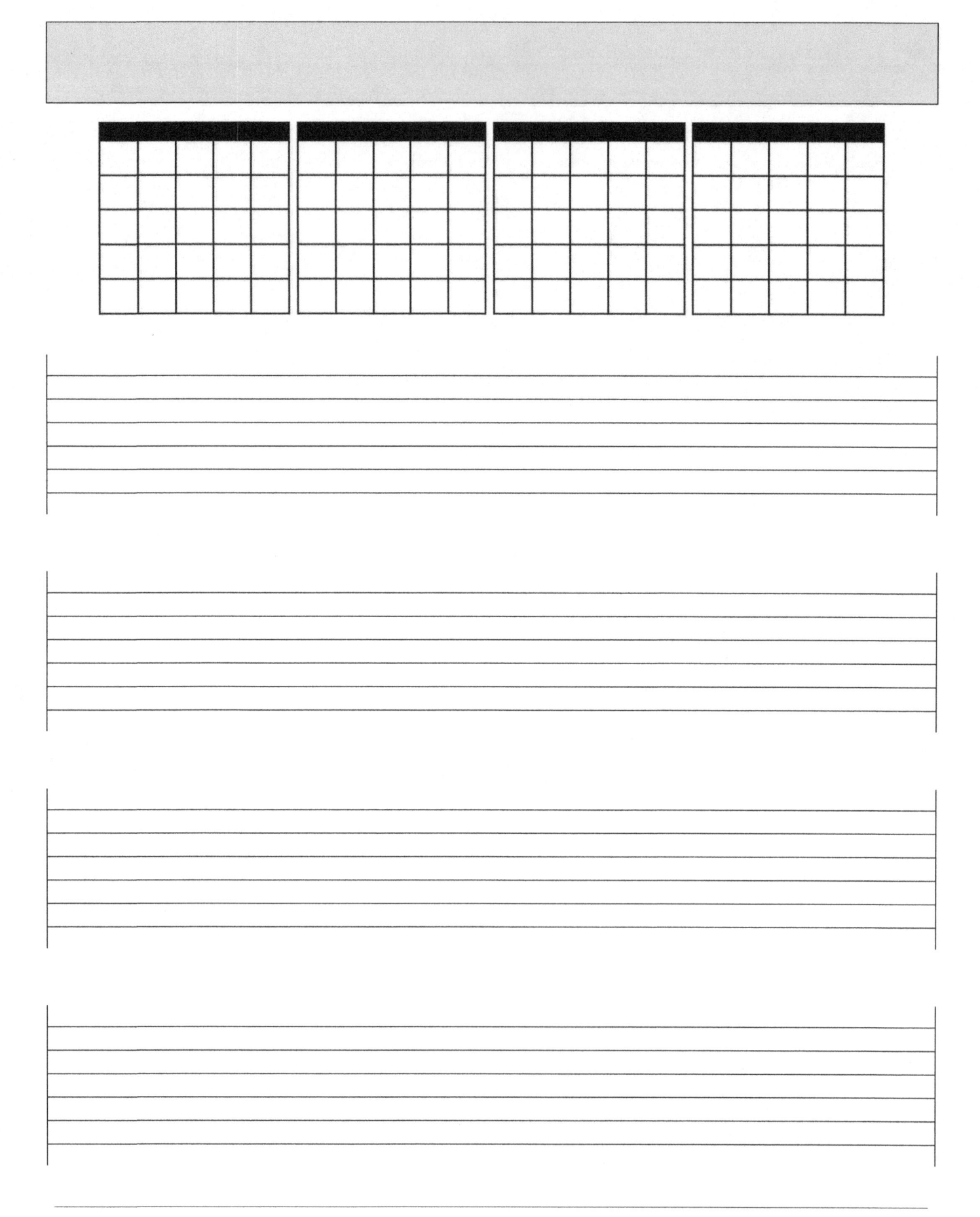

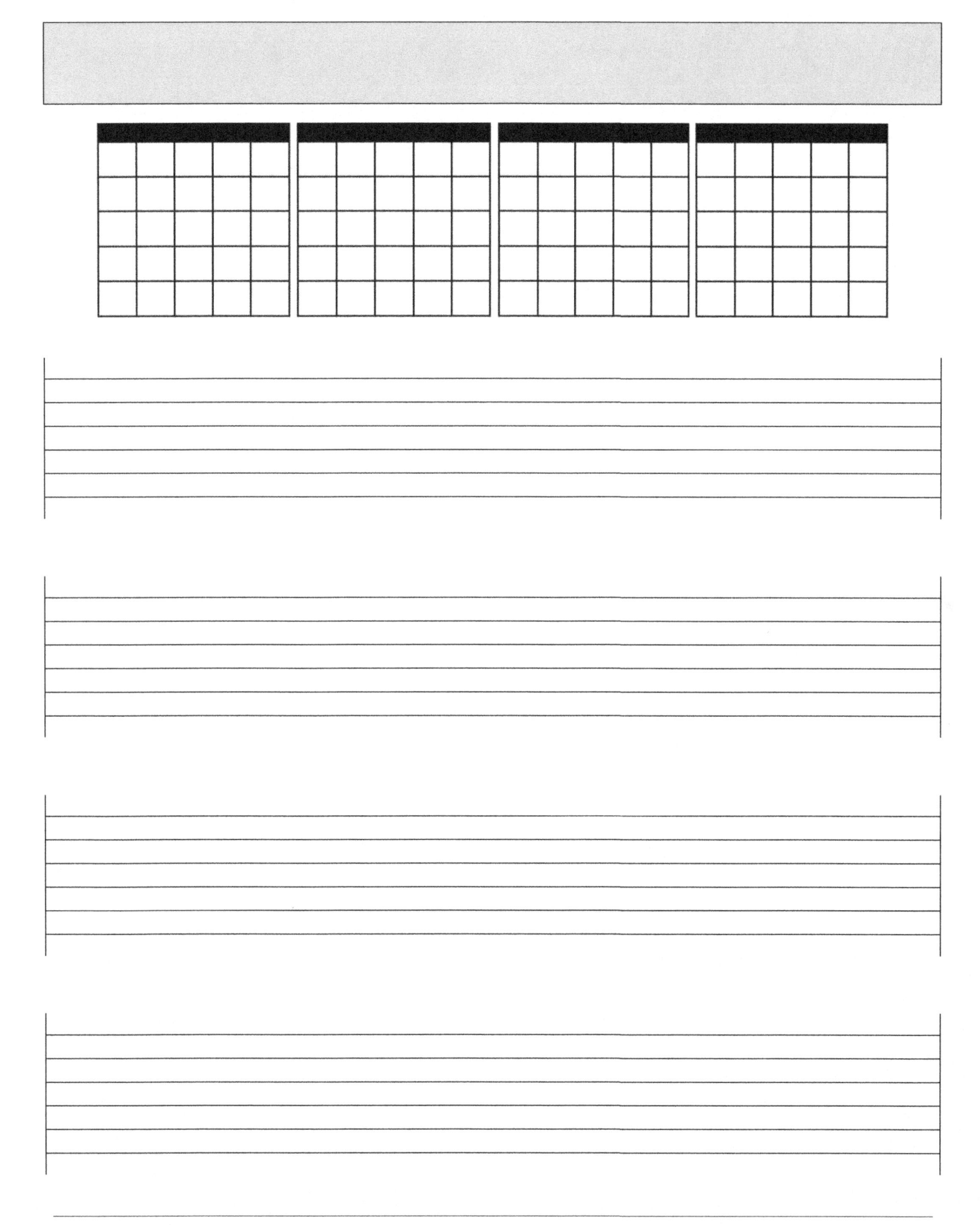

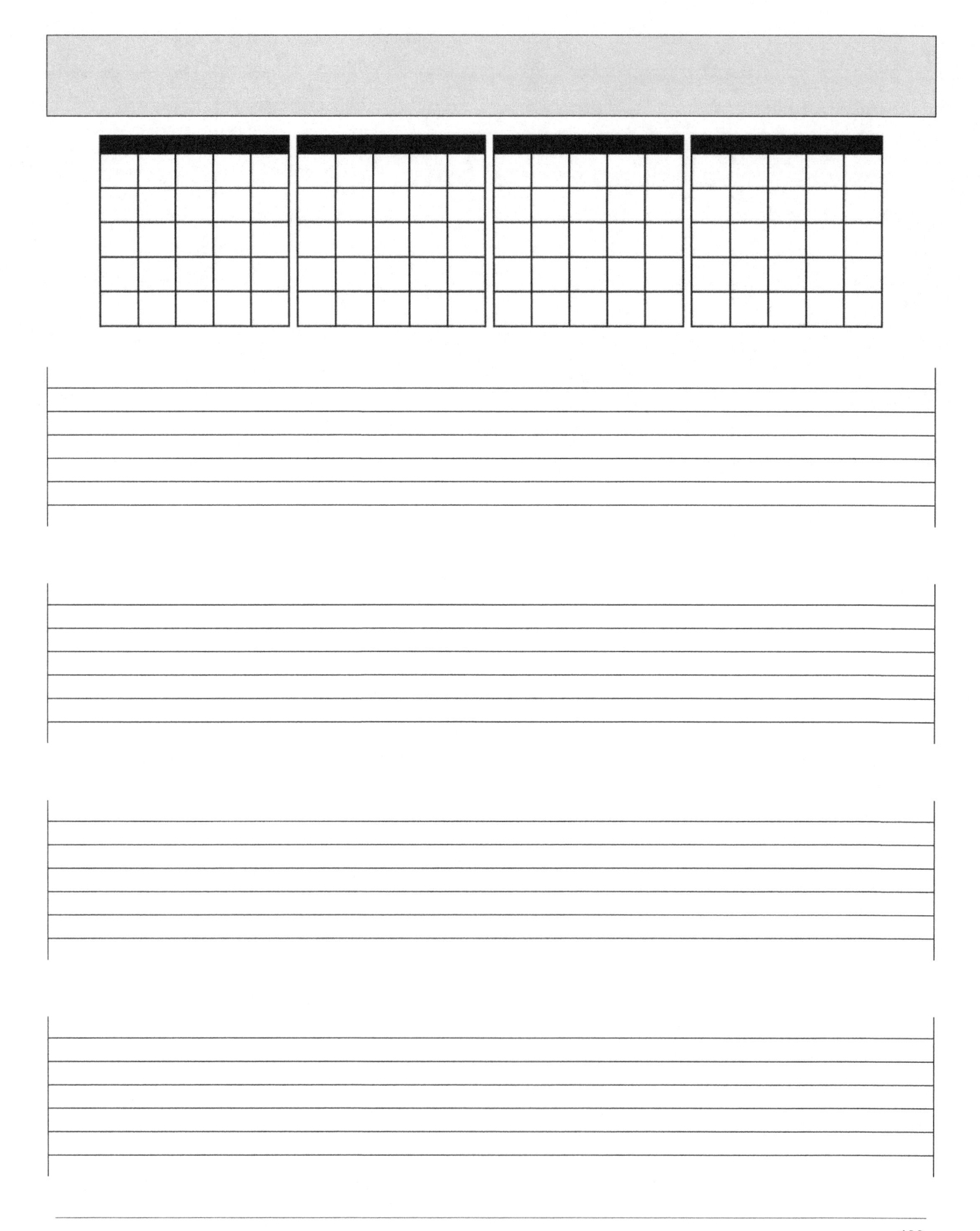

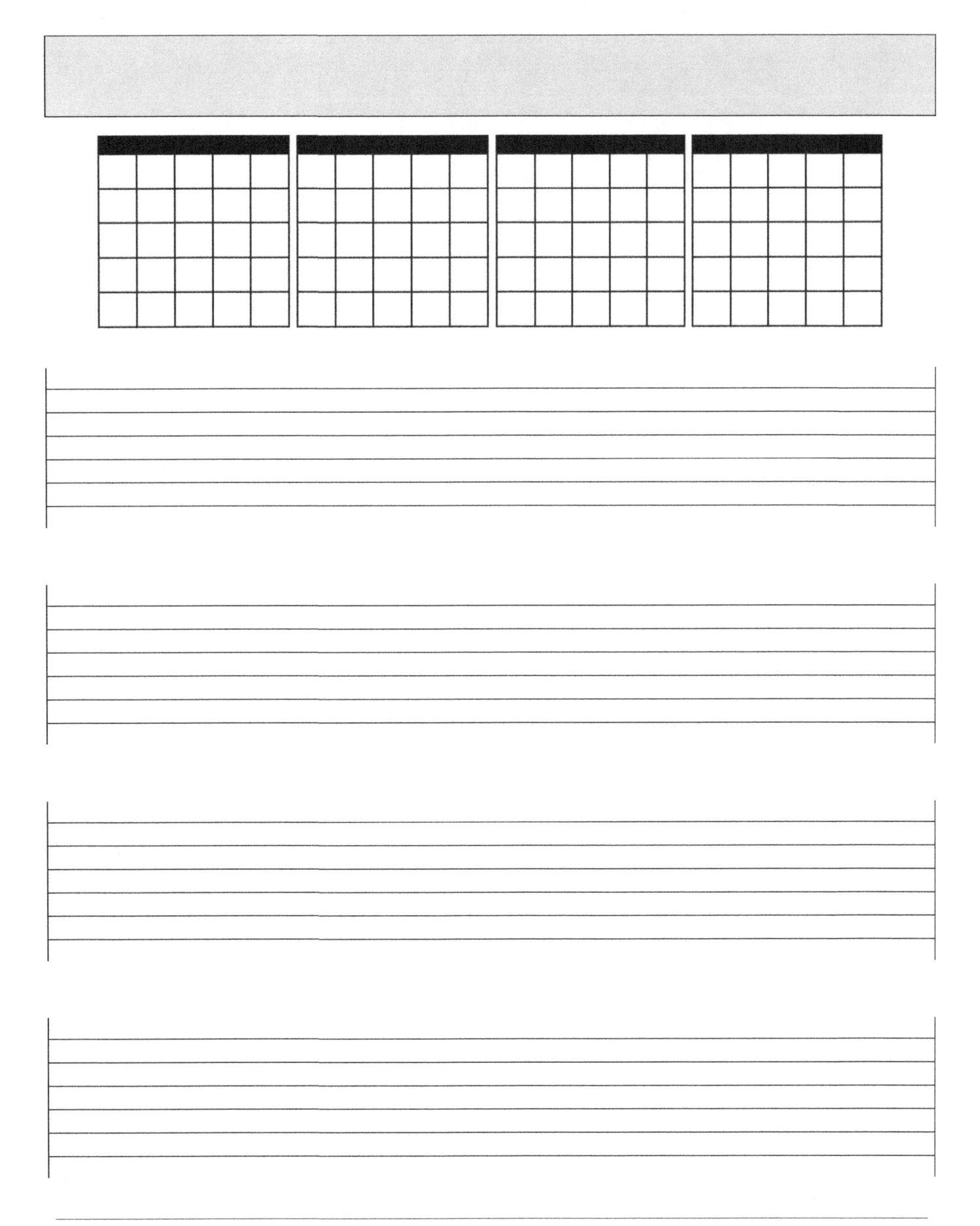

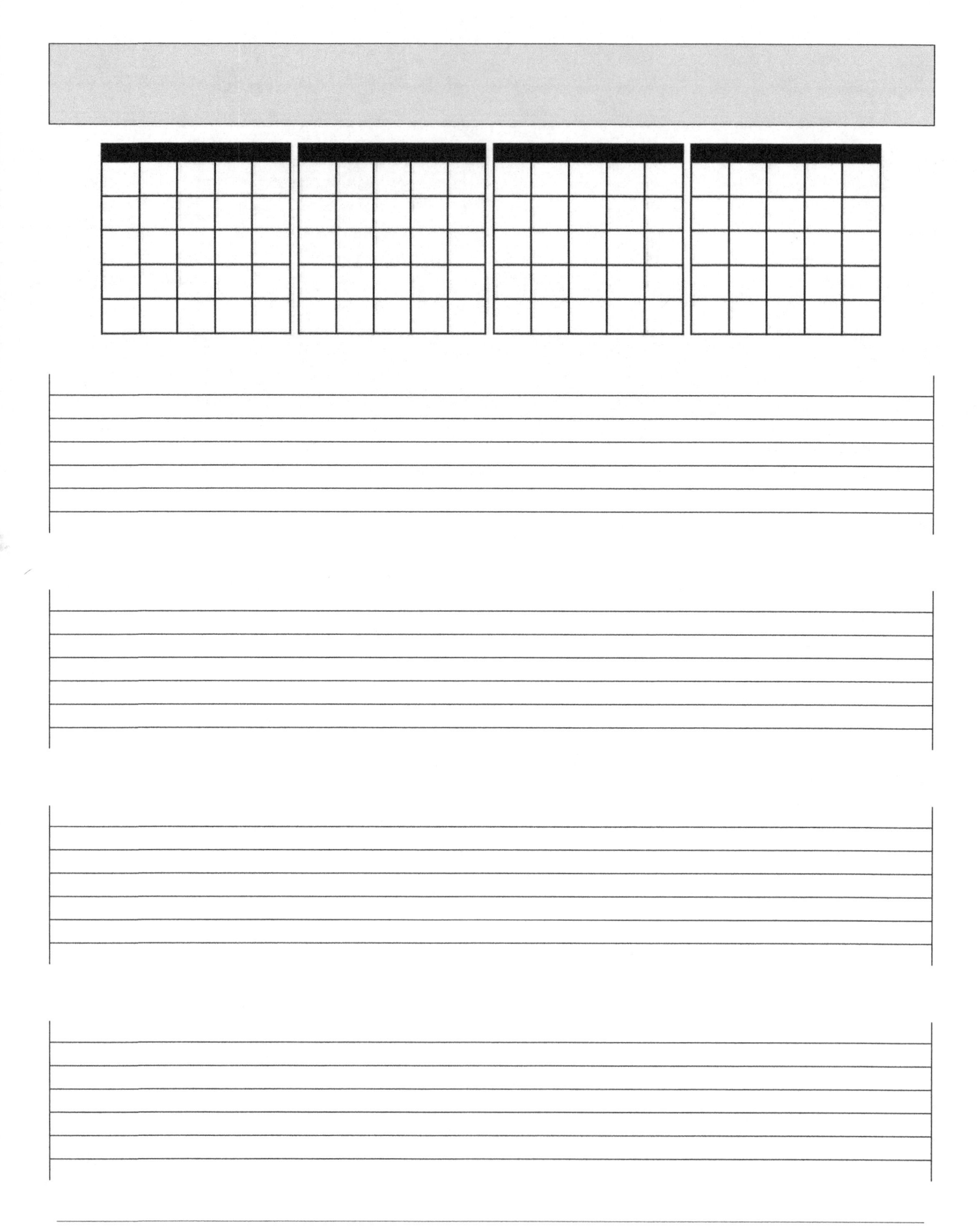

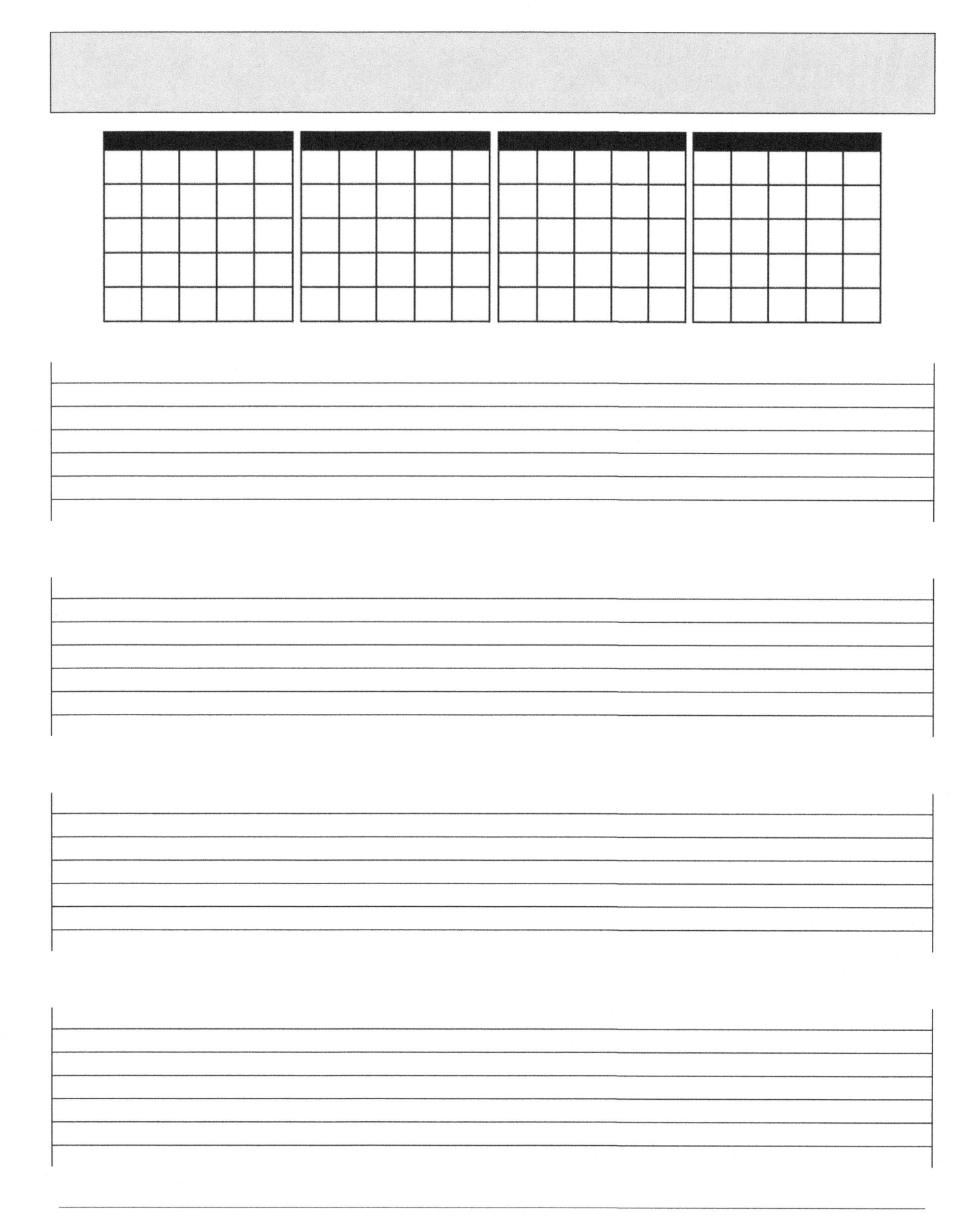

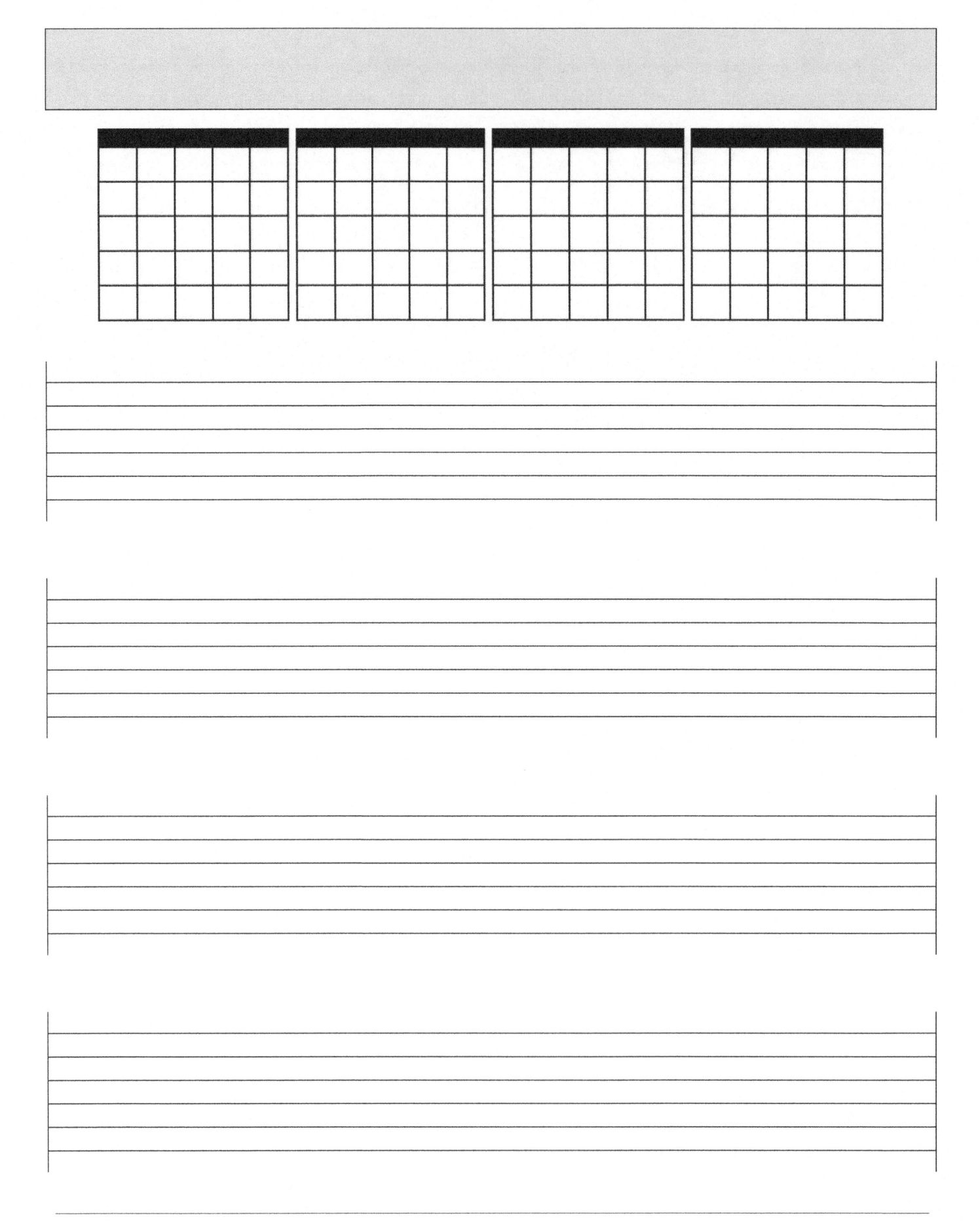

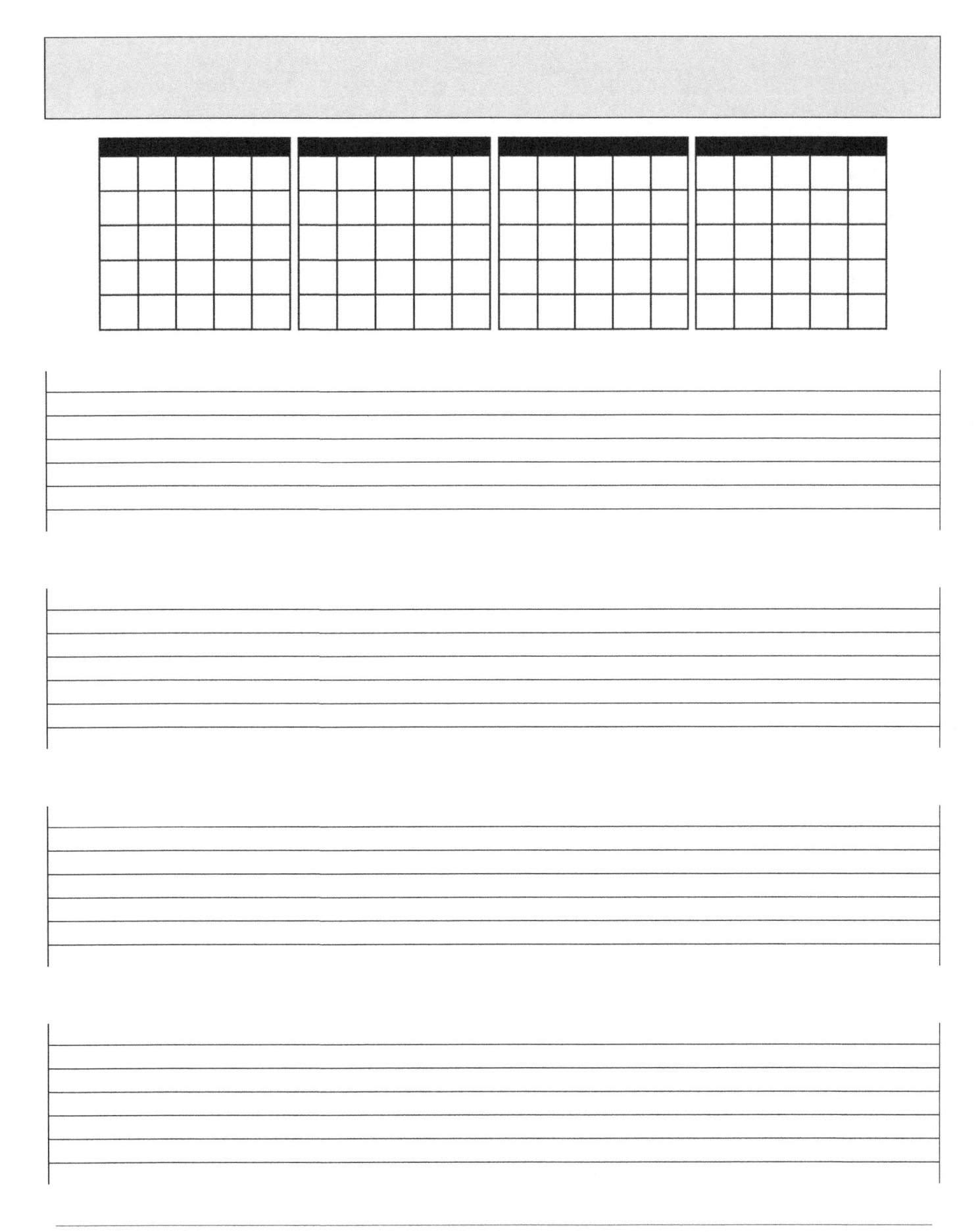

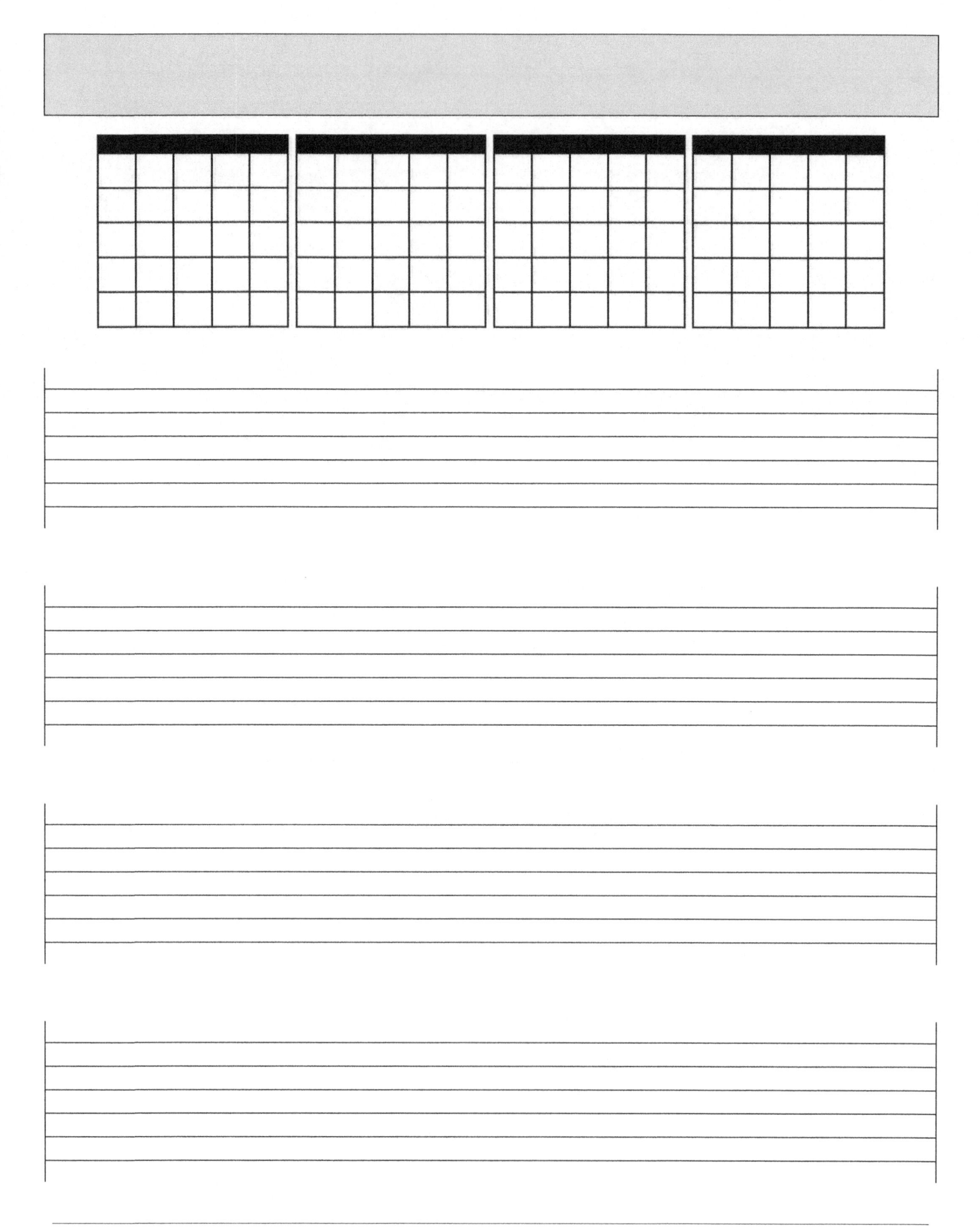

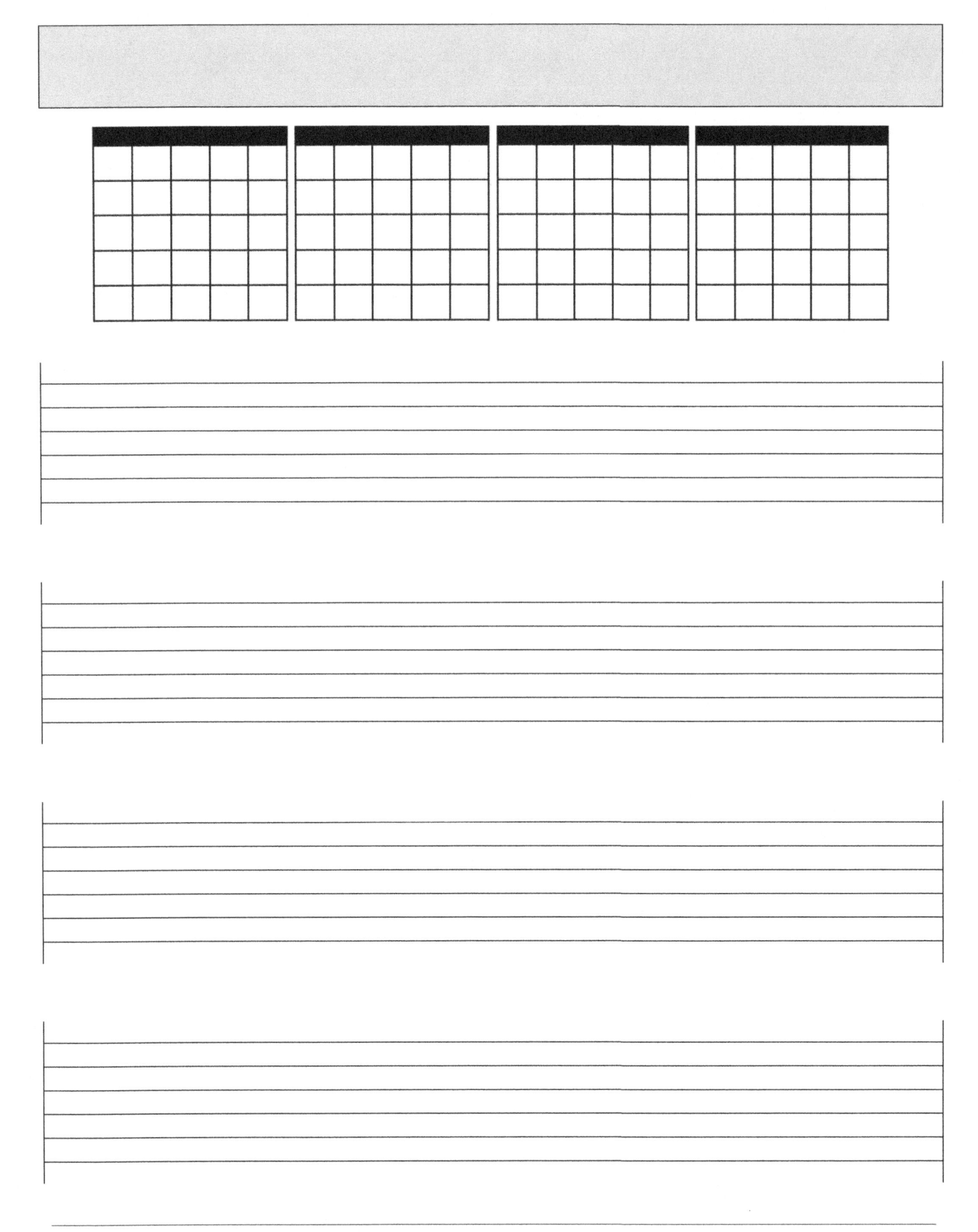

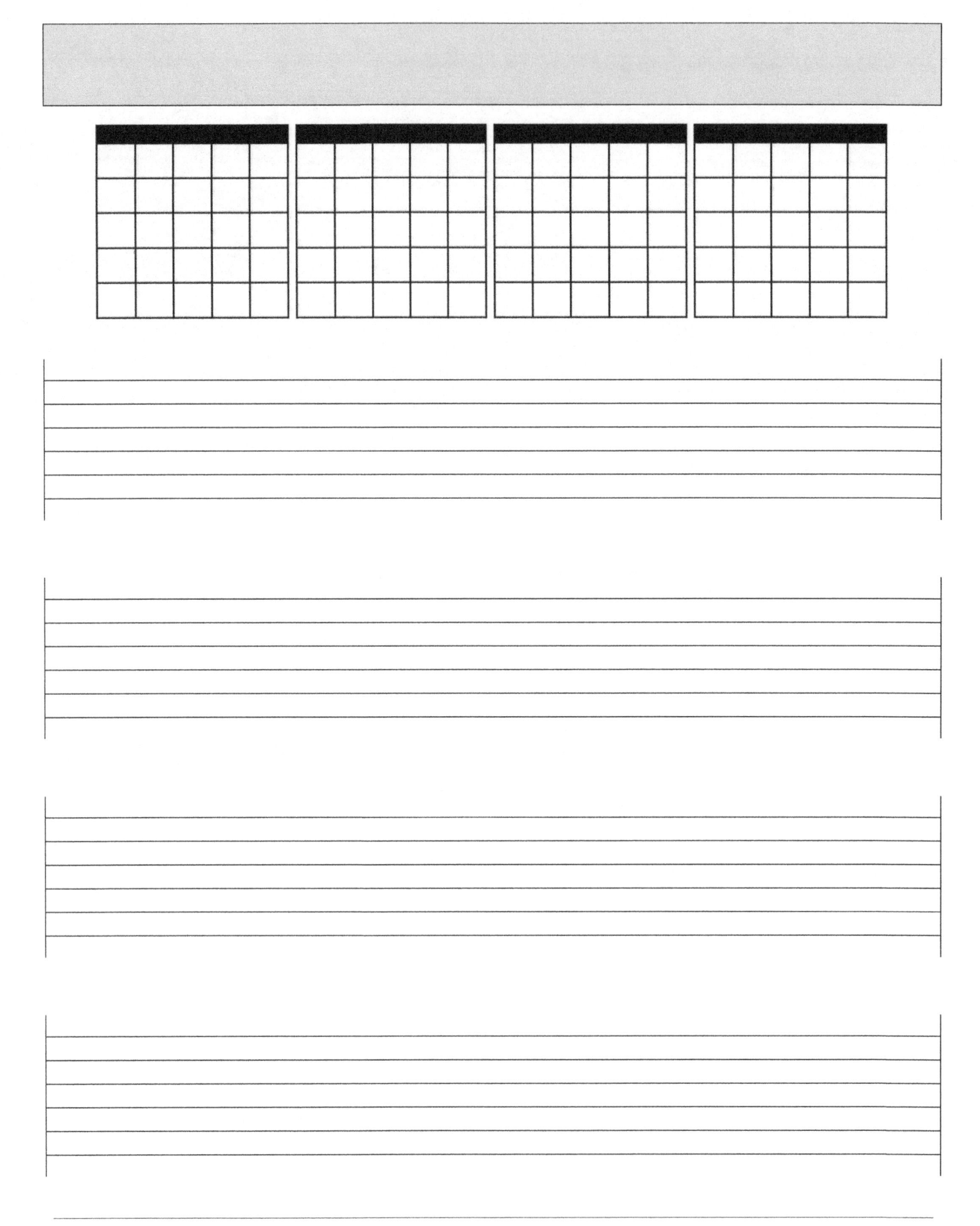

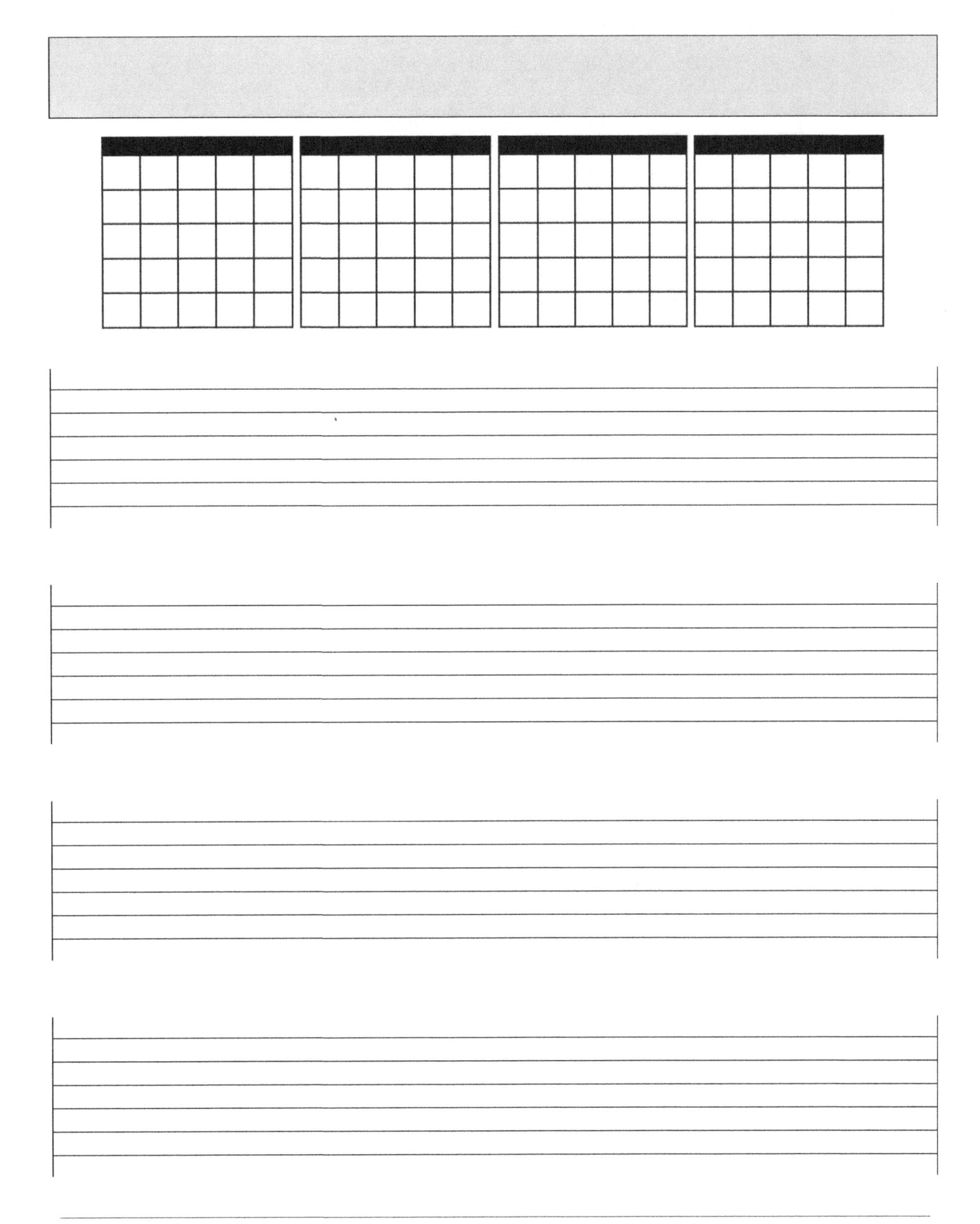

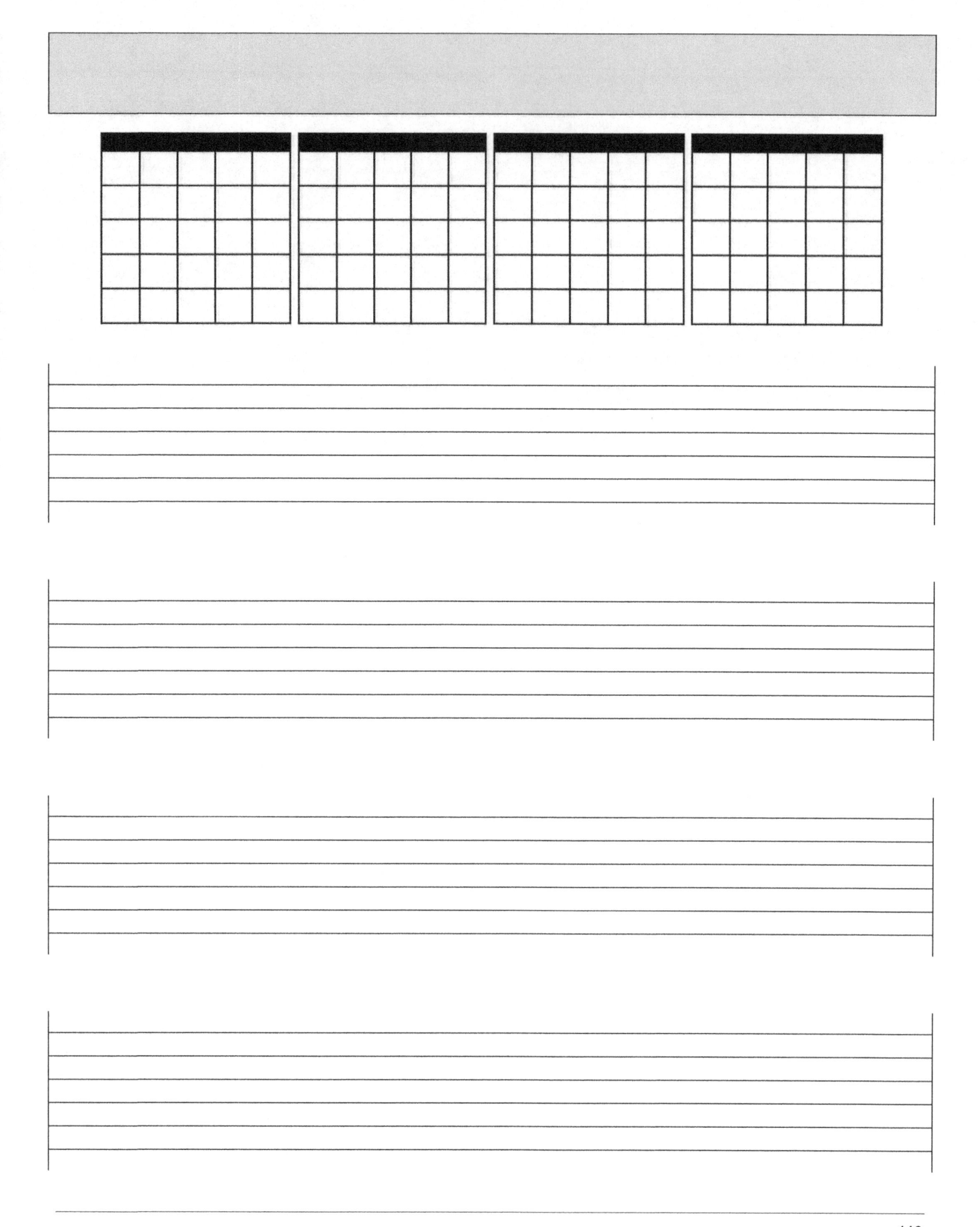

Find more on Amazon under Dexter Lives.
Instagram: @dextersworld
Facebook: @dexterlpm
YouTube: Dexter Lives
Website: Paradigmpublishingconsulting.com

Made in United States
Orlando, FL
04 December 2023